A Guide to Sources of Texas Criminal Justice Statistics

R. Scott Harnsberger

A Guide to Sources of Texas Criminal Justice Statistics

R. Scott Harnsberger

Number 6 in the North Texas Crime and Criminal Justice Series

University of North Texas Press

Denton, Texas

10 9 8 7 6 5 4 3 2 1

Permissions:
University of North Texas Press
1155 Union Circle #311336
Denton, TX 76203-5017

The paper used in this book meets the minimum requirements of the American National Standard for Permanence of Paper for Printed Library Materials, z39.48.1984. Binding materials have been chosen for durability.

Library of Congress Cataloging-in-Publication Data

Harnsberger, R. Scott.
    A guide to sources of Texas criminal justice statistics / R. Scott Harnsberger. — 1st ed.
    p. cm. — (Number 6 in the North Texas crime and criminal justice series)
    Includes bibliographical references and index.
    ISBN 978-1-57441-308-3 (cloth : alk. paper) -- ISBN 978-1-57441-314-4 (pbk. : alk. paper)
    1. Criminal statistics--Texas--Bibliography. I. Title. II. Series:
North Texas crime and criminal justice series ; no. 6.
    HV9955.T4H37 2011
    016.364976402'1—dc22

                                                    2010052453

A Guide to Sources of Texas Criminal Justice Statistics
is Number 6 in the North Texas Crime and Criminal Justice Series

Contents

Acknowledgments

I received valuable advice from Susan D. Strickland, Associate Professor and Criminal Justice Bibliographer, Newton Gresham Library, Sam Houston State University, during the preparation of this book. Timothy Kearley, Technology Specialist, Bureau of Justice Statistics, U.S. Department of Justice, provided me with pertinent information. I would also like to thank Ron Chrisman and Karen DeVinney of the UNT Press for their editorial assistance and expertise.

Introduction

This book was compiled as a resource for those needing assistance in locating Texas criminal justice statistics, including students, faculty, researchers, government officials, and individuals in the law enforcement, correctional, and judicial professions. The following types of publications are included: annual, biennial, and biannual reports; reports issued in series; analytic and research reports; statistical compilations; budgets and other fiscal documents; audits, inspections, and investigations; census publications; polls; projections; rankings; surveys; continuously updated online resources; and datasets. The sources for these statistics originate primarily, but not exclusively, from federal and State of Texas agencies, boards, bureaus, commissions, and departments.

The beginning publication date for inclusion is 2000, although many resources contain data from earlier years. It should be noted that a considerable number of important criminal justice statistical resources do not contain data at the level of individual states. These are therefore not included in the book as main entries, although a few examples of this type are mentioned in the research notes. Also, peer reviewed journal articles are not included. These can be accessed through databases such as *Criminal Justice Abstracts* (EBSCO) and *Criminal Justice Periodicals* (ProQuest).

This book reflects data availability as of late 2010. However, it is likely that changes in policies and procedures regarding the dissemination of governmental information will be implemented in the future at both the state and federal levels. Whether this results in an expansion or a contraction in the public availability of criminal justice statistics remains to be seen. In any event, the archiving and preservation of criminal justice statistical reports, in both electronic and tangible formats, is of paramount importance to researchers. As a case in point, some back editions of statistical reports disappeared from governmental websites during the preparation of this book (adjustments in the corresponding entries were made accordingly).

Resources have been listed as "online only" when they either reside on continuously updated websites or are no longer issued in a tangible format, except perhaps for internal agency use or for distribution to legislators and policymakers. Certain online resources have been excluded, including those whose access is restricted to duly authorized criminal justice agencies (e.g., the National Crime Information Center) and statistical gateways of a general nature (e.g., FedStats and LexisNexis® Statistical Insight).

The annotations were written with the goal of providing sufficient detail to enable users to decide whether the listed resources merit further investigation. The research notes contain information regarding the scope of the published data; title changes; related publications; and the availability of earlier data, previous editions, online tables, and datasets.

The *National Criminal Justice Thesaurus: Descriptors for Indexing Law Enforcement and Criminal Justice Information* was the principal source for terminology used in the chapter subdivisions and subject index. Some indexing terminology (e.g., mental defectives, physically handicapped) does not conform to current practice. Supplemental terminology was supplied by Library of Congress subject headings. Numbers in the indexes refer to entry numbers, not page numbers.

How to Use This Book

This book contains twelve chapters that cover sources for statistics on Texas crime, juvenile delinquency, law enforcement, courts, sentencing, capital punishment, corrections, victimization, driving/boating under the influence, substance abuse, governmental finances, and related subjects. Each chapter is arranged by topical subheadings. The subject index is the key to finding statistical data on specific subjects, whether they relate to criminal justice, corrections, and law enforcement, or to individual federal and State of Texas agencies. The listed resources report data either at the level of geographical areas (e.g., state, county, and city), or administrative/jurisdictional units (e.g., federal judicial district).

Statistical sources for many subjects will appear in more than one chapter. For example, data on illicit drugs can be found in Chapter 1 (arrests), Chapter 2 (production and trafficking), Chapter 3 (seizures), Chapter 4 (judicial caseloads and sentencing), Chapter 5 (use among adult inmates), Chapter 6 (use among juvenile inmates), Chapter 9 (driving under the influence), Chapter 10 (substance abuse and treatment), and Chapter 12 (state rankings for several of the foregoing topics).

Although the majority of the annotations are fairly detailed, researchers are advised to use the URLs provided and connect directly online to any resource that looks promising. The abstract, table of contents, list of tables, and statistical appendixes can then be evaluated for relevance. Complete sets of statistical reports, particularly those published before the digital era, are generally not available on governmental websites. Researchers seeking historical statistics will often need to consult the print editions (WorldCat can be checked for the holdings of individual libraries). For those requiring in-depth statistics, the research notes provide information on locating related datasets (where available).

Researchers should be aware that some of the publication series listed in this book may undergo title changes as new editions are published.

Abbreviations

P.L.	Public Law
Stat.	United States Statutes at Large
Tex. Civ. Prac. & Rem. Code Ann.	Texas Civil Practice and Remedies Code Annotated
Tex. Code Crim. Proc. Ann.	Texas Code of Criminal Procedure Annotated
Tex. Const.	Texas Constitution
Tex. Educ. Code Ann.	Texas Education Code Annotated
Tex. Fam. Code Ann.	Texas Family Code Annotated
Tex. Gov't Code Ann.	Texas Government Code Annotated
Tex. Health & Safety Code Ann.	Texas Health and Safety Code Annotated
Tex. Hum. Res. Code Ann.	Texas Human Resources Code Annotated
Tex. Occ. Code Ann.	Texas Occupations Code Annotated
U.S.	United States Reports
U.S.C.	United States Code

Format of the Entries

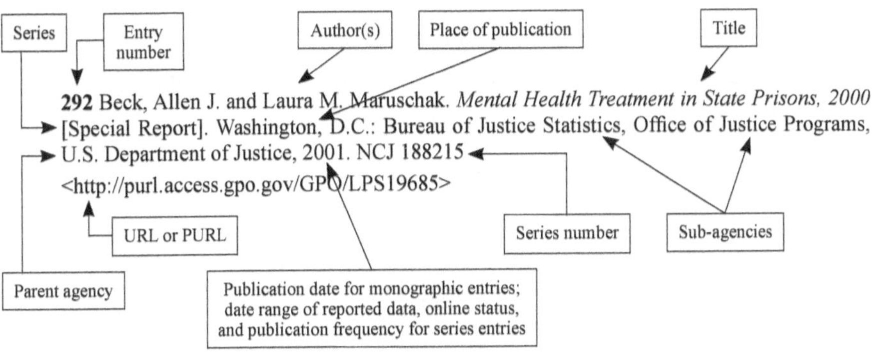

• Entries preceded with a bullet are basic or primary resources that are recommended as starting points for research within each chapter.

Important Federal Websites

Administrative Office of the U.S. Courts <http://www.uscourts.gov/>

Bureau of Alcohol, Tobacco, Firearms and Explosives <http://www.atf.gov/>

Bureau of Justice Statistics <http://bjs.ojp.usdoj.gov/>

Centers for Disease Control and Prevention <http://www.cdc.gov/>

Drug Enforcement Administration <http://www.justice.gov/dea/index.htm>

Federal Bureau of Investigation <http://www.fbi.gov/>

Federal Bureau of Prisons <http://www.bop.gov/>

National Criminal Justice Reference Service <http://www.ncjrs.gov/>

National Highway Traffic Safety Administration <http://www.nhtsa.gov/>

Office for Victims of Crime <http://www.ovc.gov/>

Office of Juvenile Justice and Delinquency Prevention <http://ojjdp.ncjrs.gov/>

Office of National Drug Control Policy <http://www.whitehousedrugpolicy.gov/

Substance Abuse and Mental Health Services Administration <http://www.samhsa.gov/>

U.S. Census Bureau, Governments Division <http://www.census.gov/govs/>

U.S. Department of Homeland Security <http://www.dhs.gov/index.shtm>

U.S. Department of Justice <http://www.justice.gov/>

U.S. Marshals Service <http://www.justice.gov/marshals/>

U.S. Sentencing Commission <http://www.ussc.gov/>

Important State of Texas Websites

Attorney General of Texas <http://www.oag.state.tx.us/>

Legislative Budget Board <http://www.lbb.state.tx.us/>

Office of Court Administration <http://www.courts.state.tx.us/oca/>

Office of the Governor, Criminal Justice Division <http://governor.state.tx.us/cjd/>

Texas Board of Pardons and Paroles <http://www.tdcj.state.tx.us/bpp/>

Texas Commission on Jail Standards <http://www.tcjs.state.tx.us/>

Texas Commission on Law Enforcement Officer Standards and Education <http://www.tcleose.state.tx.us/>

Texas Comptroller of Public Accounts <http://www.window.state.tx.us/>

Texas Criminal Justice Statistical Analysis Center <http://governor.state.tx.us/txsac/>

Texas Department of Criminal Justice <http://www.tdcj.state.tx.us/>

Texas Department of Family and Protective Services <http://www.dfps.state.tx.us/>

Texas Department of Public Safety <http://www.txdps.state.tx.us/>

Texas Department of State Health Services <http://www.dshs.state.tx.us/>

Texas Department of Transportation <http://www.dot.state.tx.us/>

Texas Juvenile Probation Commission <http://www.tjpc.state.tx.us/>

Texas Legislature Online <http://www.capitol.state.tx.us/>

Texas Youth Commission <http://www.tyc.state.tx.us/>

Chapter 1

Starting Points

Basic Resources

•**001** *Crime in Texas.* Austin: Uniform Crime Reporting Section, Crime Information Bureau, Crime Records Service, Texas Department of Public Safety [annual, 1976–date].

<http://www.txdps.state.tx.us/administration/crime_records/pages/crimestatistics.htm> [full report]

<http://www.txdps.state.tx.us/director_staff/public_information/reports.htm> [summary report]

The State of Texas officially adopted the Uniform Crime Reporting (UCR) Program on January 1, 1976. The Texas Department of Public Safety has the responsibility for collecting, validating, and tabulating UCR data received from over 1,000 law enforcement agencies in the state. Each annual report is organized as follows:

Chapter 1: The UCR Program;
Chapter 2: Texas Crime Analysis (including the Texas Crime Clock);
Chapter 3: Index Crime Analysis (murder, forcible rape, robbery, aggravated assault, burglary, larceny-theft, motor vehicle theft, and arson);
Chapter 4: Selected Non-Index Crimes (DUI arrests, drug abuse arrests, drug seizures, and weapons arrests);
Chapter 5: Family Violence (by jurisdiction);
Chapter 6: Hate Crime (by jurisdiction);
Chapter 7: Law Enforcement Personnel (law enforcement employee data, law enforcement officers assaulted, and law enforcement officers killed);
Chapter 8: Texas Arrest Data (summary by UCR categories, juvenile male arrests, juvenile female arrests, adult male arrests, adult female arrests, arrests by race, and arrests by ethnicity);
Chapter 9: Crime by Jurisdiction (summary, municipal crime by population, county crime by population, and index crimes by agency and county).

Research Note: Reports are available online back to 1999 on the DPS website under the title *The Texas Crime Report.* This designation, however, was dropped from the 2005–2008 print editions. Reports are disseminated in electronic format only beginning with the 2009 edition. The DPS also publishes an annual summary UCR report under the identical title, *Crime in Texas.* The previous annual reports, which were published by the DPS under the title *Texas Crime Report* (1947–1975), cannot always be accurately compared year-to-year because changes in the Texas Penal Code affected the categories of offenses reported during this time period. The DPS is in the process of implementing the Texas Incident-Based Reporting System (TIBRS), which contains all the data elements of the National Incident-Based Reporting System (see entry 002), supplemented with Texas-specific data. The program is currently collecting data from fifty-six TIBRS-certified jurisdictions, which is then converted to summary data for inclusion in *Crime in Texas*.

•002 *Crime in the United States: Uniform Crime Reports.* Washington, D.C.: Federal Bureau of Investigation, U.S. Department of Justice [annual, 1998–date].

<http://purl.access.gpo.gov/GPO/LPS3082> [Crime in the United States]

<http://www.ucrdatatool.gov/> [UCR Data Tool]

The FBI's Uniform Crime Reporting (UCR) Program was initiated in 1930 (the title of the annual report was changed beginning with the 1998 edition). The program currently gathers and compiles data reported by over 17,000 law enforcement agencies nationwide on violent crime, property crime, hate crime, persons arrested, offenses cleared by arrest or exceptional means, law enforcement officers feloniously or accidentally killed, law enforcement officers assaulted, and full-time law enforcement employees. The UCR Program divides offenses known to law enforcement into Part I and Part II offenses. Part 1 offenses, which are also known as index crimes, encompass violent crime (murder and nonnegligent manslaughter, forcible rape, robbery, and aggravated assault) and property crime (burglary, larceny-theft, motor vehicle theft, and arson). Congress designated arson as a Part I offense in October 1978 and data collection began the following year. Part II offenses comprise all other crimes, with the exception of traffic violations, and only arrest data is collected. Hate crime was added as an additional data reporting category in 1990. *Crime in the United States* reports data at the following levels: national, regional, state, county agency, city agency, universities and colleges, cities and counties grouped by size (population groups), and Metropolitan Statistical Areas (MSAs). The following data is reported at the sub-regional level: offenses known to law enforcement (Part I offenses); type of weapon used for murder, aggravated assault, and robbery (under Expanded Data by Offense); persons arrested (Part I and Part II offenses, under age eighteen and total all ages); hate crime; law enforcement officers feloniously killed; law enforcement officers accidently killed; law enforcement officers assaulted; and full-time law enforcement employees. In January 1989 the UCR Program began transitioning from a summary reporting system to an enhanced data collection program called the National Incident-Based Reporting System (NIBRS), which includes forty-six Group A crimes organized into twenty-two broad offense categories. Group B comprises eleven offense categories for which only arrest data is reported. Currently thirty-two states, including Texas, are certified to provide their UCR data in the expanded NIBRS format.

Research Note: Previously published under the title *Uniform Crime Reports for the United States* (1930–1997). Editions are available online back to 1995. The 2004 edition was the last to be published in a tangible format (print or CD-ROM). Beginning with the 2005 edition,

Crime in the United States: Uniform Crime Reports is disseminated in electronic format only. Printable files are available for downloading (topic pages, resource pages, data tables, data declarations, data overviews, and figures). Bernan Press reproduces and assembles these files in an unofficial print edition. Hate crime statistics and data on law enforcement officers killed and assaulted (LEOKA), while collected under the auspices of the UCR Program, are currently reported in separate publications linked from the *Crime in the United States* website (see entries 048, 098, and 149). The Crime Index was reported in the 1959 through 2002 editions and discontinued thereafter. Datasets are available through the Inter-university Consortium for Political and Social Research (ICPSR), Institute for Social Research, University of Michigan (NIBRS data is archived as thirteen separate data files, which can be merged by using linkage variables).

<http://www.icpsr.umich.edu/icpsrweb/ICPSR/series/00057> [UCR]

<http://www.icpsr.umich.edu/icpsrweb/ICPSR/series/00128> [NIBRS]

•**003** *Sourcebook of Criminal Justice Statistics.* Washington, D.C.: Bureau of Justice Statistics, Office of Justice Programs, U.S. Department of Justice [1973–date].

<http://purl.access.gpo.gov/GPO/LPS3909> [current edition]

<http://purl.access.gpo.gov/GPO/LPS320> [archived editions]

Provides over 1,000 statistical tables based on reports of federal and state agencies, research centers, universities, private companies, and other organizations. The tables are arranged in six sections as follows: characteristics of the criminal justice systems (Sec. 1); public attitudes toward crime and criminal justice-related topics (Sec. 2); nature and distribution of known offenses (Sec. 3); characteristics and distribution of persons arrested (Sec. 4); judicial processing of defendants (Sec. 5); and persons under correctional supervision (Sec. 6).

Research Note: Editions are available online back to 1994. Not all tables contain state-level data. Some tables are adapted or constructed by the sourcebook staff. The 2003 edition was the last to be published in a tangible format (print or CD-ROM). It is now available online only in the form of a continuously updated website sponsored and managed by the Utilization of Criminal Justice Statistics Project, Hindelang Criminal Justice Statistics Project, Hindelang Criminal Justice Research Center, School of Criminal Justice, University at Albany.

General Statistical Compendia

004 *The Book of the States.* Lexington, Ky: Council of State Governments [annual, 1935–date].

Provides data on state prison populations; sentenced prisoners admitted and released from state and federal jurisdiction; state prison capacities; adults on parole and probation; and capital punishment.

Research Note: See also *Almanac of the 50 States: Comparative Data Profiles and Guide to Government Data.* Woodside, Calif.: Information Publications [annual, 1985–date].

005 *County and City Data Book: A Statistical Abstract Supplement.* Washington, D.C.: U.S. Census Bureau, U.S. Department of Commerce [irregular, 1949–date].

<http://purl.access.gpo.gov/GPO/LPS29932>

Provides data on violent and property index crimes at the state, county, and city levels.

Research Note: Datasets are available through the Inter-university Consortium for Political and Social Research (ICPSR), Institute for Social Research, University of Michigan. <http://www.icpsr.umich.edu/icpsrweb/ICPSR/series/00023>

006 *State and Metropolitan Area Data Book.* Washington, D.C.: U.S. Census Bureau, U.S. Department of Commerce [irregular, 1979–date].

<http://purl.access.gpo.gov/GPO/LPS2647>

Provides crime and corrections data at the state level only.

Research Note: Datasets are available through the Inter-university Consortium for Political and Social Research (ICPSR), Institute for Social Research, University of Michigan. <http://www.icpsr.umich.edu/icpsrweb/ICPSR/series/00134>

•007 *Statistical Abstract of the United States.* Washington, D.C.: U.S. Census Bureau, U.S. Department of Commerce [annual, 1878–date].

<http://purl.access.gpo.gov/GPO/LPS2878>

State-level statistics relating to criminal justice are located in the Law Enforcement, Courts, and Prisons section (Sec. 5). See also the Transportation section (Sec. 23) for data on driving under the influence and traffic fatalities; and the Health and Nutrition section (Sec. 3) for data on substance abuse.

008 *Texas Almanac.* Denton, Tex.: Texas State Historical Association; Distributed by Texas A&M University Press Consortium [biennial, 2000–date].

Provides state-level data for the most recent twenty years, and county-level data for the most recent reporting year, for violent and property index crimes. State-level summary statistics are provided for arson, family violence, hate crimes, and law enforcement death and injuries. County-level totals are provided for the number of law enforcement agencies and commissioned personnel.

Research Note: Previously published under the title *Texas Almanac and State Industrial Guide* (1857–1999).

009 *Texas Fact Book.* Austin: Legislative Budget Board [biennial, 1996–date].
<http://www.lbb.state.tx.us/>

Provides summary data and state rankings for selected crime and law enforcement categories; also, data on appropriations, federal funds, and personnel for state functional areas, including the judiciary and public safety/criminal justice.

Research Note: Editions are available online back to 2004.

010 *USA Counties*. Washington, D.C.: U.S. Census Bureau, U.S. Department of Commerce [annual, 1981-date].
<http://purl.access.gpo.gov/GPO/LPS22642>

Provides data on violent and property index crimes at the state and county levels.

Chapter 2

Crime, Criminals, and Juvenile Delinquency

Acquaintance Rape

011 Negrusz, Adam, Matthew Juhascik, and R. E. Gaensslen. *Estimate of the Incidence of Drug-Facilitated Sexual Assault in the U.S.* [Final Report]. Chicago: Department of Biopharmaceutical Sciences, College of Pharmacy, University of Illinois at Chicago, 2005. NCJ 212000

<http://www.ncjrs.gov/pdffiles1/nij/grants/212000.pdf>

Presents the results of toxicological analyses performed at four regional clinical facilities on subjects who alleged that they were victims of drug-facilitated sexual assault (DFSA). Two definitions of DFSA were used—one only included presumed surreptitious drugging, while the second included subjects whose voluntary drug use may been a contributing factor in the assault. The estimated prevalence of DFSA was then assessed. Demographic profiles, questionnaire responses, and laboratory results are reported for 144 subjects, including thirty-one at the Texas site (Scott & White Memorial Hospital, Temple).

Alcohol-Related Crimes

012 *Annual Report of Nonfinancial Data for Fiscal Year [year]*. Austin: Texas Alcoholic Beverage Commission [2001–date].

<http://www.tabc.state.tx.us/publications/index.asp>

Addendum C.3 reports data from the Field Operations Division on the number of criminal cases filed and criminal warnings issued by TABC enforcement agents and their disposition (when known). The number of still seizures is also reported.

012A Rand, Michael R., William J. Sabol, Michael Sinclair, and Howard N. Snyder. *Alcohol and Crime: Data from 2002 to 2008*. Washington, D.C.: Bureau of Justice Statistics, Office of Justice Programs, U.S. Department of Justice, 2010.

<http://bjs.ojp.usdoj.gov/index.cfm?ty=pbdetail&iid=2313>

Presents state-level data on the number and percentage of violent incidents known to law enforcement involving alcohol as reported in the 2007 National Incident-Based Reporting System (NIBRS) sample (Appendix Table 2).

Research Note: The Uniform Crime Reporting (UCR) Program provides statistics on persons arrested for liquor law violations, driving under the influence, and drunkenness (see entries 001–003). See entries 465–490 for statistics on fatalities resulting from driving/boating under the influence.

Arson

•013 *Fires in Texas: Annual Fire Statistics.* Austin: State Fire Marshal's Office, Texas Department of Insurance [1991–date].

<http://www.tdi.state.tx.us/fire/fmbrochures.html>

Provides data extracted from the Texas Fire Incident Reporting System (TEXFIRS) on "incendiary/suspicious" fires in the following categories: total, structure, residential, vehicle, and outside/other. Additional details are provided for dollar loss, civilian injuries/deaths, firefighter injuries/deaths, alarm time intervals (for structure), and heat source (for outside/other).

Research Note: Reports are available online back to 2000. See also entries 001–003.

Bank Robbery

•014 *Bank Crime Statistics (BCS): Federal Insured Financial Institutions.* Washington, D.C.: Federal Bureau of Investigation, U.S. Department of Justice [annual, 1992–date].

<http://purl.access.gpo.gov/GPO/LPS126896>

Reports data on bank robbery statute violations (robberies, burglaries, larcenies, and extortions), by regions, geographic divisions, states, and territories (Sec. III).

Research Note: Reports are available online back to 2003 (data is posted quarterly with annual cumulations).

Bombings

•015 *Explosives Incidents.* Washington, D.C.: U.S. Bomb Data Center, Bureau of Alcohol, Tobacco, Firearms and Explosives, U.S. Department of Justice [annual, 2004–date].

<http://www.atf.gov/>

The establishment of the U.S. Bomb Data Center (USBDC) was authorized by the Omnibus Consolidated Appropriations Act, 1997 (P.L. 104-208, 110 Stat. 3009). It serves as the sole official repository for data on domestic arson- and explosives-related incidents. State-level statistics are reported on explosives incidents (bombings, attempted bombings, incendiary bombings, and attempted incendiary bombings), and the total number killed and injured for each category.

Research Note: The Homeland Security Act of 2002 (P.L. 107-296, 116 Stat. 2135) transferred certain functions and responsibilities of the ATF from the Department of the Treasury to the Department of Justice. Access to the USBDC's Bomb Arson Tracking System (BATS) is restricted to authorized law enforcement personnel and fire department investigators. For earlier data, see the ATF's *Explosives Incidents Report* (1985–1993) and *Arson and Explosives Incidents Report* (1994–1997). See also the FBI's *Bomb Summary* (1973–1993) and *Bombing Incidents* (1994–1999). The latter were published as special issues of the FBI Bomb Data Center's *General Information Bulletin.*

Child Pornography

016 Finkelhor, David, and Richard Ormrod. *Child Pornography: Patterns from NIBRS* [Juvenile Justice Bulletin]. Washington, D.C.: Office of Juvenile Justice and Delinquency Prevention, Office of Justice Programs, U.S. Department of Justice, 2004. NCJ 204911

<http://purl.access.gpo.gov/GPO/LPS57686>

Contains pornography offenses with juvenile involvement reported to the FBI's National Incident-Based Reporting System (NIBRS), per 100,000 offenses of all types, by state, 1997–2000 (Table 5).

Child Sexual Abuse

017 Estes, Richard J., and Neil Alan Weiner. *The Commercial Sexual Exploitation of Children in the U. S., Canada and Mexico: Full Report (of the U.S. National Study).* Philadelphia, Pa.: Center for the Study of Youth Policy, School of Social Work, University of Pennsylvania, 2001 (rev. 2002). NCJ 218461

<http://www.sp2.upenn.edu/~restes/CSEC.htm>

Provides the number and type of commercial sexual exploitation of children (CSEC) incidents reported in 1999 by selected organizations in focus group states and cities (including Dallas, El Paso, and San Antonio) as follows: total of all types of CSEC; agency type; pornography subjects; involuntary pornography exposure; children at home—in prostitution to get luxuries; street children engaged in prostitution; children in sex rings run by local pimps; and children in sex rings run by national entities (Exhibit 4.2).

Research Note: Datasets are available through the National Archive of Criminal Justice Data, Inter-university Consortium for Political and Social Research (ICPSR), Institute for Social Research, University of Michigan.

<http://dx.doi.org/10.3886/ICPSR03366>

017A Small, Kevonne, William Adams, Colleen Owens, and Kevin Roland. *An Analysis of Federally Prosecuted CSEC Cases since the Passage of the Victims of Trafficking and Violence Prevention Act of 2000* [Final Report]. Washington, D.C.: Justice Policy Center, Urban Institute, 2008. NCJ 222023

<http://www.ncjrs.gov/pdffiles1/ojjdp/grants/222023.pdf>

Reports the results of a study, sponsored by the Office of Juvenile Justice and Delinquency Prevention, U.S. Department of Justice, which examined the effects of the passage of the Victims of Trafficking and Violence Protection Act of 2000 (P.L. 106-386,114 Stat. 1464) on the federal prosecution of commercial sexual exploitation of children (CSEC) cases. Maps provide statistics on defendants in cases filed in U.S. district court with a CSEC charge, 1998–2005 (Fig. 3-10); mean number of cases filed in U.S. district court with a CSEC charge, 1998–2005 (Fig. 3-11); change in number of defendants in cases filed in U.S. district court charged with a CSEC offense, 1998–2005 (Fig. 3-12). The cases involved sexual exploitation of children; child pornography; and child prostitution/sex trafficking.

Research Note: Texas is in the U.S. Court of Appeals Fifth Circuit and has four districts: Eastern, Northern, Southern, and Western. For a summary of this study, see William Adams, Colleen Owens, and Kevonne Small, "Effects of Federal Legislation on the Commercial Sexual Exploitation of Children," *Juvenile Justice Bulletin* (July 2010), 1–12. <http://www.ncjrs.gov/pdffiles1/ojjdp/228631.pdf>

Computer Related Crime

•018 *Internet Crime Report.* Washington, D.C.: National White Collar Crime Center; Federal Bureau of Investigation [annual, 2006–date].

<http://purl.access.gpo.gov/GPO/LPS80681>

The Internet Crime Complaint Center (IC3) was established in 2000 as a partnership between the National White Collar Crime Center (NW3C) and the Federal Bureau of Investigation. The center's annual report summarizes the complaints of Internet crime it received that merited further investigation by federal, state, and local law enforcement and regulatory agencies. Individual state sections provide statistics on complaint characteristics (top ten complaint categories, percentage of referrals by monetary loss, and amount lost by fraud type for individuals reporting monetary loss); perpetrator characteristics; and complainant characteristics.

Research Note: Earlier editions were published under varying titles (2001–2005).

Construction and Farm Equipment

019 *Equipment Theft Report.* Jersey City, N.J.: National Equipment Register; Des Plaines, Ill.: National Insurance Crime Bureau [annual, 2003–date].

<http://www.nerusa.com/>

Reports data on the top ten states, counties, and cities for construction and farm equipment theft and equipment recovery. Statistics from the equipment rental industry are included beginning with the 2005 edition.

Crime in Schools

•020 *Indicators of School Crime and Safety*. Washington, D.C.: National Center for Education Statistics, Institute of Education Sciences, U.S. Department of Education; Bureau of Justice Statistics, Office of Justice Programs, U.S. Department of Justice [annual, 1998-date].
<http://purl.access.gpo.gov/GPO/LPS9947>

This publication reports statistics from several sources, including the School Survey on Crime and Safety; School Crime Supplement to the National Crime Victimization Survey; School and Staffing Survey; and Youth Risk Behavior Surveillance. The Supplemental Tables contain state-level data on the percentage of students in grades nine through twelve who reported being threatened or injured with a weapon on school property during the previous twelve months; percentage and number of public school teachers who reported that they were threatened with injury by a student from school during the previous twelve months; percentage and number of public school teachers who reported that they were physically attacked by a student from school during the previous twelve months; percentage of students in grades nine through twelve who reported that drugs were made available to them on school property during the previous twelve months; percentage of students in grades nine through twelve who reported having been in a physical fight during the previous twelve months; percentage of students in grades nine through twelve who reported carrying a weapon at least one day during the previous thirty days; percentage of students in grades nine through twelve who reported using alcohol during the previous thirty days; and percentage of students in grades nine through twelve who reported using marijuana during the previous thirty days.

021 *The National School Safety Center's Report on School Associated Violent Deaths*. Westlake Village, Calif.: National School Safety Center [online only, 1992–date].
<http://www.schoolsafety.us/pubfiles/savd.pdf>

The National School Safety Center was established by presidential directive in 1984 as a partnership between the U.S. Department of Justice, the U.S. Department of Education, and Pepperdine University. This continuously updated report provides a chronological record (and cumulative state totals) for all homicides, suicides, and weapons-related violent deaths in the United States in which the fatal injury occurred: (1) on the property of a functioning public, private, or parochial elementary or secondary school, grades K-12 (including alternative schools); (2) on the way to or from regular sessions at such a school; (3) while person was attending or was on the way to or from an official school-sponsored event; or (4) as obvious direct result of school incidents, functions or activities, whether on or off school bus/vehicle or school property.

Crime Rates

022 *State of the Cities Data Systems.* Washington, D.C.: Policy Development and Research Information Service, U.S. Department of Housing and Urban Development [online only, 1992, 1997–date].

<http://socds.huduser.org/>

This database provides UCR violent and property index crime rates for metropolitan central/principal cities and metropolitan suburban places. Searches can be conducted by state or Metropolitan Statistical Area (utilizing the 1990 Metropolitan Standard), or by state or Core Based Statistical Area (utilizing the 2000 Metropolitan Standard).

Crime Trends

•023 *Large Local Agency Reported Crime by Locality.* Washington, D.C.: Federal Bureau of Investigation, U.S. Department of Justice, [annual, online only, 1985–date].

<http://www.ucrdatatool.gov/Search/Crime/Local/LocalCrimeLarge.cfm>

This website contains data extracted from the FBI's Uniform Crime Reporting (UCR) Program on violent and property index crimes reported by local agencies with population coverage of over 100,000 (approximately 3,900 agencies). Three types of tabular output are available: (1) single agency trends (one jurisdiction with multiple variables and years); (2) trends in one variable (with multiple jurisdictions and years); and (3) one year of data (with multiple jurisdictions and variables).

•024 *Local Level Reported Crime.* Washington, D.C.: Federal Bureau of Investigation, U.S. Department of Justice, [annual, online only, 1985–date].

<http://www.ucrdatatool.gov/Search/Crime/Local/LocalCrime.cfm>

This website contains data extracted from the FBI's Uniform Crime Reporting (UCR) Program on violent and property index crimes reported by local agencies with population coverage of over 10,000 (approximately 5,100 agencies). Three types of tabular output are available: (1) single agency trends (one jurisdiction with multiple variables and years); (2) trends in one variable (with multiple jurisdictions and years); and (3) one year of data (with multiple jurisdictions and variables).

•**025** *State and National Crime Estimates by Year(s).* Washington, D.C.: Federal Bureau of Investigation, U.S. Department of Justice, [annual, online only, 1960–date].

<http:/www.ucrdatatool.gov/Search/Crime/State/StateCrime.cfm>

This website contains data extracted from the FBI's Uniform Crime Reporting (UCR) Program on violent and property index crimes at the state and national levels. Three types of tabular output are available: (1) state-by-state and national trends (one jurisdiction with multiple variables and years); (2) trends in one variable (with multiple jurisdictions and years); and (3) one year of data (with multiple jurisdictions and variables).

Criminal Justice System Planning

026 *Biennial Report to the . . . Texas Legislature.* Austin: Criminal Justice Division, Office of the Governor [2001–date].

<http://www.governor.state.tx.us/cjd>

Reports data relating to the efforts of the Office of the Governor's Criminal Justice Division to develop coordinated strategic approaches and partnerships to prevent and deter crime; reduce criminal behavior; administer state and federal justice-related funds that support criminal justice, juvenile justice, and victim restoration efforts; and increase the accountability, efficiency, and effectiveness of the Texas criminal justice system.

027 *Biennial Report to the Governor and the . . . Texas Legislature.* Austin: Criminal Justice Policy Council [1999-2003].

<http://www.lbb.state.tx.us/PubSafety_CrimJustice/6_Links/Documents_Alpha_Links.htm>

This report, subtitled "The Big Picture in Adult and Juvenile Justice Issues," was legislatively mandated and required the CJPC to submit to the governor and legislature "a plan detailing the actions necessary to promote an effective and cohesive criminal justice system." It contains statistics on adult and juvenile crime and arrest rates.

Research Note: The council disbanded in 2003 after the governor's line-item veto of its legislative appropriation.

Disaster Related Crimes

028 *Hurricane Katrina Fraud Task Force: Report to the Attorney General.* Washington, D.C.: Office of the Attorney General, U.S Department of Justice, 2007.

<http://www.justice.gov/criminal/katrina/about/progress-reports.html>

The second year report contains a map showing statistics, by federal judicial district, on the total number of federal criminal prosecutions for fraud related to the Gulf Coast hurricane recovery efforts (i.e., hurricanes Katrina, Rita, and Wilma of 2005). The reports also provide brief summaries of selected cases.

Research Note: See also *Oversight of Gulf Coast Hurricane Recovery: A Semiannual Report to Congress*, issued by the Executive Council on Integrity and Efficiency, President's Council on Integrity and Efficiency.

<http://purl.access.gpo.gov/GPO/LPS77554>

029 Pullin, Mark. "Impact of Katrina Evacuees Upon Law Enforcement." *TELEMASP Bulletin* [Texas Law Enforcement Management and Administrative Statistics Program] 13, no. 5 (September/October 2006): 1–8.

<http://www.lemitonline.org/telemasp/>

Presents data from a survey of fifty-two Texas law enforcement agencies on their law-enforcement-related problems with Hurricane Katrina evacuees.

Drug Law Offenses

030 *Domestic Cannabis Cultivation Assessment.* Johnstown, Pa.: National Drug Intelligence Center, U.S. Department of Justice [annual, 2007-date].

<http://purl.access.gpo.gov/GPO/LPS113898>

Provides state-level data from the Drug Enforcement Administration's Domestic Cannabis Eradication/Suppression Program on the number of outdoor and indoor marijuana plant seizures.

Research Note: See also the Office of National Drug Control Policy's *Marijuana Sourcebook.*

<http://www.ncjrs.gov/ondcppubs/publications/pdf/Marijuana_2008.pdf>

•031 *Drug Market Analyses.* Johnstown, Pa.: National Drug Intelligence Center, U.S. Department of Justice [annual, 2007–date].

<http://www.usdoj.gov/ndic/topics/dmas.htm>

These specialized reports provide data on all aspects of illicit drug production and trafficking, including seizures, gang activity, substance abuse trends, treatment admissions, drug related deaths, and money laundering. Data is reported for High Intensity Drug Trafficking Areas (HIDTAs), which include North Texas, South Texas, West Texas, and Houston. The reports cover cocaine, heroin, marijuana, methamphetamine, MDMA, PCP, and controlled prescription drugs.

•032 *Federal Justice Statistics—Statistical Tables*. Washington, D.C.: Bureau of Justice Statistics, Office of Justice Programs, U.S. Department of Justice [annual, online only, 2005–date].

<http://purl.access.gpo.gov/GPO/LPS113898>

Reports fiscal year statistics from the Federal Justice Statistics Program (FJSP) and includes a United States map (along with an accompanying spreadsheet) that provides data on suspects arrested by the Drug Enforcement Administration, by state (Map 1.1).

Research Note: This publication series supersedes *Compendium of Federal Justice Statistics* (1984–2004). Datasets are available through the Inter-university Consortium for Political and Social Research (ICPSR), Institute for Social Research, University of Michigan. <http://www.icpsr.umich.edu/icpsrweb/ICPSR/series/00073>

•033 *National Drug Threat Assessment*. Johnstown, Pa.: National Drug Intelligence Center, U.S. Department of Justice [annual, 2004-date].

<http://purl.access.gpo.gov/GPO/LPS78669>

The Appendixes contain data on trends in the availability, production and cultivation, transportation, and distribution of illicit drugs gathered from over 3,000 state and local law enforcement agencies that participate in the annual NDIC National Drug Threat Survey and also give interviews to NDIC Field Program Specialists. Profiles of each Organized Crime Drug Enforcement Task Force (OCDETF) region are provided along with selected statistics on drug availability and use. Drugs covered include cocaine, heroin, marijuana, MDMA, methamphetamine, and controlled prescription drugs.

Research Note: Texas is in the Southwest OCDETF region.

034 *National Methamphetamine Threat Assessment*. Johnstown, Pa.: National Drug Intelligence Center, U.S. Department of Justice [annual, 2005–date].

<http://purl.access.gpo.gov/GPO/LPS78669>

Provides data on trends in methamphetamine availability, demand, clandestine laboratories, trafficking, seizures, positive workplace drug test results, and treatment admissions, by Organized Crime Drug Enforcement Task Force (OCDETF) region. The data is gathered from over 3,000 state and local law enforcement agencies that participate in the annual NDIC National Drug Threat Survey and also give interviews to NDIC Field Program Specialists.

Research Note: Texas is in the Southwest OCDETF region.

035 *National Prescription Drug Threat Assessment.* Johnstown, Penn.: National Drug Intelligence Center, U.S. Department of Justice [annual, 2009–date].

<http://purl.access.gpo.gov/GPO/LPS78669>

Provides data on the domestic diversion of controlled prescription drugs and the current nonmedical use of prescription-type psychotherapeutic drugs (opioid pain relievers, tranquilizers, sedatives, and stimulants). Table B1 reports city/county-level data on diverted controlled prescription drug prices reported by federal, state, and local law enforcement agencies, by drug (high and low prices by quantity/weight). Maps provide additional data by Organized Crime Drug Enforcement Task Force (OCDETF) region.

Research Note: Texas is in the Southwest OCDETF region.

•036 *State & Local Resources.* Washington, D.C.: Drug Policy Information Clearinghouse, Office of National Drug Control Policy, Executive Office of the President [online only].

<http://www.whitehousedrugpolicy.gov/statelocal/index.html>

This website features an interactive map that links to regularly updated Profiles of Drug Indicators for states and selected cities (including Austin, Dallas, El Paso, Houston, and San Antonio). These provide statistics on drug abuse, narcotics trafficking and seizures, gang activity, correctional populations, drug overdoses, substance abuse treatment, and related topics.

Federal Law Violations

•037 *Federal Justice Statistics—Statistical Tables.* Washington, D.C.: Bureau of Justice Statistics, Office of Justice Programs, U.S. Department of Justice [annual, 2005–date].

<http://purl.access.gpo.gov/GPO/LPS113898>

Reports fiscal year statistics from the Federal Justice Statistics Program (FJSP), drawing on source files of the Drug Enforcement Administration, U.S. Marshals Service, Executive Office for U.S. Attorneys, Administrative Office of the U.S. Courts, U.S. Sentencing Commission, and Federal Bureau of Prisons. It includes United States maps (along with accompanying spreadsheets) that provide data on suspects arrested by the Drug Enforcement Administration, by state (Map 1.1); suspects referred to U.S. attorneys, by federal judicial district (Map 2.1); and defendants under federal supervision, by federal judicial district (Map 7.1).

Research Note: This publication series supersedes *Compendium of Federal Justice Statistics* (1984–2004). Texas is in the U.S. Court of Appeals Fifth Circuit and has four districts: Eastern, Northern, Southern, and Western. Datasets are available through the Inter-university Consortium for Political and Social Research (ICPSR), Institute for Social Research, University of Michigan. <http://www.icpsr.umich.edu/icpsrweb/ICPSR/series/00073>

Financial Institutions

•**038** *Financial Institution Fraud and Failure Report.* Washington, D.C.: Federal Bureau of Investigation, U.S. Department of Justice [online only, 2000–date].

<http://purl.access.gpo.gov/GPO/LPS25141>

Reports fiscal year data from FBI field offices on financial institution failure investigations (banks, savings and loans, and credit unions); financial institution fraud cases by institution type and major case; and seizures and forfeitures. Also, state-level data on financial institutions as follows: fraud convictions and pretrial diversions, fraud indictments/informations, fraud recoveries, fraud restitutions, and fraud fines.

Firearms

039 *The Bureau of Alcohol, Tobacco, Firearms and Explosives' Investigative Operations at Gun Shows.* [Washington, D.C.]: Evaluation and Inspections Division, Office of the Inspector General, U.S. Department of Justice, 2007. I-2007-007

<http://www.usdoj.gov/oig/reports/ATF/e0707/final.pdf>

Reports the results of the general investigative operations at gun shows aimed at reducing regional and cross-border firearms trafficking between the United States and Mexico, including investigations conducted by the ATF's Houston Field Division.

•**040** *Conviction Rates for Concealed Handgun License Holders.* Austin: Concealed Handgun Licensing Bureau, Regulatory Licensing Service, Texas Department of Public Safety [annual, online only, 1996–date].

<http://www.txdps.state.tx.us/administration/crime_records/chl/convrates. htm>

Statistics on conviction rates are listed alphabetically by offense (total convictions in Texas, convictions of concealed handgun license holders, and percentage of total).

041 *Federal Firearms Cases, FY[year].* St. Louis, Mo.: Regional Justice Information Service [annual, 2007–date].

<http://www.ncjrs.gov/App/Publications/alphaList.aspx?alpha=F>

Provides fiscal year data on defendants in cases filed and concluded in U.S. district court with 18 U.S.C. § 922G (2007) as most serious charge.

Research Note: Texas is in the U.S. Court of Appeals Fifth Circuit and has four districts: Eastern, Northern, Southern, and Western. 18 U.S.C. § 922G (2007) pertains to unlawful acts stipulated by the Gun Control Act of 1968, specifically the provision making it unlawful for a prohibited person to ship, transport, possess, or receive a firearm.

042 *Gun Control: Opportunities to Close Loopholes in the National Instant Criminal Background Check System* [Report to the Ranking Member, Committee on the Judiciary, House of Representatives]. Washington, D.C.: U.S. Government Accountability Office, 2002. GAO-02-720

<http://purl.access.gpo.gov/GPO/LPS34735>

Provides Texas data from a survey on crimes committed by persons after their gun ownership rights were restored by pardon between January 1, 1992, and December 31, 2001 (Table 1), and reasons for concealed carry permit revocations between January 1, 1996, and October 25, 2001 (Table 2).

043 *Gun Crime Trace Reports: National Reports* [Youth Crime Gun Interdiction Initiative (YCGII)]. Washington, D.C.: Bureau of Alcohol, Tobacco and Firearms, U.S. Department of the Treasury [annual, online only, 1997–2000].

<http://www.atf.gov/publications/historical/>

The Youth Crime Gun Interdiction Initiative (YCGII) is a project developed by the ATF in collaboration with police chiefs, local prosecutors, and U.S. attorneys, to monitor illegal firearms trafficking to juveniles. The 2000 annual report includes detailed information from forty-seven cities including Austin, Dallas, Houston, and San Antonio. Data in these reports includes crime gun trace requests (age of possessor and relationship to purchaser; crime type by age of possessor; and type of firearm by age of possessor); most frequent crime gun trace requests (manufacturer, caliber, and type by age of possessor); time-to-crime for most frequently traced crime guns by manufacturer, caliber, and type; most frequent source states for crime guns traced to a firearms dealer; dealer trace frequency and distance to recovery; crime guns with obliterated serial numbers; and results of crime gun traces (age of possessor and detailed analyses).

Research Note: Provisions of the Science, State, Justice, Commerce, and Related Agencies Appropriations Act, 2006 (P.L. 109-108,119 Stat. 2290) prohibit future release of data from the Firearms Trace System database ". . . to anyone other than a Federal, State, or local law enforcement agency or a prosecutor solely in connection with and for use in a bona fide criminal investigation or prosecution and then only such information as pertains to the geographic jurisdiction of the law enforcement agency requesting the disclosure . . ."

Gangs

044 *Gangs in Texas 2001: An Overview.* Austin: Attorney General of Texas [2002].
<http://www.oag.state.tx.us/AG_Publications/pdfs/2001gangrept.pdf>

Reports the results of a survey of 429 Texas police chiefs, school district police departments, sheriffs, district attorneys, criminal district attorneys, and county attorneys. Data includes statistics on the composition, criminal activities, and influence of gangs; intelligence gathering and information sharing; enforcement, intervention, and prevention strategies; and the effectiveness of curfews.

Research Note: Earlier editions are available.

•045 *National Gang Threat Assessment.* Washington, D.C.: National Gang Intelligence Center; Johnstown, Pa.: National Drug Intelligence Center [biennial, 2005–date].
<http://purl.access.gpo.gov/GPO/LPS78669>

This report represents a collaboration between the National Gang Intelligence Center (NGIC) and the National Drug Intelligence Center (NDIC). It contains maps showing the Southwest Region gang membership by county; gang membership per capita, by state; and gang members per law enforcement officer, by state.

Research Note: No report for 2007 was published.

Hate Crimes

046 *Active U.S. Hate Groups.* Montgomery, Ala.: Intelligence Project, Southern Poverty Law Center [online only].
<http://www.splcenter.org/get-informed/hate-map>

An interactive United States map enables users to access information and profiles of active hate groups by state and city. The categories of hate groups monitored include Ku Klux Klan, neo-Nazi, white nationalist, racist skinhead, Christian Identity, neo-Confederate, black separatist, and general hate. A chronology of apparent hate crimes and hate group activities, by state and city, is provided in the "For the Record" section (2003–date). This website continuously updates the annual hate group list published in the Spring issue of the SPLC's quarterly periodical *Intelligence Report*, which also contains lists of hate group websites, patriot groups, and patriot group websites, by state and city.

Research Note: Some groups have objected that their inclusion on this list is unwarranted.

047 *Audit of Anti-Semitic Incidents.* New York: Anti-Defamation League [annual, online only, 1998–date].

<http://www.adl.org/main_Anti_Semitism_Domestic/default.htm>

Provides state-level data on reported anti-Semitic incidents (harassment and vandalism).

Research Note: Audits are posted in the "Trends in Anti-Semitism" section. Data is compiled from official crime statistics as well as information provided to and evaluated by the ADL's regional offices by victims, law enforcement officers, and community leaders.

•048 *Hate Crime Statistics* [Uniform Crime Reporting Program]. Washington, D.C.: Federal Bureau of Investigation. U.S. Department of Justice [annual, 1990–date].

<http://purl.access.gpo.gov/GPO/LPS9179>

The Hate Crime Statistics Act of 1990 (P.L. 101-275, 104 Stat. 140) mandated that the attorney general collect statistics on hate crime. The task of collecting, managing, and disseminating this data was assigned to the FBI's Uniform Crime Reporting (UCR) Program. This report provides aggregate state totals and individual agency data for bias-motivated incidents, which are defined as criminal offenses that are motivated, in whole or in part, by the offender's bias against a race, religion, sexual orientation, ethnicity/national origin, or disability, and are committed against persons, property, or society. Annual state-level statistics are reported for total offenses, crimes against persons, crimes against property, and crimes against society. Quarterly statistics are reported for individual agencies at the following levels: cities, universities and colleges, metropolitan counties, nonmetropolitan counties, other agencies (e.g., school districts), and agencies reporting zero data.

Research Note: Reports are available online back to 1995. Print editions were published under slightly varying titles. Beginning with the 2004 edition, *Hate Crime Statistics* is only available through the FBI's website in electronic format. Printable data tables are available for downloading. Summary data is reported in *Uniform Crime Reports for the United* States (1996–1997) and *Crime in the United States: Uniform Crime Reports* (1998–date) (see entry 002). Datasets are available through the National Archive of Criminal Justice Data, Inter-university Consortium for Political and Social Research (ICPSR), Institute for Social Research, University of Michigan. <http://www.icpsr.umich.edu/NACJD/ucr.html#desc_al>

049 *Hate Violence Against Lesbian, Gay, Bisexual and Transgender People in the United States.* New York: National Coalition of Anti-Violence Programs [annual, 1998–date].

<http://www.ncavp.org/publications/NationalPubs.aspx>

Contains data provided by the Montrose Counseling Center on violence against lesbian, gay, bisexual, and transgender (LGBT) individuals in Houston, including total number of victims, demographics of victims, victim medical/injury information, details of crimes and offenses, total number of offenders, demographics of offenders, relationship of offenders to victims, police response information, bias classification, and immigration and disability status of victims.

Research Note: Published under varying titles.

050 Kercher, Glen, Claire Nolasco, and Ling Wu. *Hate Crimes.* Huntsville: Crime Victims' Institute, Criminal Justice Center, Sam Houston State University, 2008.

<http://www.crimevictimsinstitute.org/pubs.html>

Contains graphs showing 1999–2006 statistics (nationally and for six states, including Texas) for the following: percentage of hate crimes against persons (Figure 1); percentage of hate motivated aggravated assault (Figure 2); percentage of hate motivated simple assault (Figure 3); percentage of bias motivated intimidation (Figure 4); and percentage of hate motivated vandalism (Figure 5).

Homeless Persons

051 *Hate, Violence and Death on Main Street USA: A Report on Hate Crimes and Violence Against People Experiencing Homelessness.* Washington, D.C.; National Coalition for the Homeless [annual, 1999–date].

<http://www.nationalhomeless.org/publications/#reports>

Provides a list of states and cities/counties where crimes against homeless persons occurred during the reporting year, including the number of incidents along with an indication as to whether they were lethal or non-lethal. Brief case descriptions are listed by category (deaths, non-lethal rape/sexual assault, non-lethal setting on fire, non-lethal beatings, non-lethal shootings, and non-lethal police harassment/brutality). Sources are documented in Appendix A.

Homicide

•052 *CDC WONDER* [Wide-ranging Online Data for Epidemiologic Research]. Atlanta, Ga.: Centers for Disease Control and Prevention, U.S. Department of Health and Human Services [online only, 1979–date].

<http://purl.access.gpo.gov/GPO/LPS18322>

This database contains a Compressed Mortality File that allows user generated state- or county-level reports for number of deaths, crude death rates, or age-adjusted death rates utilizing the *International Classification of Diseases—Tenth Revision (ICD-10)*. Output can be customized utilizing the following variables: underlying cause of death (e.g., assault, intentional self-harm, or legal intervention and operations of war); age group; gender; race; Hispanic origin; urbanization; and year.

Research Note: Data prior to 1999 is presented in tables utilizing the *International Classification of Diseases—Ninth Revision (ICD-9).*

•**053** "Deaths: Final Data for [year]." *National Vital Statistics Reports.* Hyattsville, Md.: National Center for Health Statistics, Centers for Disease Control and Prevention, U.S. Department of Health and Human Services [annual, 1997–date].

<http://purl.access.gpo.gov/GPO/LPS2365>

One report is published annually under this title (authors and cover dates vary). It presents state-level data for number of deaths, death rates, and age-adjusted death rates for major causes of death utilizing the *International Classification of Diseases—Tenth Revision (ICD-10).* Major causes of death listed include assault (homicide), intentional self-harm (suicide), and injury by firearms.

Research Note: This series supersedes *Monthly Vital Statistics Reports (MVSR).*

•**054** *Easy Access to the FBI's Supplementary Homicide Reports.* Washington, D.C.: Office of Juvenile Justice and Delinquency Prevention, Office of Justice Programs, U.S. Department of Justice [online only, 1980–date].

<http://ojjdp.ncjrs.org/ojstatbb/ezashr/>

Provides access to data from the FBI's Supplementary Homicide Reports (SHR). The National Center for Juvenile Justice modifies the contents of the FBI files by deleting incompatible data and recoding values into more general categories; in addition, they construct and add weights to the records so that weighted analyses yield national estimates. State-level tables can be constructed using the following variables: year of incident; characteristics of victim (age, sex, and race); offender-victim relationship; weapon used; number of offenders; and characteristics of oldest offender (age, sex, and race).

Research Note: This website is sponsored by the Office of Juvenile Justice and Delinquency Prevention, Office of Justice Programs, U.S. Department of Justice, and is maintained by the National Center for Juvenile Justice, which is the research division of the National Council of Juvenile and Family Court Judges. Datasets are available through the National Archive of Criminal Justice Data, Inter-university Consortium for Political and Social Research, Institute for Social Research, University of Michigan.

<http://www.icpsr.umich.edu/NACJD/ucr.html#desc_al>

055 Finkelhor, David, and Richard Ormrod. *Homicides of Children and Youth* [Juvenile Justice Bulletin]. Washington, D.C.: Office of Juvenile Justice and Delinquency Prevention, Office of Justice Programs, U.S. Department of Justice, 2001. NCJ 187239

<http://purl.access.gpo.gov/GPO/LPS16240>

Reports data for 1996–1997 on homicides of juveniles (average state rates per 100,000 juveniles, ages zero to seventeen), as calculated by the Crimes against Children Research Center (Table 1).

•**056** *Local Level Homicide Trends and Characteristics.* Washington, D.C.: Bureau of Justice Statistics, Office of Justice Programs, U.S. Department of Justice [annual, online only, 1985–date].

<http://bjs.ojp.usdoj.gov/index.cfm?ty=daa>

This website provides statistics from two FBI sources: Uniform Crime Reports (UCR) and Supplementary Homicide Reports (SHR). Three types of tabular output are available: (1) single agency trends (one jurisdiction with multiple variables and years); (2) trends in one variable (with multiple jurisdictions and years); and (3) one year of data (with multiple jurisdictions and variables). Variables include number of homicide victims, age of victim (in age groups), race of victim, gender of victim, race and gender of victim, and weapon used. Data is available from Texas agencies that each have a population coverage of more than 250,000 and also provide both UCR and SHR.

057 Patel, Reshma N., L. J. David Wallace, and Len Paulozzi. *Atlas of Injury Mortality Among American Indian and Alaska Native Children and Youth, 1989–1998.* [Atlanta, Ga.]: National Center for Injury Prevention and Control, Centers for Disease Control and Prevention, U.S. Department of Health and Human Services, 2005.

<http://purl.access.gpo.gov/GPO/LPS62935>

Presents injury mortality data from 1989 through 1998 for Native American children and youth from birth to nineteen years of age who resided in the twelve Indian Health Service (IHS) Areas. The following eight major causes of injury-related death are covered: motor vehicle crashes, pedestrian-related, firearm-related, suicide, homicide, drowning, fire, and suffocation. Composite maps of the IHS area rates and individual maps are included for each category, which allow for rate comparisons among areas and with national rates for all races. Trends in death rates by race, age-specific rates, and subtype distributions of cause are also provided for each of the eight causes of injury.

Research Note: American Indians in Texas are under the jurisdiction of three IHS Areas: Albuquerque (Ysleta Del Sur Reservation); Oklahoma City (Kickapoo Reservation); and Nashville (Alabama-Coushatta Reservation). An earlier edition is available that covers all age groups.

058 Snyder, Howard N., and Monica H. Swahn. "Juvenile Suicides, 1981–1998." *Youth Violence Research Bulletin* (March 2004): 1–8. NCJ 196978

<http://purl.access.gpo.gov/GPO/LPS46387>

Reports state-level data for the juvenile suicide rate and the juvenile suicide/homicide ratio, 1981–1998.

Research Note: The report defines "juveniles" as youth ages seven to seventeen. The authors note that "The reasons for variations in the numbers of juvenile suicides and homicides among states are beyond the scope of this Bulletin. States with the largest suicide/homicide ratios tend to have low homicide rates."

•059 *State Level Homicide Trends and Characteristics*. Washington, D.C.: Bureau of Justice Statistics, Office of Justice Programs, U.S. Department of Justice [annual, online only, 1976–date].

<http://bjs.ojp.usdoj.gov/index.cfm?ty=daa>

This website provides statistics from two FBI sources: Uniform Crime Reports (UCR) and Supplementary Homicide Reports (SHR). Three types of tabular output are available: (1) state-by-state trends (one jurisdiction with multiple variables and years); (2) trends in one variable (with multiple jurisdictions and years); and (3) one year of data (with multiple jurisdictions and variables). Variables include number of homicide victims, age of victim (in age groups), race of victim, gender of victim, race and gender of victim, and weapon used.

060 "Surveillance for Homicide Among Intimate Partners—United States, 1981–1998" [Surveillance Summaries]. *Morbidity and Mortality Weekly Report,* 50, no. SS-3 (October 12, 2001), 1–[18].

<http://www.cdc.gov/mmwr/PDF/ss/ss5003.pdf>

Presents estimated age-adjusted rates of intimate partner homicide/100,000 population among white females by state—United States, 1981–1998 (Fig. 3); and estimated age-adjusted rates of intimate partner homicide/100,000 population among black females by state—United States, 1981–1998 (Fig. 4).

•061 *Texas Health Data: Death Data*. Austin: Center for Health Statistics, Texas Department of State Health Services [annual, online only, 1990–date].

<http://soupfin.tdh.state.tx.us/deathdoc.htm>

Annual death data collected from the Texas Certificate of Death is coded and presented in tables utilizing the *International Classification of Diseases— Tenth Revision (ICD-10)*. Query output can be customized to display optional variables (race/ethnicity, gender, and age group); focus at the county level; or range over multiple years. Causes of death reported include assault (homicide), legal intervention, and intentional self-harm (suicide).

Research Note: Death data prior to 1999 is presented in tables utilizing the *International Classification of Diseases—Ninth Revision (ICD-9)*.

062 *Texas Selected Health Facts.* Austin: Center for Health Statistics, Texas Department of State Health Services [annual, online only, 2000–date].

<http://www.dshs.state.tx.us/chs/cfs/>

Provides statistics on homicide and suicide at the state, public health region, county levels. Beginning with 2006 data, an array of other geographical limiters are also available, including Metropolitan Statistical Areas (MSAs).

•**063** *WISQARS*™ [Web-based Injury Statistics Query and Reporting System]. Atlanta, Ga.: National Center for Injury Prevention and Control, Centers for Disease Control and Prevention, U.S. Department of Health and Human Services [online only, 1981–date].

<http://www.cdc.gov/injury/wisqars/index.html>

This database allows users to generate reports on injury mortality utilizing the *International Classification of Diseases—Tenth Revision (ICD-10).* Output can be customized using the following variables: intent or manner of the injury (e.g., violence-related—homicide, legal intervention, or suicide), cause or mechanism of the injury, census region or state, race, Hispanic origin, sex, age group, and year(s). Injury rates can be compared using the age-adjusting option. Reports can also be generated utilizing the same variables for the leading cause of death for all causes (with drill down to ICD codes) or for violence-related injuries only (1994–date).

Research Note: Data prior to 1999 is presented in tables utilizing the *International Classification of Diseases—Ninth Revision (ICD-9).*

Human Trafficking

064 Kyckelhahn, Tracey, Allen J. Beck, and Thomas H. Cohen. *Characteristics of Suspected Human Trafficking Incidents, 2007–08* [Special Report]. Washington, D.C.: Bureau of Justice Statistics, Office of Justice Programs, U.S. Department of Justice, 2009. NCJ 224526

<http://bjs.ojp.usdoj.gov/index.cfm?ty=pbdetail&iid=550>

This report fulfills the requirements of the Trafficking Victims Protection Reauthorization Act of 2005 (P.L. 109-164, 119 Stat. 3558), which mandates biennial reporting on human trafficking using available data from state and local authorities. The report contains a map showing the number (by range) of human trafficking incidents reported by task force locations, which include four in Texas.

Identity Theft

•**065** *Identity Theft Consumer Complaint Data: Texas.* Washington, D.C.: Identity Theft Data Clearinghouse, Federal Trade Commission [annual, on-line only, 2002–date].
<http://www.ftc.gov/bcp/edu/microsites/idtheft/reference-desk/state-data. html>

This database presents statistics on how victims' information is misused; complaints by consumer age; and a ranking of identity theft complaints by state, per 100,000 population. Types of fraud reported include credit card, government documents or benefits, phone or utilities, employment-related, bank, and loan.

Research Note: Published under slightly varying titles.

066 Morris, Robert, Glen Kercher, and Matthew Johnson. *Identity Theft: A Research Report.* Huntsville: Crime Victims' Institute, Criminal Justice Center, Sam Houston State University [undated].
<http://www.crimevictimsinstitute.org/pubs.html>

Reports the results of two 2005 identity theft surveys: (1) the Identity Theft Survey (ITS), a mail survey of a random sample of 4,500 Texas residents, and (2) the annual Crime Victims' Institute's Crime Victimization Survey (CVS), which utilized an Internet computer assisted telephone interviewing system (iCATI) to conduct interviews with 751 Texas residents. The data reported includes demographic characteristics of identity theft victims; income of identity theft victims compared to other crime victims; and method of identity theft discovery.

Immigration Offenses

•**067** *Estimates of the Unauthorized Immigrant Population Residing in the United States: January [year]* [Population Estimates]. Washington, D.C.: Policy Directorate, Office of Immigration Statistics, U.S. Department of Homeland Security [annual, 2005–date].
<http://www.dhs.gov/files/statistics/publications/>

Contains data for the top ten states of residence of the unauthorized immigrant population in the United States for January 2000 and January of the reporting year (estimated population, percentage of total, percentage change, and average annual change).

Research Note: For earlier data see *Estimates of the Unauthorized Immigrant Population Residing in the United States: 1990 to 2000.* <http://www.dhs.gov/files/statistics/publications/archive.shtm>

•**068** *Immigration Enforcement Actions* [Annual Report]. Washington, D.C.: Office of Immigration Statistics, U.S. Department of Homeland Security [online only, 2004–date].
<http://www.dhs.gov/ximgtn/statistics/publications/index.shtm>

Contains data on the top Southwest border sectors for alien apprehensions by the Border Patrol as reported by the Enforcement Case Tracking System (ENFORCE).

Research Note: The individual titles in the *Annual Report* series have now replaced the separate chapters that appeared in earlier editions of the *Yearbook of Immigration Statistics* (see entry 071).

069 Passel, Jeffrey. *Unauthorized Migrants in the United States: Estimates, Methods, and Characteristics* [OECD Social, Employment and Migration Working Papers]. Paris, France: Directorate for Employment, Labour and Social Affairs, Organisation for Economic Co-operation and Development, 2007.
<http://www.oecd.org/dataoecd/41/25/39264671.pdf>

Presents adjusted residual estimates of the unauthorized foreign-born population, by state of residence (Table 2), which are based on March 2006 *Current Population Survey* (CPS) and the *1990 Census of Population and Housing.*

070 Passel, Jeffrey S., and D'Vera Cohn. *A Portrait of Unauthorized Immigrants in the United States.* Washington, D.C.: Pew Hispanic Center, Pew Research Center, 2009.
<http://pewhispanic.org/reports/report.php?ReportID=107>

Provides data on states with the largest unauthorized immigrant populations, 2008 (Table 1); states with the largest share of unauthorized immigrants in the labor force, 2008 (Table 2); estimated unauthorized immigrant population and range of estimates by state, 2008 (Table 3); estimated unauthorized immigrant population by state, 2008, 2005, 2000, and 1990 (Table B1); and number and share of unauthorized immigrants for labor force and total population by state, 2008 (Table B2). The report also contains maps showing state-level 2008 statistics (by range) for estimated unauthorized immigrant population (Map 1); share of K–12 students with at least one unauthorized immigrant parent (Map 2); unauthorized immigrant workers as share of labor force (Map 3); share of Mexicans among unauthorized immigrants (Map 4); unauthorized immigrant share of population (Map A1); and unauthorized immigrants as share of foreign born (Map A2).

Research Note: Earlier editions are available. See also the PHC's interactive map, *Unauthorized Immigrants in the U.S.* <http://pewhispanic.org/unauthorized-immigration/>

•**071** *Yearbook of Immigration Statistics.* Washington, D.C.: Office of Immigration Statistics, U.S. Department of Homeland Security [2002–date].
<http://purl.access.gpo.gov/GPO/LPS40400>

The Enforcement section provides statistics (for the current and previous nine fiscal years) on deportable aliens located by program and Border Patrol Sector and Investigations Special Agent in Charge (SAC) jurisdiction.

Research Note: Online tables in the Enforcement section are added, reviewed, and revised online throughout the reporting year (date of the last revision is noted). Previously published under the title *Statistical Yearbook of the Immigration and Naturalization Service* (1978–2001).

Juvenile Delinquency

•**072** Snyder, Howard N. *Juvenile Arrests* [Juvenile Justice Bulletin]. Washington, D.C.: Office of Juvenile Justice and Delinquency Prevention, Office of Justice Programs, U.S. Department of Justice [annual, 1995–date].
<http://purl.access.gpo.gov/GPO/LPS3190>

This report summarizes and analyzes national and state juvenile UCR arrest data, including reporting coverage, violent index offenses, property index offenses, drug abuse, and weapons law violations.

•**073** Snyder, Howard N., and Melissa Sickmund. *Juvenile Offenders and Victims: 2006 National Report.* Washington, D.C.: Office of Juvenile Justice and Delinquency Prevention, Office of Justice Programs, U.S. Department of Justice, 2006. NCJ 212906
<http://www.ojjdp.ncjrs.gov/ojstatbb/nr2006/index.html>

Chapter 1 provides juvenile population characteristics as follows: juvenile population demographics; juveniles in poverty; living arrangement of juveniles; births to teens; and school dropouts. Chapter 3 provides data on juvenile offenders as follows: self-reports vs. official data, homicides by juveniles, juvenile homicide offender characteristics, juvenile offending behavior demographics, offending into the adult years, juvenile offending behavior and associated factors, school crime, weapons use, drug and alcohol use, drug and alcohol use trends, co-occurrence of substance use behaviors, gangs, and time-of-day analysis of juvenile offending. Chapter 5 provides data on gender, age, and racial variations in juvenile arrests; juvenile proportion of arrests; juvenile arrest trends (ten-year, female juveniles, young juveniles); violent index offenses; property index offenses; simple assault; vandalism; weapons law violations; drug abuse violations; juvenile crime vs. adult crime; clearance statistics; violent crime arrest rates (by state and county); property crime arrest rates (by state and county); and police disposition of juvenile arrests.

Research Note: Earlier editions are available. Not all subsections contain state-level data. This report incorporates data from some earlier specialized OJJDP reports individually authored by Sickmund and Snyder that are not otherwise included in this book.

074 Snyder, Howard N. *Law Enforcement and Juvenile Crime* [Juvenile Offenders and Victims: National Report Series Bulletin]. Washington, D.C.: Office of Juvenile Justice and Delinquency Prevention, Office of Justice Programs, U.S. Department of Justice, 2001. NCJ 191031

<http://purl.access.gpo.gov/GPO/LPS40438>

Provides state-level 1999 data for arrests per 100,000 juveniles, ages ten to seventeen, for violent index offenses and property index offenses.

•075 *Statistical Briefing Book.* Washington, D.C.: Office of Juvenile Justice and Delinquency Prevention, Office of Justice Programs, U.S. Department of Justice [online only, 1993–date].

<http://purl.access.gpo.gov/GPO/LPS73143>

This website provides access to a wide array of publications, data analysis tools, and national datasets, covering the following topics: juvenile population characteristics, juveniles as victims, juveniles as offenders, juvenile justice system structure and process;,law enforcement and juvenile crime, juveniles in court, juveniles on probation, juveniles in corrections, and juvenile reentry and aftercare.

•076 "Youth Risk Behavior Surveillance—United States." [Surveillance Summaries]. *Morbidity and Mortality Weekly Report* (*MMWR*) [biennial, 1993–date].

<http://www.cdc.gov/mmwr/mmwr_ss/ss_cvol.html>

One report is published biennially under this title (authors and cover dates vary). It provides survey results (total, male, and female) by state and selected local areas, for the following categories: percentage of high school students who carried a weapon or a gun; percentage of high school students who were in a physical fight or who were injured in a physical fight; and percentage of high school students who carried a weapon on school property or were threatened or injured with a weapon on school property.

Research Note: The survey is conducted in odd-numbered years and the report is published the following year. Online access to current and past editions is also available on the website of the Division of Adolescent and School Health, National Center for Chronic Disease Prevention and Health Promotion, Centers for Disease Control and Prevention, U.S. Department of Health and Human Services. <http://www.cdc.gov/healthyyouth/yrbs/index.htm>

Land Sale Fraud

•077 *Mortgage Fraud Report: Year in Review*. Washington, D.C.: Federal Bureau of Investigation, U.S. Department of Justice [annual, 2006–date].
<http://purl.access.gpo.gov/GPO/LPS125189>

Reports data on mortgage fraud activity, cases, and investigations, which is derived from the FBI, state and local law enforcement, mortgage industry sources, and open-source reporting. Information is also provided by other government agencies, including the Office of Inspector General; Department of Housing and Urban Development; Federal Housing Administration; Federal National Mortgage Association; and the Treasury Department's Financial Crimes Enforcement Network. Industry reporting is obtained from the LexisNexis® Mortgage Asset Research Institute (MARI), RealtyTrac, Inc., Mortgage Bankers Association (MBA), and Interthinx®. Data is provided for states and major metropolitan areas for the most prevalent mortgage fraud schemes reported by law enforcement and industry sources, including loan origination, foreclosure rescue, builder bailout, equity skimming, short sale, home equity line of credit, illegal property flipping, reverse mortgage fraud, credit enhancement, and schemes associated with loan modifications.

Money Laundering

078 Motivans, Mark. *Money Laundering Offenders, 1994–2001* [Special Report]. Washington, D.C.: Bureau of Justice Statistics, Office of Justice Programs, U.S. Department of Justice, 2003. NCJ 199574
<http://purl.access.gpo.gov/GPO/LPS53206>

Contains a chart showing the ten federal judicial districts with largest number of matters referred with money laundering as most serious charge (2001), which includes the Southern District of Texas (total number of matters referred, number of money laundering matters referred, and number of money laundering matters as a percentage of all matters referred).

•079 *National Money Laundering Strategy*. Washington, D.C.: U.S. Department of the Treasury, U.S. Department of Justice, and U.S. Department of Homeland Security [annual, 1999–date].
<http://purl.access.gpo.gov/GPO/LPS15921>

The appendixes contain rankings for Suspicious Activity Report (SAR) filing locations including all SAR forms, all currency transaction reports; currency transaction reports from casinos, Form 8300, and outbound and inbound Reports of International Transportation of Currency or Monetary Instruments

(CMIR). The report also provides recorded seizures of cash and monetary instruments (origins and destinations), and rankings of states based on Federal Drug Seizure System data.

School Discipline

080 Carmichael, Dottie, Guy Whitten, and Michael Voloudakis. *Study of Minority Over-Representation in the Texas Juvenile Justice System: Final Report*. College Station: Public Policy Research Institute, Texas A&M University, 2005.

<http://dmcfinalreport.tamu.edu/>

This study, which was submitted to the Office of the Governor's Criminal Justice Division, focuses on the factors associated with the over-representation of minorities in the Texas juvenile justice system. It considered the following risk factors commonly associated with referral to the juvenile justice system: gender, low income status, academic giftedness, limited English proficiency, school disciplinary contact, gang affiliation, race/ethnicity, disability status, offense type, living arrangements, school attendance rate, and age. It concluded that the single most important predictor for involvement with the juvenile justice systems was a history of disciplinary referrals at school and, furthermore, the more severe the disciplinary history, the higher the probability of such a referral.

081 *Texas' School-to-Prison Pipeline: Dropout to Incarceration—The Impact of School Discipline and Zero Tolerance*. Austin: Texas Appleseed, 2007.

081A *Texas' School-to-Prison Pipeline: School Expulsion–The Path from Lockout to Dropout*. Austin: Texas Appleseed, 2010.

<http://www.texasappleseed.net/>

These reports explore the relationship between school disciplinary referrals and expulsions in Texas public schools and future involvement with the juvenile and adult justice systems. Referrals range from in-school suspension (ISS), out-of-school suspension (OSS), Disciplinary Alternative Education Centers (DAEPs), and—for the more serious offenders—Juvenile Justice Alternative Education Programs (JJAEPs). DAEPs have five times the dropout rate of mainstream schools and, furthermore, one in three juveniles sent to the Texas Youth Commission, and more than 80 percent of Texas prison inmates, are school dropouts. Statistics are presented for Texas school districts relating to their rate of both discretionary and mandatory referrals to DAEPs and expulsions, including data for African-American students, Hispanic students, and special education students.

Research Note: Entry 081 has updated data available for 2008–2009.

Sex Offender Registration

082 Adams, Devon B. *Summary of State Sex Offender Registries, 2001* [Fact Sheet]. Washington, D.C.: Bureau of Justice Statistics, Office of Justice Programs, U.S. Department of Justice, 2002. NCJ 192265

<http://bjs.ojp.usdoj.gov/content/pub/pdf/sssor01.pdf>

Presents state-level data on the number of offenders in state sex offender registries for 1998 and 2001 (Appendix Table 2).

Research Note: Earlier editions are available.

083 *Dru Sjodin National Sex Offender Public Website.* Washington, D.C.: Office of Sex Offender Sentencing, Monitoring, Apprehending, Registering, and Tracking, Office of Justice Programs, U.S. Department of Justice [online only, 2005–date].

<http://www.nsopw.gov/Core/Conditions.aspx>

The Dru Sjodin National Sex Offender Public Website (NSOPW) was established by the Sex Offender Registration and Notification Act, which comprises Title I of the Adam Walsh Child Protection and Safety Act of 2006 (P.L. 109-248, Title I, 120 Stat. 590). It is coordinated by the U.S. Department of Justice and represents a cooperative effort between the state agencies hosting public sex offender registries and the federal government.

Research Note: Searches for Texas offenders link to the Sex Offender Registry maintained by the Texas Department of Public Safety (see entry 086).

084 *Long-Term Care Facilities: Information on Residents Who Are Registered Sex Offenders or Are Paroled for Other Crimes* [Report to Congressional Requestors]. Washington, D.C.: U.S. Government Accountability Office, 2006. GAO-06-326

<http://purl.access.gpo.gov/GPO/LPS70466>

Presents state-level statistics, based on the FBI's National Sex Offender Registry (NSOR), on the number of sex offenders living in nursing homes and intermediate care facilities for people with mental retardation (ICFs-MR) as of January 3, 2005 (Appendix IV).

085 *Review of the Department of Justice's Implementation of the Sex Offender Registration and Notification Act.* [Washington, D.C.]: Evaluation and Inspections Division, Office of the Inspector General, U.S. Department of Justice, 2008. I-2009-001

<http://purl.access.gpo.gov/GPO/LPS110459>

A review of the U.S. Department of Justice's implementation of the Sex Offender Registration and Notification Act (SORNA), which comprises Title I of the Adam Walsh Child Protection and Safety Act of 2006 (P.L. 109-248, Title I, 120 Stat. 587). It provides a state-by-state breakdown of registered sex offenders in public registries and the Federal Bureau of Investigation's National Sex Offender Registry (NSOR) as follows: number of sex offenders in OIG sample registered in public registry; number of sex offenders in OIG sample registered in public registry and in NSOR; and percentage of sex offenders in OIG sample listed in public registry also contained in NSOR (Appendix V).

•**086** *Sex Offender Registry.* Austin: Crime Records Service, Texas Department of Public Safety [online].

<https://records.txdps.state.tx.us/DPS_WEB/SorNew/index.aspx>

Adult and juvenile sex offenders are required to register with the local law enforcement authority of the city in which they reside or, if the offender does not reside in a city, with the local law enforcement authority of the county in which they reside (Tex. Code Crim. Proc. Ann. arts. 62.001–.408 (Vernon 2006 & Supp. 2010)). Searches can be conducted by name, city, or zip code (the mapping feature allows searches by county or street address). The registry provides the following information: name and known aliases, current address, date of birth, gender, physical description (including photographs), registrations/verifications, risk level, and offense (including the victim's age and gender, and case disposition).

Terrorism

•**087** *Worldwide Incidents Tracking System.* [Washington, D.C.]: National Counterterrorism Center, Office of the Director of National Intelligence [online only, 2004–date].

<https://wits.nctc.gov/FederalDiscoverWITS/index.do?N=0>

A worldwide database of reported terrorist incidents that is searchable at the level of region, country, state/province, or city. The advanced search mode allows the user to narrow their search utilizing the following criteria: incident (subject, summary, date, event type, weapon, assassination, suicide, or IED); location; victim (type, nationality, defining characteristics, targeting characteristics, combatant, indicator, child, dead count, wounded count, hostage count, and total victims); facility (type, nationality, defining characteristics, targeting characteristics, combatant, indicator, and damage); and perpetrator (characteristic and nationality).

Research Note: The center publishes an annual report on terrorism (under slightly varying titles) that extracts information from this database (2004–date). <http://purl.access.gpo.gov/GPO/LPS110287> For databases of earlier terrorist incidents, see *Global Terrorism Database 1.1, 1970–1997* and *Global Terrorism Database II, 1998–2004*, which were compiled by Gary LaFree and Laura Dugan with funding provided by the Human Factors Division, Science and Technology Directorate, U.S. Department of Homeland Security and the National Institute of Justice, U.S. Department of Justice.

<http://dx.doi.org/10.3886/ICPSR22541> [1970–1997]

<http://dx.doi.org/10.3886/ICPSR22600> [1998–2004]

Violence in the Workplace

•**088** *Fatal Occupational Injury Data.* Austin: Division of Workers' Compensation, Texas Department of Insurance [annual, online only, 2003–date].

<http://www.tdi.state.tx.us/wc/safety/sis/fathomepage.html>

Reports Texas statistics from the annual Census of Fatal Occupational Injuries (CFOI), which is conducted by the Bureau of Labor Statistics, U.S. Department of Labor. Data is provided on incidents of workplace fatalities resulting from assaults and violent acts (violence by persons, self-inflicted injury, and attacks by animals) and homicides (total, homicides by shooting, and all other homicides).

Research Note: Due to changes to the OSHA recordkeeping logs and the transition from the Standard Industrial Classification (SIC) system to the North American Industry Classification System (NAICS), pre-2003 data cannot be compared to data from subsequent years, although it is available to researchers upon request.

•**089** *State Occupational Injuries, Illnesses, and Fatalities.* Washington, D.C.: Bureau of Labor Statistics, U.S. Department of Labor [annual, online only, 2003–date].

<http://www.bls.gov/iif/oshstate.htm>

Texas data from the Census of Fatal Occupational Injuries (CFOI) is reported under "Profile of Occupational Fatalities" as follows: by selected demographic characteristics and major events or exposures (including assaults and violent acts); by selected events and employee status and sex (including homicides, homicides–shooting, and self-inflicted injuries); and by selected industries and occupations by major events or exposures (including assaults and violent acts). The link labeled "Get detailed statistics for occupational fatalities" allows queries to be conducted utilizing multiple parameters.

Research Note: *Fatal Workplace Injuries in [year]: A Collection of Data and Analysis* (Washington, D.C.: Bureau of Labor Statistics, U.S. Department of Labor, 1991–date) also reports statistics from the CFOI on assaults/violent acts and homicides by state and selected metropolitan areas. See the State and Area Data (Appendix B) in the Tables and Appendixes CD-ROM that supplements the main report. <http://purl.access.gpo.gov/GPO/LPS105819>

090 *Texas Workplace Fatalities in [year].* Dallas: Southwest Information Office, Bureau of Labor Statistics, U.S. Department of Labor [annual, online only, 1992–date].

<http://www.bls.gov/ro6/fax/cfoi_tx.htm>

Chart B shows the four most frequent work-related fatal events (including homicide) and Table A shows the distribution of fatal occupational injuries by selected event (including homicide), for 1992–date. Tables 1–4 provides data for Texas extracted from the Census of Fatal Occupational Injuries (CFOI) on fatal occupational injuries by event or exposure (including assaults and violent acts), and major private industry sector, for the most recent reporting year.

Violent Crime

091 *A Gathering Storm—Violent Crime in America* [Chief Concerns]. Washington, D.C.: Police Executive Research Forum, 2006.

<http://www.policeforum.org/library.asp?MENU=1624>

Contains "Updated Violent Crime Statistics (CY2004–2005/Jan–June 2005—Jan–June 2006)" for homicide, robbery, and aggravated assault (total and percentage change) as reported directly from law enforcement agencies in Arlington, Dallas, Houston, and San Antonio.

092 *Violent Crime in America: "A Tale of Two Cities"* [Critical Issues in Policing]. Washington, D.C.: Police Executive Research Forum, 2007.

<http://www.policeforum.org/library.asp?MENU=1624>

Contains "Violent Crime Statistics: January–June 2006 and January–June 2007" for homicide, robbery, aggravated assault, and aggravated assault with a firearm (totals and percentage change) as reported directly from law enforcement agencies in Abilene, Arlington, Dallas, Farmers Branch, Fort Worth, Garland, Houston, and San Antonio, and Tarrant County.

093 *Violent Crime in America: 24 Months of Alarming Trends* [Chief Concerns]. Washington, D.C.: Police Executive Research Forum [2007].

<http://www.policeforum.org/library.asp?MENU=1624>

Contains "Violent Crime Statistics 2004–2006" for homicide, robbery, aggravated assault, and aggravated assault with a firearm (totals and percentage change) as reported directly from law enforcement agencies in Arlington, Dallas, Houston, and San Antonio.

White Collar Crimes

•094 *Annual Report.* Glen Allen, Va: National White Collar Crime Center, Bureau of Justice Assistance, Office of Justice Programs, U.S. Department of Justice [annual, 2005–date].

<http://www.nw3c.org/research/site_files.cfm>

The National White Collar Crime Center (NW3C) is a congressionally funded, non-profit corporation. Since 1978 it has provided support services to state and local law enforcement for the prevention, investigation, and prosecution of high-tech and economic crime. This report provides state-level statistics by fiscal year on complaints filed with the NW3C (number of complaints and suspects).

Chapter 3

Law Enforcement

Agricultural Crime

095 *Special Ranger Statistical Information.* Fort Worth, Tex.: Texas and Southwestern Cattle Raisers Association [annual].

<http://www.texascattleraisers.org/theftProtectionstats.asp>

The Texas and Southwestern Cattle Raisers Association (TSCRA) is a 130-year-old trade organization whose 14,500 members manage approximately 5.4 million cattle on 70.3 million acres of range and pasture land, primarily in Texas and Oklahoma. The TSCRA employs twenty-nine investigators, who are commissioned as Special Rangers by the Oklahoma State Bureau of Investigation or the Texas Department of Public Safety (Tex. Code Crim. Proc. Ann. art. 2.125 (Vernon Supp. 2010)). This report provides statistics by calendar year on the number of cases investigated that involved cattle and livestock related theft. The dispositions of those cases brought to trial are also reported (sentences, court costs assessed, fines assessed, and restitution made). In addition, property recovered or accounted for by the Special Rangers is reported as follows: number and value of steers and bulls, cows and heifers, calves, yearlings, horses, trailers, saddles, and miscellaneous ranch property.

Research Note: These reports are unpublished, but available to researchers upon request. The association's website posts the annual press release announcing and summarizing the annual data.

Aircraft

•096 Langton, Lynn. *Aviation Units in Large Law Enforcement Agencies, 2007.* Washington, D.C.: Bureau of Justice Statistics, Office of Justice Programs, U.S. Department of Justice, 2009. NCJ 226672

<http://purl.access.gpo.gov/GPO/LPS126122>

Provides statistics on law enforcement agencies with 100 or more sworn personnel and aviation units, by state and unit characteristics, including type of agency, planes, helicopters, pilots, and flight hours (Appendix Table 1).

Research Note: Datasets are available through the National Archive of Criminal Justice Data, Inter-university Consortium for Political and Social Research (ICPSR), Institute for Social Research, University of Michigan.

<http://dx.doi.org/10.3886/ICPSR25482>

Arrest Statistics

•097 *Easy Access to FBI Arrest Statistics.* Washington, D.C.: Office of Juvenile Justice and Delinquency Prevention, Office of Justice Programs, U.S. Department of Justice [online only, 1994–date].

<http://ojjdp.ncjrs.org/ojstatbb/ezaucr/>

Provides access to detailed adult and juvenile arrest statistics for Part I and Part II offense categories from the FBI's Uniform Crime Reporting (UCR) program, whose datasets are maintained by the National Archive of Criminal Justice Data (NACJD). The NACJD, in consultation with the UCR project staff, developed a procedure to impute arrest counts using an imputation algorithm to adjust for incomplete reporting by individual law enforcement jurisdictions. Data is available at the state and county levels. Display options include counts, rates, percentage of total, and time period.

Research Note: This website is maintained by the National Center for Juvenile Justice, which is the research division of the National Council of Juvenile and Family Court Judges, and sponsored by the Office of Juvenile Justice and Delinquency Prevention, Office of Justice Programs, U.S. Department of Justice. The county-level estimates are not official FBI releases and are provided for research purposes only. Datasets are available for index crimes (except arson) through the National Archive of Criminal Justice Data, Inter-university Consortium for Political and Social Research (ICPSR), Institute for Social Research, University of Michigan (under Offenses Known and Clearances by Arrest).

<http://www.icpsr.umich.edu/NACJD/ucr.html#desc_al>

Assaults on Police

•098 *Law Enforcement Officers Killed and Assaulted.* Washington, D.C.: Federal Bureau of Investigation, U.S. Department of Justice [annual, 1982-date]. <http://purl.access.gpo.gov/GPO/LPS700>

Provides state-level statistics reported to the FBI's Uniform Crime Reporting (UCR) Program for assaults on law enforcement officers and federal officers, with additional data provided on the type of weapon involved.

Research Note: See also entry 149. Reports are available online back to 1996 and have been disseminated in electronic format only beginning with the 2004 edition. Printable data tables are available for downloading. Regional data for 1960–1981 is reported in *Uniform Crime Reports for the United States* (see entry 002). See also *Assaults on Federal Officers* (1976–1981). Datasets are available through the National Archive of Criminal Justice Data, Inter-university Consortium for Political and Social Research (ICPSR), Institute for Social Research, University of Michigan (under Police Employee (LEOKA) Data). <http://www.icpsr.umich.edu/NACJD/ucr.html#desc_al>

Asset Forfeiture

099 Bowman, Lisa. "Asset Forfeitures." *TELEMASP Bulletin* [Texas Law Enforcement Management and Administrative Statistics Program] 15, no. 6 (November/December 2008): 1–12. <http://www.lemitonline.org/telemasp/>

Reports data from a survey of fifty-two Texas law enforcement agencies on their civil forfeiture policies, procedures, and statistics for FY2005 through FY2007.

Bicycle Police

100 Swindell, Sam. "Policing on Bicycles and Horses." *TELEMASP Bulletin* [Texas Law Enforcement Management and Administrative Statistics Program] 14, no. 6 (November/December 2007): 1–12.

<http://www.lemitonline.org/telemasp/>

Reports data from a survey of fifty-two Texas law enforcement agencies on their bicycle patrol units including criteria for bicycle officer selection (Figure 1); initial and additional training required for bicycle officers (Figures 2 and 3); percentage of seasonal bicycle patrol deployment by month (Figure 4); most frequent type of all injuries reported in 1998 and 2006 (Figure 5); injuries reported as a percentage of primary bicycle officers in 1998 and 2006; a comparison of deployment areas for police cyclists and mounted officers (Figure 7); and a comparison of bicycle brands used in 1998 and 2006 (Table 1).

Border Control

101 *An Audit Report on Border Security Funds* [SAO Report]. Austin: State Auditor's Office, 2009.

<http://www.sao.state.tx.us/reports/main/09-022.html>

Reports the results of an audit of state and federal funds awarded or appropriated to the Governor's Division of Emergency Management for border security operations for FY2006 through FY2009, and funds appropriated by the 80th Texas Legislature to the Texas Department of Public Safety and the Texas Parks and Wildlife Department.

Campus Police

•**102** Reaves, Brian A. *Campus Law Enforcement, 2004–05* [Special Report]. Washington, D.C.: Bureau of Justice Statistics, Office of Justice Programs, U.S. Department of Justice, 2008. NCJ 219374

<http://purl.access.gpo.gov/GPO/LPS121384>

Provides data on total employees and sworn personnel (full-time, part-time, and per 1,000 students) for campus law enforcement agencies serving the 100 largest enrollments in the United States, 2004–2005 (Appendix Table 2).

Research Note: Appendix Tables are available in the online edition only. Earlier editions are available.

Citizen Patrols

103 Marks, John M., Jr. "Citizens on Patrol Programs." *TELEMASP Bulletin* [Texas Law Enforcement Management and Administrative Statistics Program] 15, no. 3 (May/June 2008): 1–12.

<http://www.lemitonline.org/telemasp/>

Reports data from a survey of forty-nine Texas law enforcement agencies on their Citizens on Patrol (COP) programs, including the impetus for initiating such a program, membership requirements, office locations, age ranges of volunteers, training requirements, those with whom volunteers ride along, duties, types of insignia or uniforms worn, program funding sources, equipment used, and the degree to which volunteers "over-step" their role or authority.

Community Policing

104 Garcia, Hector. "Bilingual Police Officers: Policing in a Diverse America." *TELEMASP Bulletin* [Texas Law Enforcement Management and Administrative Statistics Program] 13, no. 4 (July/August 2006): 1–12.

<http://www.lemitonline.org/telemasp/>

Reports data from a survey of forty-five Texas law enforcement agencies on their bilingual policies, training, and specialized services.

105 Mindel, Charles, Richard F. Dangel, Wayne Carson, and Maria L. Mays. *An Evaluation of the Dallas Police Department's Interactive Community Policing Program 1995–1999: Final Report*. Arlington, Tex.: Center for Research, Evaluation, and Technology, University of Texas at Arlington, 2000. NCJ 193429

<http://www.ncjrs.gov/pdffiles1/nij/grants/193429.pdf>

Reports data from an evaluation of implementation and impact of the Interactive Community Policing (ICP) program of the Dallas Police Department from 1995 to 1999. Citizen survey results from both low and high ICP areas include changes in perceptions of social disorder; changes in fear of crime; use of security measures by citizens to make them feel safer; changes in citizen crime victimization; citizen familiarity with the ICP Program; changes in perceptions of police activity; changes in citizen assessment of how well police are doing in Dallas; and police availability for neighborhood problems.

Police survey results for ICP and non-ICP Program officers are also reported on a variety of community policing issues.

Complaints Against Police

106 Sarver, Mary. "Citizen Complaints." *TELEMASP Bulletin* [Texas Law Enforcement Management and Administrative Statistics Program] 14, no. 5 (September/October 2007): 1–8.

<http://www.lemitonline.org/telemasp/>

Presents data on citizen complaints from a survey of thirty-three Texas law enforcement agencies that reported all complaints received (data for an additional six agencies that only reported formal complaints received is summarized separately). Data presented includes citizen complaints by gender (Figure 1); internal complaints versus external complaints (Figure 2); ratio of citizen complaints to sworn officers in 2006 (Table 1); number of citizen complaints received for officers within each age range (Table 2) and rank (Table 3); number of citizen complaint ranges to total number of officers (Table 4); citizen complaints for specific behaviors (Table 5); citizen complaints reported in the context of specific activities (Table 6); outcomes of citizen complaints (Table 7); and processes utilized to handle citizen complaints (Table 8).

Computer Related Crime

107 Murff, Karon. "Digital Crime." *TELEMASP Bulletin* [Texas Law Enforcement Management and Administrative Statistics Program] 12, no. 5 (September/October 2005): 1–12.

<http://www.lemitonline.org/telemasp/>

Presents data from a survey of forty-nine Texas law enforcement agencies on the characteristics of their computer-related criminal investigations, focusing on the training and educational requirements of investigators.

•108 *RCFL Annual Report for Fiscal Year [year].* Quantico, Va.: Regional Computer Forensics Laboratory, Federal Bureau of Investigation, U.S. Department of Justice [2003-date].

<http://purl.fdlp.gov/GPO/gpo96>

The Regional Computer Forensics Laboratory (RCFL) Program is a network of fourteen FBI-sponsored digital forensics laboratories and training centers that provide support and services to law enforcement agencies nationwide. This report provides statistics for the Greater Houston RCFL and the North Texas RCFL as follows: number of agencies in service area; number of agencies that requested assistance (federal, state, and local); number of service requests received; number of pieces of media examined; number of examinations completed; number of law enforcement officers trained in various digital forensics tools and techniques; and top five customer requests by crime classification.

Criminal Histories

109 *2008 Study of Criminal Records: Analysis of the Reliability of Texas Department of Public Safety's Computerized Criminal History Database.* [Fort Worth, Tex.]: Imperative Information Group, 2008.

<http://www.imperativeinfo.com/pdfs/DPS_Criminal.pdf>

This audit of the Texas Department of Public Safety's Computerized Criminal History (CCH) database showed that it was missing 36 percent of criminal history records as of October 2008. The report includes the percentage of missing records by case type (capital murder, felony, and misdemeanor); the percentage of missing records by county (top ten counties); and a list of death row inmates who were either missing from the database or whose offense that put them on death row was not listed.

110 *An Audit Report on State Agencies' Use of Criminal History Records* [SAO Report]. Austin: State Auditor's Office, 2006. 06-049

<http://www.sao.state.tx.us/reports/main/06-049.html>

The objectives of this audit were to determine (1) whether criminal history background check requests submitted by state agencies and processed by the Texas Department of Public Safety permit those agencies to correctly identify individuals who do not meet standards for activities such as licensing or employment, and (2) the extent to which state agencies with authorized access to state and national criminal history records for licensing or permitting rely on this data for these activities.

•**111** *Computerized Criminal History.* Austin: Crime Records Service, Texas Department of Public Safety [online only].

<https://records.txdps.state.tx.us/DPS_WEB/Cch/index.aspx>

The Computerized Criminal History (CCH) system serves as the official statewide repository of criminal history information as reported to the DPS by local criminal justice agencies in Texas. It is used extensively by state licensing agencies and private sector employers as their primary source for criminal history information on applicants for employment and occupational licensing.

Research Note: The CCH is one component of the Texas Criminal Justice Information System (Tex. Code Crim. Proc. Ann. art. 60.01–.21 (Vernon 2006 & Supp. 2010)). The other is the

Corrections Tracking System (CTS), which is managed by the Texas Department of Criminal Justice. Public criminal histories are searchable (registration and account creation is required), but searches of secure criminal histories are restricted to legislatively authorized criminal justice agencies, governmental entities, and private entities.

112 *Report of the National Focus Group on the Retention of Civil Fingerprints by Criminal History Record Repositories.* Washington, D.C.: Bureau of Justice Statistics, Office of Justice Programs, U.S. Department of Justice [2007]. NCJ 225204.

<http://www.ncjrs.gov/pdffiles1/bjs/225204.pdf>

Provisions of federal law allow non-criminal justice governmental agencies and private entities within states to obtain access to FBI-maintained criminal history record information when conducting fingerprint-based criminal record background checks to determine, for example, the fitness of an employee, volunteer, or a person with unsupervised access to children, the elderly, or individuals with disabilities (42 U.S.C. 5119a, 5119c (2003)). This publication reports the results of a survey of the civil fingerprint retention policies and practices of the forty-five responding states (including Texas).

•**113** *Survey of State Criminal History Information Systems [year]: A Criminal Justice Information Policy Report.* Washington, D.C.: Bureau of Justice Statistics, Office of Justice Programs, U.S. Department of Justice [biennial, 1989–date].

<http://purl.access.gpo.gov/GPO/LPS26394>

Reports data on state criminal history information systems as follows: overview of state criminal history record systems (Table 1); overview of state criminal history record system functions (Table 1a); number of subjects (individual offenders) in state criminal history file (Table 2); biometric and image data collection by state criminal history repository (Table 3); protection order information and records (Table 4); state registry of sex offenders (Table 5); community notification services and public access to records (Table 5a); number of final dispositions reported to state criminal history repository (Table 6); final disposition reporting (Table 6a); automation of disposition reporting to state criminal history repository (Table 7); arrest records submitted electronically (Table 8); criminal and noncriminal justice background checks submitted electronically (Table 9); noncriminal justice applicant information (Table 9a); certification and privatization of fingerprint capture services (Table 10); number of felony arrests and current status of backlog (Table 11); length of time to process disposition data submitted to state criminal history repository and current status of backlog (Table 12); length of time to process correctional admission data submitted to state criminal history repository and current status of backlog (Table 13); length of time to process correctional admission data submitted to state criminal history repository and current status of backlog (Table 14); noncriminal justice name-based background checks (Table 14a); noncriminal justice name-based background check processing, (Table 14b); noncriminal justice name-based background check results (Table 14c); noncriminal justice name-based background check authorizations/fees (Table 15); noncriminal justice fingerprint-based background checks (Table 15a); noncriminal justice fingerprint-based background check requirements (Table 15b); Federal Bureau of Investigation (FBI) fee retention (Table 16); fingerprint record processing by state criminal history repository (Table 17); state criminal history repository operating hours, (Table 18); fees charged by state criminal history repository for noncriminal justice purposes (Table 19); fees charged for additional services by state criminal history repository (Table 20); fees charged for web-based services by state criminal history repository or other entity for noncriminal justice purposes (Table 21); and criminal history records of Interstate Identification Index (III) participants maintained by the state criminal history repository and the Federal Bureau of Investigation (FBI) (Table 22).

Custody Deaths

•**114** Mumola, Christopher J. *Arrest-Related Deaths in the United States, 2003–2005* [Special Report]. Washington, D.C.: Bureau of Justice Statistics, Office of Justice Programs, U.S. Department of Justice, 2007. NCJ 219534

<http://bjs.ojp.usdoj.gov/index.cfm?ty=dcdetail&iid=243>

In order to implement the mandates of the Death in Custody Reporting Act of 2000 (P.L. 106-297, 114 Stat. 1045), the Bureau of Justice Statistics implemented a nationwide data collection program that includes all arrest-related deaths reported by state authorities. Forty-seven states and the District of Columbia reported over 2,000 such deaths during the initial collection period (2003–2005). These reports contain data on both the cause of death and characteristics of the deceased. All manners of death during an arrest are reported, including homicides (both those by officers and other persons), suicides, alcohol or drug intoxication, accidental injuries, and fatal medical problems. The Appendix Tables contain data for the number of arrest-related deaths and data reporting sources, by state (Table 1); number of arrest-related deaths, by state and cause of death (Table 2); comparative counts of law enforcement homicides in Supplemental Homicide Reports (SHR) and Deaths in Custody Reporting Program (DCRP) data collections, by state (Table 3); and law enforcement officers killed and assaulted, and arrestees killed in the process of arrest, by state (Table 11).

Research Note: Appendix Tables are available in the online edition only. Datasets are available through the Inter-university Consortium for Political and Social Research (ICPSR), Institute for Social Research, University of Michigan.

<http://www.icpsr.umich.edu/icpsrweb/ICPSR/series/00225>

•**115** Mumola, Christopher J., and Margaret E. Noonan. *Deaths in Custody Statistical Tables: State and Local Law Enforcement Arrest-Related Deaths.* Washington, D.C.: Bureau of Justice Statistics, Office of Justice Programs, U.S. Department of Justice [annual, online only, 2003–date].

<http://bjs.ojp.usdoj.gov/content/dcrp/dictabs.cfm>

In order to implement the mandates of the Death in Custody Reporting Act of 2000 (P.L. 106-297, 114 Stat. 1045), the Bureau of Justice Statistics implemented a nationwide data collection program that includes all arrest-related deaths reported by state authorities. The State and Local Law Enforcement Arrest-Related Deaths subsection reports the number of arrest-related deaths, by state (Table 7); number of arrest-related deaths by state and cause of death (Table 8); and number of arresting agencies with at least one reported arrest-related death, by state (Table 9).

Research Note: Datasets are available through the Inter-university Consortium for Political and Social Research (ICPSR), Institute for Social Research, University of Michigan.

<http://www.icpsr.umich.edu/ICPSR/series/00225>

DNA Fingerprinting

•**116** *CODIS–NDIS Statistics.* Washington, D.C.: Federal Bureau of Investigation, U.S. Department of Justice [online].

<http://www.fbi.gov/hq/lab/codis/stats.htm>

The DNA Identification Act of 1994 (P.L. 103-322, Title XXI, Subtitle C, 108 Stat. 2065) formally authorized the FBI to establish the National DNA Index System (NDIS), which is a repository of DNA profile records submitted by criminal justice agencies (including state and local law enforcement agencies). The Combined DNA Index System (CODIS) is the automated DNA information processing and telecommunication system that supports NDIS. State-level statistics are provided for the number of offender profiles, forensic samples, CODIS labs, NDIS participating labs, and investigations aided.

117 Schnurbush, Kim. "DNA Evidence Collection and Analysis." *TELEMASP Bulletin* [Texas Law Enforcement Management and Administrative Statistics Program] 15, no. 5 (September/October 2008): 1–8.

<http://www.lemitonline.org/telemasp/>

Presents results from a survey of fifty Texas law enforcement agencies on their DNA evidence collection policies and procedures.

Domestic Assault

118 Johnson, Matthew. "Law Enforcement Response to Domestic Violence." *TELEMASP Bulletin* [Texas Law Enforcement Management and Administrative Statistics Program] 14, no. 2 (March/April 2007): 1–8.

<http://www.lemitonline.org/telemasp/>

Presents results from a survey of forty-seven Texas law enforcement agencies on their domestic violence units including policies, functions, and officers (number, selection, experience, and training).

Drug Seizures

•**119** *Annual Report.* Austin: Texas Department of Public Safety [1980–date].

<http://www.txdps.state.tx.us/director_staff/public_information/reports.htm>

The Criminal Law Enforcement section reports drug seizures and arrests made by DPS Narcotics Service officers.

Research Note: Reports are online back to 2000. Published as *Biennial Report* prior to 1980 (the 1980 *Annual Report* was included with 1978/1979 *Biennial Report*).

120 *Cocaine Smuggling in 2007.* Washington, D.C.: Office of National Drug Control Policy, Executive Office of the President, 2008. NCJ 225372

<http://purl.access.gpo.gov/GPO/LPS111609>

Provides a map showing Southwest Border Area port of entry cocaine seizure incidents for 2007 and percentage of cocaine seized by border region.

Research Note: Earlier editions are available.

121 *High Intensity Drug Trafficking Areas.* Washington, D.C.: High Intensity Drug Trafficking Area Program, Office of National Drug Control Policy, Executive Office of the President [annual, 2005-date].

<http://purl.access.gpo.gov/GPO/LPS102923>

The High Intensity Drug Trafficking Area program was authorized within the Office of National Drug Control Policy (ONDCP) by the Anti-Drug Abuse Act of 1988 (P.L. 100-690, 102 Stat. 4181) and became operational in 1990. It was designed to coordinate federal, state, local, and tribal law enforcement efforts to curtail illegal drug production and distribution. The Office of National Drug Control Policy Reauthorization Act of 2006 reaffirmed the previously amended section 707 of the original act by stipulating that "The [ONDCP]

Director, in consultation with the Attorney General, the Secretary of the Treasury, the Secretary of Homeland Security, heads of the National Drug Control Program agencies, and the Governor of each applicable State, may designate any specified area of the United States as a high intensity drug trafficking area" (P.L. 109-469, 120 Stat. 3502 § 301). This website provides access to annual reports from individual HIDTAs (including North Texas, Southwest Border Region—South Texas, Southwest Border Region—West Texas, and Houston), which were submitted in accordance with the ONDCP's Performance Management Process (PMP). They contain data on efforts to disrupt and dismantle drug trafficking and money laundering organizations in each designated area, including statistics on drug and asset seizures.

122 *National Drug Control Strategy: Data Supplement.* Washington, D.C.: Office of National Drug Control Policy, Executive Office of the President [annual, 2004–date].

<http://purl.access.gpo.gov/GPO/LPS6500> [current edition]

<http://purl.access.gpo.gov/GPO/LPS94333> [archived editions]

The State Data section provides statistics on eradicated domestic cannabis, total cultivated plants; eradicated plots of domestic outdoor cannabis; eradicated domestic outdoor cultivated cannabis plants; eradicated domestic indoor cannabis grow sites; eradicated domestic indoor cannabis plants; methamphetamine seizure incidents; seizure of methamphetamine small toxic labs; and methamphetamine seizures of super labs.

123 *Pushing Back Against Meth: A Progress Report on the Fight Against Methamphetamine in the United States.* [Washington, D.C.]: Office of National Drug Control Policy, Executive Office of the President, 2006.

<http://purl.access.gpo.gov/GPO/LPS78406>

Includes individual state profiles that provide comparisons of the standards mandated by the Combat Methamphetamine Epidemic Act of 2005 (P.L. 109-177, Title VII, 120 Stat. 256) with individual state precursor laws. Data is reported on methamphetamine laboratory incident seizures and amphetamine workplace drug testing.

•124 *Stats & Facts—State Fact Sheets.* Washington, D.C.: Drug Enforcement Administration, U.S. Department of Justice [annual, online only].

<http://www.usdoj.gov/dea/statistics.html>

These state fact sheets report data on federal drug seizures in kilograms (cocaine, heroin, methamphetamine, marijuana, hashish, and MDMA); methamphetamine lab incidents (DEA, state, and local); and drug violation arrests.

Electronic Surveillance

•**125** *Wiretap Report.* Washington, D.C.: Administrative Office of the United States Courts [annual, 1993-date].

<http://purl.access.gpo.gov/GPO/LPS2679>

Presents state-level data for number of orders authorized for jurisdictions with statutes authorizing the interception of wire, oral, or electronic communications (Table 1). Also provides jurisdiction-level data for the following: intercept orders issued by judges—number, average length (in days), and location authorized in original application (Table 2); major offenses for which court-authorized intercepts were granted pursuant to 18 U.S.C. § 2519 (2007) (Table 3); summary of interceptions of wire, oral, or electronic communications—number authorized, orders for which intercepts were installed, and average number per order when installed (Table 4); average cost per order (Table 5); types of surveillance used, arrests, and convictions for intercepts installed (Table 6); summary of supplementary reports for intercepts terminated since 1991 (Table 8); and summary of intercept orders issued by federal judges (Table 10). The Appendix provides a report by judges (Table A-1), and a supplemental report by prosecutors (Table A-2), of court-authorized intercepts of wire, oral, or electronic communications pursuant to 18 U.S.C. § 2519 (2007) by U.S. District Court region (Table A-1); a report by judges of court-authorized intercepts of wire, oral, or electronic communications pursuant to 18 U.S.C. § 2519 (2007) by state courts (Table B-1); and a supplementary report of prosecutors for intercepts terminated by state courts (Table B-2).

Research Note: Reports are available online back to 1997.

Firearm Tracing

•**126** *Firearms Trace Data.* Washington, D.C.: Bureau of Alcohol, Tobacco, Firearms and Explosives, Office of Strategic Intelligence and Information, U.S. Department of Justice [annual, online only, 2006–date].

<http://www.atf.gov/statistics/>

The ATF traces the sale and possession of specific firearms for federal, state, local, and foreign law enforcement agencies. Individual state reports provide the following data: total number of firearms recovered and traced, recovered firearm types, top categories reported on recovered firearm traces, top fifteen source states for recovered firearms, time-to-crime rates for recovered firearms, and top cities for recovered firearms.

Research Note: Data is reported by calendar year.

Gun Control

127 *Active License/Certified Instructor Counts as of December 31 [year].* Austin: Concealed Handgun Licensing Bureau, Regulatory Licensing Service, Texas Department of Public Safety [annual, online only, 1996–date].

<http://www.txdps.state.tx.us/administration/crime_records/chl/demographics.htm>

Provides the total number of active license holders (i.e., individuals who, as of the date listed at the top of each report, are licensed by the Concealed Handgun Licensing Bureau (CHLB) to carry a concealed handgun), and certified instructors (i.e., individuals, who, as of the date listed at the top of each report, are certified by CHLB as instructors).

Research Note: Published under slightly varying titles.

128 *Background Checks for Firearm Transfers—Statistical Tables.* Washington, D.C.: Bureau of Justice Statistics, Office of Justice Programs, U.S. Department of Justice [annual, 1999-date].

<http://purl.access.gpo.gov/GPO/LPS26421>

The Brady Handgun Violence Prevention Act of 1993 (P.L. 103-159, 107 Stat. 1536) mandates that anyone applying to purchase firearms from a Federal Firearm Licensee (FFL) undergo a criminal history background check. The act, which established the National Instant Criminal Background Check System (NICS), requires a background check by the Federal Bureau of Investigation, a state point of contact (POC), or a combination of the two. The Bureau of Justice Statistics' Firearm Inquiry Statistics Program (FIST) gathers information on background checks conducted by state and local agencies, and combines this information with the FBI's NICS transaction data. This report provides data on the number of firearm purchase applications received and denied by selected state agencies (Table 3a); appeals by type of checking agency (Table 6); and reported arrests of denied persons, by type of agency (Table 7). The Appendix provides lists of agencies conducting firearm background checks (Appendix Table 1); checking agencies—FBI or state point of contact—for firearm transfers under the National Instant Criminal Background Check System (NICS) (Appendix Table 2); and forums for appeals of denials (Appendix Table 3).

Research Note: Available online only in the form of data tables on the BJS website beginning with the 2006 edition ("Statistical Tables" was added to the title beginning with that edition). Texas is currently not included in Tables 3a, 6, or 7, although data is available on rejection rates for years prior to 2006. Statistics for the so-called Brady Interim period prior to the enactment of the permanent provisions can be found in *Presale Handgun Checks, the Brady Interim Period, 1994–98* (NCJ 175034). <http://purl.access.gpo.gov/GPO/LPS4565>

129 *Demographic Reports for Calendar Year [year].* Austin: Concealed Handgun Licensing Bureau, Regulatory Licensing Service, Texas Department of Public Safety [annual, online only, 1995–date].

<http://www.txdps.state.tx.us/administration/crime_records/chl/demographics.htm>

Concealed handgun license and instructor applications (issued, denied, suspended, and revoked) are reported by race/sex, age, zip code, and county.

Research Note: Statistics are also available by fiscal year (2006-date).

•130 *Survey of State Procedures Related to Firearm Sales.* Washington, D.C.: Bureau of Justice Statistics, Office of Justice Programs, U.S. Department of Justice [annual, 1995-date].

<http://purl.access.gpo.gov/GPO/LPS2865>

Reports state-level data on applications for firearm transfers and permits processed (received, rejected, and rejection rate). Information is also provided on state rules and procedures relating to prohibited persons (statutory basis for denial of firearm sale or possession); minors (restrictions based on age or juvenile offender status); regulation of dealer, private, and gun show sales; background check and permit procedures; fees, record retention, and appeals; prohibited and restricted firearms; notification procedures of state agencies regarding denied persons subject to arrest; data accessed for firearm background checks (domestic violence and other prohibitions); and revisions of sales regulations and other significant changes in state firearm laws.

Research Note: The surveys are conducted by the Regional Justice Information Service, St. Louis, Missouri, under the auspices of the Bureau of Justice Statistics' Firearm Inquiry Statistics (FIST) project. "Midyear" was added to the title from 1999 through 2004. See also Peter Brien, *Survey of State Records Included in Presale Firearm Background Checks: Mental Health Records, Domestic Violence Misdemeanor Records, and Restraining Orders, 2003* (NCJ 206042), which reports the findings from a special BJS survey of state repository directors on the quality and availability of state records pertaining to background checks on individuals prohibited by federal law from firearm transfers (18 U.S.C. § 922 (2007)).

Hypnotism in Investigation

131 Nix, Christine. "Investigative Hypnosis." *TELEMASP Bulletin* [Texas Law Enforcement Management and Administrative Statistics Program] 16, no. 6 (November/December 2009): 1–8.

<http://www.lemitonline.org/telemasp/>

Presents data on investigative hypnosis from a survey of forty-eight Texas law enforcement agencies as follows: agencies that have employed investigative hypnosis (Fig. 2); future use of investigative hypnosis by agencies not already employing it (Fig. 3); regular duty assignments of investigative hypnotists (Fig. 4); additional investigative specialties (Fig. 5); educational background (Fig. 6); additional hypnosis training (Fig. 7); types of investigative hypnosis interviews (Fig. 8); location of investigative hypnosis interviews (Fig. 9); recording method (Fig. 10); induction technique (Fig. 11); and information obtained (Fig. 12).

International Cooperation

132 Parker, J. Edward. "Utilization of International Police Cooperation for Criminal Investigations." *TELEMASP Bulletin* [Texas Law Enforcement Management and Administrative Statistics Program] 7, no. 6 (February/March 2001): 1–8.

<http://www.lemitonline.org/telemasp/>

Presents data on the nature and extent of international police cooperation in criminal investigations from a survey of thirty-two Texas law enforcement agencies.

Lawful Use of Force

133 Alford, Andy, and Erik Rodriguez. "Unequal Force." *Austin American-Statesman,* January 25–28, 2004.

<http://www.statesman.com/specialreports/content/specialreports/useofforce/index.html>

The *Austin American-Statesman* requested information under the Texas Public Information Act from the City of Austin in July 2003 regarding police use of force. This included police reports, statistical information, and an electronic database of every use of force report filed by the Austin Police Department from 31 October 1998 to 11 May 2003. The complete four-part series that presented and analyzed this data is linked from this website, as well as a follow-up explanation of the methodology the authors employed to reach their conclusions. Responses to the series from the Mayor of Austin, the Austin Police Chief, and others are also included.

Research Note: This series received a Silver Gavel Award Honorable Mention in the newspapers category from the American Bar Association in 2005.

134 Frasier. Margo L. "The Use of Conducted Energy Devices (Tasers)." *TELEMASP Bulletin* [Texas Law Enforcement Management and Administrative Statistics Program] 12, no. 6 (November/December 2005): 1–12.

<http://www.lemitonline.org/telemasp/>

Presents data on Tasers from a survey of fifty-nine Texas law enforcement agencies regarding usage (authorization, circumstances, and restrictions), reporting requirements, EMS responses, placement on use of force continuum, percentage of time malfunctioned or failed, lawsuits, and newspaper coverage.

135 Garner, Joel H., and Christopher D. Maxwell. *Understanding the Use of Force By and Against the Police in Six Jurisdictions: Final Report.* Williamston, Mich.: Joint Center for Justice, 2002. NCJ 196694

<http://www.ncjrs.gov/pdffiles1/nij/grants/196694.pdf>

Contains a site specific report for the Dallas Police Department, which was one of the six jurisdictions studied (Appendix C). Statistics are based on a systematic survey of 1,456 adult custody arrests made during two weeks in October 1996, which evaluated the extent to which fifty-five characteristics of offense situations, police officers, and arrested suspects are associated with increases and decreases in four measures of force.

Management and Administration

•**136** *Law Enforcement Management and Administrative Statistics (LEMAS).* Washington, D.C.: Bureau of Justice Statistics, Office of Justice Programs, U.S. Department of Justice [1987-date].

<http://bjs.ojp.usdoj.gov/index.cfm?ty=daa>

This database provides access to LEMAS survey results gathered from law enforcement agencies at the state level (state police or highway patrols) and the local level (local police and sheriffs' agencies with 100 or more sworn officers and fifty or more uniformed officers assigned to respond to calls for service). The data can be accessed in the following categories utilizing the indicated variables (either for single agency overviews or for additional details on one or more agencies):

Budgets: annual operating budgets (total, per employee, per sworn officer, per resident; calls for service; and number and percentage of full-time sworn employees responding to calls for service).

Community policing: community policing activities and policies; formal, written community policing plan; full-time community policing units; number of community substations; number of full-time community policing officers; and full-time school resource officers.

Computers: types of in-field computers/terminals used by patrol officers, total vehicle-mounted, and other computers.

Demographics: percentage of full-time sworn employees by race/ethnicity and gender.

Digital imaging: digital imaging methods used by agencies (fingerprints, mug shots, and suspect composites).

Drug asset forfeitures: value of drug asset forfeiture receipts (total and per sworn officer).

Drug enforcement: number of full-time and part-time officers assigned to a drug enforcement unit or a multi-agency drug task force.

Full-time employees: sworn, civilian, and total.

Patrols: types of patrol other than automobiles (bicycle, foot, horse, marine, and motorcycle).

Personnel by function: percentage of full-time, sworn personnel assigned by function (patrol and investigations and jail and court duties—jail operations, court security, and process serving).

Salaries: base annual starting salaries for chief executive, sergeant or equivalent, and entry-level officer.

Special operations: Special and other types of operations—special operations (special weapons and tactics (SWAT), and search and rescue); and other operations (dispatching calls for service and training academy operations).

Special units: special units with full-time personnel (bias crime, child abuse, cybercrime, domestic violence, drug education in schools, drunk drivers, gangs, juvenile crime, missing children, youth outreach, victim assistance).

Training: education and training requirements (minimum educational level required; minimum recruit training hours—academy and field; and minimum annual in-service training hours required of field/patrol officers).

Vehicles: number of vehicles operated—cars (marked and unmarked) and off-land vehicles (airplanes, boats, and helicopters).

Video cameras: use of video cameras (patrol cars, fixed-site surveillance, mobile surveillance, and traffic enforcement).

Research Note: Survey is conducted triennially. Reports are available online back to 1993. <http://bjs.ojp.usdoj.gov/index.cfm?ty=dcdetail&iid=248> Datasets are available through the Inter-university Consortium for Political and Social Research (ICPSR), Institute for Social Research, University of Michigan. <http://www.icpsr.umich.edu/icpsrweb/ICPSR/series/00092>

137 Reaves, Brian A., and Matthew J. Hickman. *Law Enforcement Management and Administrative Statistics, 2000: Data for Individual State and Local Agencies with 100 or More Officers.* Washington, D.C.: Bureau of Justice Statistics, Office of Justice Programs, U.S. Department of Justice, 2004. NCJ 203350

<http://purl.access.gpo.gov/GPO/LPS4289>

A compilation of statistics from the Law Enforcement Management and Administrative Statistics (LEMAS) survey (see entry 136).

Research Note: Earlier editions are available.

Mental Defectives

138 Peck, Leonard W., Jr. "Law Enforcement Interactions with Persons with Mental Illness." *TELEMASP Bulletin* [Texas Law Enforcement Management and Administrative Statistics Program] 10, no. 1 (January/February 2003): 1–12.

<http://www.lemitonline.org/telemasp/>

Presents the results of a survey of forty-one Texas law enforcement agencies concerning their interactions with mentally ill persons (frequency, perceived victimization threat, problematic behaviors, referrals, and training).

Missing Children

139 Brown, Katherine M. "Missing Child Investigations." *TELEMASP Bulletin* [Texas Law Enforcement Management and Administrative Statistics Program] 14, no. 3 (May/June 2007): 1–12.

<http://www.lemitonline.org/telemasp/>

Presents data on missing child units, policies, and investigations from a survey of forty-four Texas law enforcement agencies.

140 DeValve, Elizabeth Q. "Communication with Parents of Missing Children." *TELEMASP Bulletin* [Texas Law Enforcement Management and Administrative Statistics Program] 7, no. 5 (December 2000/January 2001): 1–8.

<http://www.lemitonline.org/telemasp/>

Presents data on the interactions between police departments and the parents of missing children from a survey of thirty-two Texas law enforcement agencies.

Motorcycles

141 Day, George J. "Motorcycle Patrol." *TELEMASP Bulletin* [Texas Law Enforcement Management and Administrative Statistics Program] 16, no. 2 (March/April 2009): 1–12.

<http://www.lemitonline.org/telemasp/>

Presents the results of a survey of fifty-nine Texas law enforcement agencies concerning the size of their motorcycle units, selection of motorcycle officers, training requirements, specific motorcycles and equipment used, patrol scheduling including consideration for inclement weather, and motorcycle safety issues.

Mounted Police Patrol

142 Swindell, Sam. "Policing on Bicycles and Horses." *TELEMASP Bulletin* [Texas Law Enforcement Management and Administrative Statistics Program] 14, no. 6 (November/December 2007): 1–12.

<http://www.lemitonline.org/telemasp/>

Reports data from a survey of forty-nine Texas law enforcement agencies on their mounted patrol units including officer experience and training, deployment hours, and a comparison of deployment areas for police cyclists and mounted officers.

Municipal Police

•**143** Police department websites of the ten most populous Texas cities:

Houston Police Department
<http://www.piersystem.com/go/doc/2133/289249/>
San Antonio Police Department
<http://www.ci.sat.tx.us/sapd/>
Dallas Police Department
<http://www.dallaspolice.net/>
Austin Police Department
<http://www.ci.austin.tx.us/police/>
Fort Worth Police Department
<http://www.fortworthpd.com/>
El Paso Police Department
<http://www.elpasotexas.gov/police/>
Arlington Police Department
<http://www.arlingtonpd.org/>
Corpus Christi Police Department
<http://www.cctexas.com/police/>
Plano Police Department
<http://www.plano.gov/departments/police/>
Laredo Police Department
<http://www.ci.laredo.tx.us/policenew/index/index.html>

The websites of most Texas municipal police departments provide current and historical crime statistics for districts, neighborhoods, or police beats. Data on violent crime and property crime is usually presented for Uniform Crime Reporting (UCR) offenses. Some departments also provide interactive maps as well as additional data for driving under the influence arrests, narcotic laws violations, racial profiling, and so forth.

144 Reaves, Brian A., and Matthew J. Hickman. *Police Departments in Large Cities, 1990–2000* [Special Report]. Washington, D.C.: Bureau of Justice Statistics, Office of Justice Programs, U.S. Department of Justice, 2002. NCJ 175703

<http://purl.access.gpo.gov/GPO/LPS75615>

Presents 1990 and 2000 data for police departments serving cities with populations of 250,000 or more, as follows: full-time employees (Appendix Table A); percentage of full-time sworn personnel who are women and minorities, and ratio of minority officers to minority residents (Appendix Table B); annual operating budget (Appendix Table C); UCR violent crime index offenses reported (Appendix Table D); and UCR property crime index offenses reported (Appendix Table E).

Neighborhood Watch Programs

145 San Miguel, Claudia. "Community Crime Prevention Programs: Neighborhood Watch." *TELEMASP Bulletin* [Texas Law Enforcement Management and Administrative Statistics Program] 11, no. 2 (March/April 2004): 1–12.

<http://www.lemitonline.org/telemasp/>

Presents the following data on neighborhood watch programs from a survey of forty-six Texas law enforcement agencies: sponsor agency of watch program (Table 1); tasks performed by officers (Table 2); officers assigned to watch programs by time equivalent (Table 3); correlation between number of officers and larger department unit (Table 4); financial support (Table 5); number of citizens/percentage of total population who attend watch meetings (Tables 6 and 7); and purpose of watch meetings (Table 8).

Police Casework

146 Reyes, Napoleon C. "Cold Case Investigation Units." *TELEMASP Bulletin* [Texas Law Enforcement Management and Administrative Statistics Program] 16, no. 1 (January/February 2009): 1–12.

<http://www.lemitonline.org/telemasp/>

Presents data from a survey of fifty-eight Texas law enforcement agencies on their cold case investigation units as follows: police agencies with cold case units (Figure 1); percentage of homicides or suspected homicides turning cold (Figure 2); selection of homicide cases assigned to cold case investigation units (Figure 3); criteria used for selection of cold cases (Figure 4); years of investigative experience required to be a cold case investigator (Figure 5); selection of potential members (Figure 6); criteria used in selecting members of cold case investigation units (Figure 7); time spent by cold case investigators (Figure 8); and primary factor in clearing cold cases (Figure 9).

Police Compensation

147 *A Report on the State's Law Enforcement Salary Schedule (Salary Schedule C)*. [SAO Report]. Austin: State Auditor's Office, 2010. 10-707

<http://www.sao.state.tx.us/reports/main/10-707.html>

This report analyzes the State's direct compensation for law enforcement positions and compares that compensation with the direct compensation paid by local Texas law enforcement departments that employ more than 1,000 commissioned law enforcement officers. Direct compensation includes base pay and various forms of supplemental pay, such as hazardous duty pay, education pay, and certification pay.

Research Note: Earlier editions are available.

Police Crisis Intervention

148 Van Aelstyn, Michael A. "Crisis Negotiation Teams." *TELEMASP Bulletin* [Texas Law Enforcement Management and Administrative Statistics Program] 14, no. 4 (July/August 2007): 1–8.

<http://www.lemitonline.org/telemasp/>

Presents the following data on crisis negotiation teams from a survey of forty-three Texas law enforcement agencies: status, unit/department where located, duties, ranks, financial bonuses, education levels, college majors, training frequency, incident types, and unsuccessful outcomes.

Police Deaths

•149 *Law Enforcement Officers Killed and Assaulted.* Washington, D.C.: Federal Bureau of Investigation, U.S. Department of Justice [annual, 1982-date].

<http://purl.access.gpo.gov/GPO/LPS700>

Presents state-level statistics reported to the FBI's Uniform Crime Reporting (UCR) Program for the following categories: law enforcement officers feloniously killed, with additional jurisdiction-level data on the type of weapon involved; law enforcement officers accidentally killed, with additional jurisdiction-level data on circumstance at the scene of incident; and federal officers killed, with additional data on the type of weapon involved.

Research Note: See also entry 098. Reports are available online back to 1996 and have been disseminated in electronic format only beginning with the 2004 edition. Printable data tables are available for downloading. Regional data for 1937–1981 is reported in *Uniform Crime Reports for the United States* (see entry 002). See also *Law Enforcement Officers Killed, Summary* (1972–1976); *Law Enforcement Officers Killed* (1977–1981); and *Assaults on Federal Officers* (1976–1981). Datasets are available through the National Archive of Criminal Justice Data, Inter-university Consortium for Political and Social Research (ICPSR), Institute for Social Research, University of Michigan (under Police Employee (LEOKA) Data). <http://www.icpsr.umich.edu/NACJD/ucr.html#desc_al>

Police Department Volunteers

150 Guglu, Timur. "Use of Volunteers in Policing." *TELEMASP Bulletin* [Texas Law Enforcement Management and Administrative Statistics Program] 17, no. 1 (January/February 2010): 1–8.

<http://www.lemitonline.org/telemasp/>

Presents data on the use of volunteers from a survey of seventy-four Texas law enforcement agencies as follows: percentage of increase or decrease in the use of volunteers, 2005–2009 (Fig. 1); use of citizen volunteers (Table 1); assessment of volunteers according to their roles (Table 2); problems related to use of volunteers (Fig. 2); incentives used to motivate volunteers (Fig. 3); required hours of volunteer training (Fig. 4); typical age of volunteers (Fig. 5); and reasons that agencies may refrain from the use of volunteers (Fig. 6).

Police Discipline

151 Arslan, Hasan. "Disciplinary Procedures." *TELEMASP Bulletin* [Texas Law Enforcement Management and Administrative Statistics Program] 12, no. 1 (January/February 2005): 1–8.

<http://www.lemitonline.org/telemasp/>

Presents the following data on disciplinary procedures from a survey of thirty-nine Texas law enforcement agencies: disciplinary rate per one hundred officers (Figure 1); conduct usually generating written reprimand (Figure 2); polygraph use for disciplinary investigations (Figure 3); days required to adjudicate minor/major disciplinary cases (Figures 4 and 5); and days from agency adjudication to civil service/other appeal determination (Figure 6).

Police Dogs

152 Kawucha, S. Kris. "K-9 Units and Policing." *TELEMASP Bulletin* [Texas Law Enforcement Management and Administrative Statistics Program] 16, no. 4 (July/August 2009): 1–8.

<http://www.lemitonline.org/telemasp/>

Presents data on K-9 units from a survey of sixty-three Texas law enforcement agencies as follows: number of K-9s per agency (Fig. 1), age at acquisition (Fig. 2), training levels at acquisition (Fig. 3), breeds (Fig. 4), where acquired (Fig. 5), assignments (Fig. 6), average annual maintenance costs (Fig. 7), range of annual costs (Table 1), and K-9 vehicles (Fig. 8).

Police Patrol

153 DiMambro, Andy. "Patrol Shift Schedules." *TELEMASP Bulletin* [Texas Law Enforcement Management and Administrative Statistics Program] 15, no. 2 (March/April 2008): 1–8.

<http://www.lemitonline.org/telemasp/>

Presents data from a survey of fifty-three Texas law enforcement agencies on patrol shift schedules (focusing on twelve-hour shifts).

Police Performance Evaluation

154 Ekici, Ahmet. "Employee Performance Evaluations." *TELEMASP Bulletin* [Texas Law Enforcement Management and Administrative Statistics Program] 15, no. 4 (July/August 2008): 1–8.

<http://www.lemitonline.org/telemasp/>

Presents data on employee performance evaluations from a survey of fifty-one Texas law enforcement agencies, including their purpose, importance, methods, frequency, input from employees, and use in personnel decision making.

Police Personnel

•155 *Census of Governments: Government Employment and Payroll.* Washington, D.C.: Governments Division, U.S. Census Bureau, U.S. Department of Commerce [quinquennial, 1957–date].

<http://purl.access.gpo.gov/GPO/LPS33151>

The Census of Governments is conducted in years ending in "2" and "7" as mandated by 13 U.S.C. § 161 (2009). The Annual Survey of Government Employment is conducted in the intervening years under the provisions of 13 U.S.C. § 182 (2009). The latter includes a sample of state and local governments, with a new sample being selected every five years (years ending in "4" and "9"). The Census Bureau website provides a Build-a-Table function, which allows users to access data at the level of state government, local government (aggregated county, municipality, township, school district, and special district), or combined state and local government. Data is presented for the government functions police protection total, police officers only, and other police employees, as follows: full-time employees and pay, part-time employees and pay, total employees, total pay, and full-time equivalent.

Research Note: Editions are available online back to 1992. The government functions are defined as follows: "police protection total" encompasses "all activities concerned, with the enforcement of law and order, including coroner's offices, police training academies, investigation bureaus, and local jails, 'lockups,' or other detention facilities not intended to serve as correctional facilities"; "police officers only" comprises persons with the power of arrest; and "other police employees" includes only persons who do not have the power of arrest. Datasets are available through the Inter-university Consortium for Political and Social Research (ICPSR), Institute for Social Research, University of Michigan. <http://www.icpsr.umich.edu/icpsrweb/ICPSR/series/00012>

•**156** *Census of State and Local Law Enforcement Agencies.* Washington, D.C.: Bureau of Justice Statistics, Office of Justice Programs, U.S. Department of Justice [quadrennial, 1992–date].

<http://purl.access.gpo.gov/GPO/LPS40398>

The main tables provide statistics for primary state law enforcement agency full-time employees, total and sworn personnel (number and per 100,000 residents), by state; full-time sworn personnel of the nation's ten largest transit system law enforcement agencies; full-time sworn personnel of the nation's ten largest airport law enforcement agencies; and full-time sworn officers of the nation's thirty largest state and local law enforcement agencies with special jurisdictions. The Appendix Tables provide statistics on state and local law enforcement agencies and employees, total and sworn personnel (number and per 100,000 residents), by state; the fifty largest state and local law enforcement agencies, by number of full-time sworn personnel; local police departments and employees, total and sworn personnel (number and per 100,000 residents), by state; the fifty largest local police departments, by number of full-time sworn personnel; sheriffs' offices and employees, by state; and the fifty largest sheriffs' offices, by number of full-time sworn personnel.

•**157** *Federal Law Enforcement Officers* [Bulletin]. Washington, D.C.: Bureau of Justice Statistics, Office of Justice Programs, U.S. Department of Justice [biennial, 1993–date].

<http://purl.access.gpo.gov/GPO/LPS23994>

Provides statistics from the Census of Federal Law Enforcement Officers on the number of full-time federal officers with arrest and firearms authority and number per 100,000 residents, by state of employment.

•**158** *Justice Expenditure and Employment.* Washington, D.C.: Bureau of Justice Statistics, Office of Justice Programs, U.S. Department of Justice [annual, 1982–date].

<http://bjs.ojp.usdoj.gov/index.cfm?ty=daa>

Presents data extracted from the Census Bureau's Annual Survey of Government Finances and Annual Survey of Government Employment, which provide estimates of full-time only and full-time equivalent employment for the government function "police protection," including both sworn and non-sworn personnel. Data is reported at the level of states, large counties (with populations of 500,000 or more), and large cities (with populations of 300,000 or more). Annual March payrolls are also reported.

Research Note: Definitions are provided for the police protection categories covered in the report. Prior data is reported in various publications series of the U.S. Department of Justice's Law Enforcement Assistance Administration and the Census Bureau's Governments Division. Datasets are available through the Inter-university Consortium for Political and Social Research (ICPSR), Institute for Social Research, University of Michigan. <http://www.icpsr.umich.edu/icpsrweb/ICPSR/series/00087>

•**159** *The Municipal Year Book.* Washington, D.C.: ICMA Press [annual, 1934–date].

Contains statistics on police department personnel, salaries, and expenditures for cities of 10,000 residents and over, based on responses to the annual *Police and Fire Personnel, Salaries, and Expenditures* survey conducted by the International City/County Management Association. Data includes full-time paid personnel, full-time uniformed personnel, duty hours per week, minimum base salary, maximum base salary, longevity pay, maximum salary with longevity, years of service for longevity, total expenditures, total personnel expenditures, total personnel expenditures as percentage of total expenditures, salaries and wages, city contribution to retirement and Social Security, city contribution to insurance, capital outlay, and all other.

Research Note: A total of 1,263 jurisdictions completed the 2009 survey, for an overall response rate of 39 percent (some jurisdictions respond to the survey in alternate years, which causes the response rate to fluctuate).

•**160** *Occupational Employment Statistics: Occupational Employment and Wage Estimates*. Washington. D.C.: Bureau of Labor Statistics, U.S. Department of Labor [annual, online only, 1999–date].
<http://purl.access.gpo.gov/GPO/LPS68663>

Provides employment and wage estimates for states, metropolitan areas, and nonmetropolitan areas, and includes the following occupations (Standard Occupational Classification codes noted): first-line supervisors/managers of police and detectives (33-1012); fire inspectors and investigators (33-2021); detectives and criminal investigators (33-3021); fish and game wardens (33-3031); police and sheriff's patrol officers (33-3051); transit and railroad police (33-3052); private detectives and investigators (33-9021); gaming surveillance officers and gaming investigators (33-9031); security guards (33-9032); forensic science technicians (19-4092); and police, fire, and ambulance dispatchers (43-5031).

Police Recruits

161 Lee, Chang-Bae. "Psychological Testing for Recruit Screening." *TELEMASP Bulletin* [Texas Law Enforcement Management and Administrative Statistics Program] 13, no. 2 (March/April 2006): 1–8.
<http://www.lemitonline.org/telemasp/>

Presents data on pre-employment psychological testing of recruits from a survey of forty-three Texas law enforcement agencies regarding their procedures and elements of psychological testing, objective tests, and psychological interviews.

Police Response

162 Lee, Won-Jae. "Patrol Workload." *TELEMASP Bulletin* [Texas Law Enforcement Management and Administrative Statistics Program] 9, no. 2 (March/April 2002): 1–12.
<http://www.lemitonline.org/telemasp/>

Presents data from a survey of twenty Texas law enforcement agencies on their Differential Police Response programs (call classification and response; calls and immediate response time according to shifts and days of the week; and immediate and delayed response according to shifts and days of the week).

163 Munson, Michelle. "Response Times." *TELEMASP Bulletin* [Texas Law Enforcement Management and Administrative Statistics Program] 13, no. 6 (November/December 2006): 1–8.

<http://www.lemitonline.org/telemasp/>

The following data is presented from a survey of forty-seven Texas law enforcement agencies: average response time for calls for service by priority (Table 1); average response time from receipt of calls for services to arrival at scene for the busiest and for the slowest shifts (Table 2); and average response times from receipt of calls for services to arrival at scene grouped by three measures of size—number of sworn officers, population served, and crime rate per 100,000 population (Table 3).

164 Zhou, Ling. "Differential Police Response." *TELEMASP Bulletin* [Texas Law Enforcement Management and Administrative Statistics Program] 8, no. 3 (August/September 2001): 1–8.

<http://www.lemitonline.org/telemasp/>

Presents data from a survey of thirty-one Texas law enforcement agencies on their Differential Police Response programs (personnel, call evaluation, offenses handled, and strategies used).

Police School Relations

165 Gulen, Engin. "School Resource Officer Programs." *TELEMASP Bulletin* [Texas Law Enforcement Management and Administrative Statistics Program] 17, no. 2 (March/April 2010): 1–8.

<http://www.lemitonline.org/telemasp/>

Presents data on the use of school resource officers (SRO) from a survey of seventy-one Texas law enforcement agencies as follows: distribution of SRO programs (Fig. 1); distribution of SRO program at each school level (Fig. 2); duration of SRO program in years (Fig. 3); assignment of school resource officers (Fig. 4); weekly time distribution spent per week at each school level (Fig. 5); required years of police experience (Fig. 6); and funding distribution rounded to the nearest percent (Fig. 7).

Police Standards

•**166** *Active Police Licenses by County/Region.* Austin: Texas Commission on Law Enforcement Officer Standards and Education [online only].

<http://www.tcleose.state.tx.us/surveytest/Agency_pubs.htm>

The Texas Commission on Law Enforcement Officer Standards and Education (TCLEOSE) develops, maintains, and enforces minimum qualifications for the selection, training, and certification of law enforcement personnel and county correctional officers (Tex. Occ. Code Ann. §§ 1701.001–.603 (Vernon

2004 & Supp. 2010)). This report provides the current number of active police licenses by TCLEOSE region and county.

167 *The Texas Commission on Law Enforcement Officer Standards and Education Self Assessment Report.* Austin: Texas Commission on Law Enforcement Officer Standards and Education, 2007.

<http://www.sunset.state.tx.us/81streports/leose/ser.pdf>

The Texas Sunset Act requires the automatic termination of designated State agencies twelve years after review unless the legislature extends the life of the agency by statute (Tex. Gov't Code Ann. §§ 325.001–.024 (Vernon 2005)). The Sunset Advisory commission assists the legislature in making these determinations by evaluating the operations of agencies scheduled for termination. As a part of the review process, each agency submits a Self-Evaluation Report (SER) to the Commission. This report provides statistics on the fiscal matters (appropriations, revenues, and expenditures); personnel; and key performance measures (e.g., number of new licenses issued, number of courses maintained, and number of academy evaluations, complaints resolved, and average license cost per individual).

Research Note: Earlier editions are available. See also the report of the commission's decisions regarding this review. <http://www.sunset.state.tx.us/81streports/leose/leose_dec.pdf>

168 Stewart, Daniel M. "Collegiate Educational Standards." *TELEMASP Bulletin* [Texas Law Enforcement Management and Administrative Statistics Program] 13, no. 3 (May/June 2006): 1–12.

<http://www.lemitonline.org/telemasp/>

The following data is presented on collegiate educational policies from a survey of forty-seven Texas law enforcement agencies: minimum entry-level requirements, exceptions/substitutions to the college education requirement and reasons for them, policies linking college education with promotion, college education required and bonus points awarded for promotion, recruitment practices and degree preferences, departmental educational programs, education pay incentive programs, and restrictions placed on officers enrolled in college courses.

Policewomen

169 Langton, Lynn. *Women in Law Enforcement, 1987–2008* [Crime Data Brief]. Washington, D.C.: Bureau of Justice Statistics, Office of Justice Programs, U.S. Department of Justice, 2010. NCJ 230521

<http://bjs.ojp.usdoj.gov/index.cfm?ty=pbdetail&iid=2274>

Presents data from the Law Enforcement Management and Administrative Statistics surveys on the percentage and number of full-time sworn female officers among the largest police departments, including Dallas and Houston, 1997 and 2007 (Table 2).

Racial/ethnic Profiling

170 Hickman, Matthew J. *Traffic Stop Data Collection Policies for State Police, 2004* [Fact Sheet]. Washington, D.C.: Bureau of Justice Statistics, Office of Justice Programs, U.S. Department of Justice, 2005. NCJ 209156

<http://bjs.ojp.usdoj.gov/index.cfm?ty=dcdetail&iid=252>

Table 2 shows circumstances during traffic stops in which state police agencies required troopers to collect race or ethnicity data about motorists, by state, 2004 (officer initiated stops, reactive traffic stops, stops resulting in citation, stops resulting in arrest, vehicle or occupant searches, officer use of force, and no stops).

Research Note: Earlier editions are available.

171 *Racial Profiling Report.* Austin: Texas Criminal Justice Coalition [annual, 2004-date].

<http://www.criminaljusticecoalition.org/public_safety_project/publications>

The Law Enforcement Policy on Racial Profiling (Tex. Code Crim. Proc. Ann. art. 2.132 (Vernon 2005 & Supp. 2010)), which became effective on September 1, 2001, requires the collection of information relating to traffic stops in which a citation is issued and to arrests resulting from those traffic stops, including information relating to (a) the race or ethnicity of the individual detained, and (b) whether a search was conducted and, if so, whether the person detained consented to the search. Furthermore, it requires the agency to submit to the governing body of each county or municipality served by the agency an annual report of this information collected if the agency is an agency of a county, municipality, or other political subdivision of the state. The Texas Criminal Justice Coalition (TCJC) has served since 2001 as the sole statewide repository and analyst of these reports. For each Texas law enforcement agency that responded to the coalition's open records request and also issued 3,000 or more citations during traffic stops, this report provides data on the number of consent searches per one hundred stops (Appendix Table 1), and the racial disparity on consent stops (Appendix Table 2).

Research Note: Each edition has an individual title. Law enforcement agencies were required to adopt and implement a policy and begin collecting information no later than January 1, 2002.

•**172** *Traffic Stop Data Report.* Austin: Texas Department of Public Safety [annual, 2000–date].

<http://www.txdps.state.tx.us/director_staff/public_information/reports.htm>

Provides DPS traffic stop data by race (number and percentage) for the following: traffic stops, citations, written warnings, consent vehicle searches, probable cause vehicle searches, all other vehicle searches, and criminal interdiction. In addition, data is also provided by race for DPS vehicle searches (citations, warnings, and combined totals), non-traffic criminal arrests resulting from vehicle searches, and vehicle searches by driver license state.

Sheriffs

•**173** Hickman, Matthew J., and Brian A. Reaves. *Sheriffs' Offices 2003* [Law Enforcement Management and Administrative Statistics]. Washington, D.C.: Bureau of Justice Statistics, Office of Justice Programs, U.S. Department of Justice, 2006. NCJ 211361

<http://purl.access.gpo.gov/GPO/LPS58821>

Presents data from the Law Enforcement Management and Administrative Statistics (LEMAS) survey on the twenty-five largest sheriffs' offices by number and function of full-time sworn personnel, i.e., percentage of officers by area of duty.

Research Note: Earlier editions are available. Published under the title *Sheriffs' Departments* prior to 1999.

•**174** Sheriffs' office websites of the ten most populous Texas counties:

Harris County Sheriff's Office
<http://www.hcso.hctx.net/>
Dallas County Sheriff's Office
<http://www.dallassheriffsoffice.com/>
Tarrant County Sheriff's Office
<http://tcweb.tarrantcounty.com/eSheriff/site/default.asp>
Bexar County Sheriff's Office
<http://www.bexar.org/bcsheriff/>
Travis County Sheriff's Office
<http://www.tcsheriff.org/index.html>
El Paso County Sheriff's Office
<http://www.epcounty.com/sheriff/>
Collin County Sheriff's Office
<http://www.co.collin.tx.us/sheriff/index.jsp>
Hidalgo County Sheriff's Office

<http://www.hidalgoso.org/>

Denton County Sheriff's Office

<http://sheriff.dentoncounty.com/main.asp?Dept=54>

Fort Bend County Sheriff's Office

<http://www.co.fort-bend.tx.us/getsitepage.asp?sitepage=3219>

The websites of many Texas sheriffs' offices provide current and historical crime statistics for their jurisdictions. Data on violent crime and property crime is usually presented for Uniform Crime Reporting (UCR) offenses. Some offices also provide interactive maps as well as data for driving under the influence arrests, narcotic laws violations, racial profiling, and so forth.

Special Weapons and Tactics Units

175 Dulin, Adam. "Special Weapons and Tactics Teams." *TELEMASP Bulletin* [Texas Law Enforcement Management and Administrative Statistics Program] 12, no. 3 (May/June 2005): 1–12.

<http://www.lemitonline.org/telemasp/>

Presents data on SWAT teams from a survey of forty-eight Texas law enforcement agencies (team selection and training; activity; and weaponry and technology).

Stress Management

176 MacMillan, Scott. "Mental Health and Stress Management Programs in Policing." *TELEMASP Bulletin* [Texas Law Enforcement Management and Administrative Statistics Program] 16, no. 5 (September/October 2009): 1–8.

<http://www.lemitonline.org/telemasp/>

Presents data on the use of mental health and stress management programs from a survey of fifty-seven Texas law enforcement agencies as follows: agency provisions for mental health, stress management and/or peer counseling (Fig. 1); internal and external services provided (Fig. 2); total mental health/stress management personnel (Fig. 3); external program services available to officers (Fig. 4); how officers are selected to be peer counselors (Fig. 5); techniques used by peer counselors (Fig. 6); and situations where peer counselors are used (Fig. 7).

Texas Department of Public Safety

177 *Agency Strategic Plan (Including Polygraph Examiners Boards), Fiscal Years [year–year]*. Austin: Office of Audit and Inspection, Texas Department of Public Safety [biennial, 1994-date].

<http://www.txdps.state.tx.us/oai/index.htm>

The Strategic Outlook section provides statistical highlights for each major DPS division (in the corresponding Accomplishments subsections): Texas Highway Patrol Division, Driver License Division, Criminal Law Enforcement Division, Texas Ranger Division, Administration Division, and Emergency Management Division.

•178 *Annual Report*. Austin: Texas Department of Public Safety [1980-date].

<http://www.txdps.state.tx.us/director_staff/public_information/reports.htm>

Selected statistics are presented within the individual reports of each major DPS division: Texas Highway Patrol Division, Driver License Division, Criminal Law Enforcement Division, Texas Ranger Division, Administration Division, and Emergency Management Division.

Research Note: Reports are available online back to 2000. Published as *Biennial Report* prior to 1980 (the 1980 *Annual Report* was included with 1978/1979 *Biennial Report*). See also entry 119.

179 *Self-evaluation Report to the Sunset Advisory Commission*. Austin: Texas Department of Public Safety, 2007.

<http://www.sunset.state.tx.us/81streports/dps/ser.pdf>

The Texas Sunset Act requires the automatic termination of designated State agencies twelve years after review unless the legislature extends the life of the agency by statute (Tex. Gov't Code Ann. §§ 325.001–.024 (Vernon 2005)). The Sunset Advisory Commission assists the legislature in making these determinations by evaluating the operations of agencies scheduled for termination. As a part of the review process, each agency submits a Self-Evaluation Report (SER) to the commission. This report provides statistics on fiscal matters (appropriations, revenues, expenditures, and federal aid); personnel; complaints against the agency received, investigated, and resolved; activities and accomplishments; and key performance measures.

Research Note: Earlier editions are available. See also the report of the commission's decisions regarding this review. <http://www.sunset.state.tx.us/81streports/dps/dps_dec.pdf>

180 *Texas Department of Public Safety: Management and Organizational Structure Study*. 2 vol. Austin: Deloitte Consulting, 2008.

<http://www.txdps.state.tx.us/director_staff/public_information/
Deloitte102808.pdf>

<http://www.txdps.state.tx.us/deloittestudy/docs/DeloitteStudy.pdf>

Although primarily a narrative report, this study contains selected statistics on the DPS's organizational structure, workforce, finances, and information systems.

Wildlife Law Enforcement

181 *Annual Report.* Austin: Texas Parks and Wildlife Department [1996-date].
<http://www.tpwd.state.tx.us/publications/business/>

The Accountability Measures, which appear in the Law Enforcement subsection, report the vehicle miles patrolled by game wardens; boat hours patrolled by game wardens; arrests (game and fish); arrests (water safety); and law enforcement contacts by game wardens.

Research Note: Data is reported by fiscal year. Published under slightly varying titles prior to 1996. Some editions also have individual titles.

182 *Annual Report.* [Washington, D.C.]: Office of Law Enforcement, Fish and Wildlife Service, U.S. Department of the Interior [1994–date].
<http://purl.access.gpo.gov/GPO/LPS66491>

The Statistical Summary (Appendix A) contains fiscal year data on wildlife inspection activity (in terms of number of shipments) for designated ports of entry (including Dallas/Fort Worth and Houston), and non-designated ports of entry (including Brownsville, El Paso, Laredo, and McAllen). The federal statutes enforced by the Office of Law Enforcement are enumerated in Appendix B.

Research Note: Reports are available online back to 1999. The office was called the Division of Law Enforcement prior to 2002.

Chapter 4

Courts and Sentencing

Adult Felony System

183 *Felony Defendants in Large Urban Counties* [Bulletin]. Washington, D.C.: Bureau of Justice Statistics, Office of Justice Programs, U.S. Department of Justice [biennial, 1988–date].

<http://purl.access.gpo.gov/GPO/LPS1754>

Reports representative sample data gathered through the State Court Processing Statistics (SCPS) program, which focuses on the processing of felony defendants in the state courts of the seventy-five most populated counties in the United States (including Dallas, El Paso, Harris, and Tarrant). These counties account for approximately one-half of the felony crimes committed nationwide. The Appendix Tables provide SCPS jurisdiction-level data as follows: population, sampling weights, and number of cases; most serious arrest charge of felony defendants; sex and age of felony defendants; race and Hispanic/Latino origin; felony defendants released before or detained until case disposition; failure-to-appear and re-arrest rates of defendants released prior to case disposition; adjudication outcome for felony defendants; and most severe type of sentence received by defendants convicted of a felony.

Research Note: The program was called the National Pretrial Reporting Program prior to 1994. Researchers should review the BJS data advisory, *State Court Processing Statistics Data Limitations* (March 2010), before using this report. <http://bjs.ojp.usdoj.gov/content/pub/pdf/scpsdl_da.pdf> Datasets are available through the Inter-university Consortium for Political and Social Research (ICPSR), Institute for Social Research, University of Michigan. <http://www.icpsr.umich.edu/icpsrweb/ICPSR/series/00079>

Aliens

184 Salant, Tanis J. *Undocumented Immigrants in U.S.–Mexico Border Counties: The Costs of Law Enforcement and Criminal Justice Services*. Tucson: Eller College of Management, School of Public Administration and Policy, University of Arizona, 2008. NCJ 223285

<http://www.bordercounties.org/>

Provides a breakdown of the costs of undocumented immigrants to law enforcement and criminal justice services in the U.S. counties bordering Mexico, which includes fifteen in Texas. County-level statistics are presented for county and district clerks, district courts, district attorneys, county district courts, county courts at law, county attorneys, justices of the peace and constables, county law magistrates, and indigent defense.

Research Note: This report was sponsored by the U.S./Mexico Border Counties Coalition. For earlier data, see Tanis J. Salant, *Illegal Immigrants in U.S.-Mexico Border Counties: Costs of Law Enforcement, Criminal Justice and Emergency Medical Services*. Tucson: Eller College of Business and Public Administration, School of Public Administration and Policy, University of Arizona, 2001. NCJ 201492

184A *Statistical Year Book.* Falls Church, Va.: Executive Office for Immigration Review, U.S. Department of Justice [annual, 2000–date].

<http://purl.access.gpo.gov/GPO/LPS31215>

An alien charged by the Department of Homeland Security (DHS) with an immigration law violation is issued a charging document, usually a Notice to Appear (NTA) or a Notice of Referral to an immigration judge. When the charging document is filed by DHS with the immigration court, jurisdiction over the case transfers from DHS to the Executive Office for Immigration Review (EOIR), which has oversight over the fifty-seven U.S. immigration courts (including eight in Texas). Once an alien has been ordered removed by the EOIR, the removal is the responsibility of DHS. This report provides fiscal year data for each immigration court as follows: total immigration court matters received; total immigration court receipts by type of matter (proceedings, bonds, motions, and total); total immigration court matters completed; total immigration court completions by type of matter; asylum receipts and completions; asylum grant rate; convention against torture completions; immigration court completions (proceedings) with applications for relief; and immigration court completions (proceedings) for detained cases.

Caseloads

•**185** *Federal Court Management Statistics: U.S. District Courts—Judicial Caseload Profiles.* Washington, D.C.: Statistics Division, Office of Judges Programs, Administrative Office of the United States Courts [annual, online only, 1997-date].

<http://purl.access.gpo.gov/GPO/LPS37887>

Provides summary statistics for the reporting year and five previous years for the following: overall caseload statistics, number of judgeships, vacant judgeship months, actions per judgeship, median times (months), and other. Data on criminal felony filings by nature of suit and offense is provided for the reporting year.

Research Note: Data is reported by fiscal year. Texas is in the U.S. Court of Appeals Fifth Circuit and has four districts: Eastern, Northern, Southern, and Western. Datasets for some categories are available through the Inter-university Consortium for Political and Social Research (ICPSR), Institute for Social Research, University of Michigan. <http://www.icpsr.umich.edu/icpsrweb/ICPSR/series/00072>

•**186** *Federal Judicial Caseload Statistics.* Washington, D.C.: Office of Human Resources and Statistics, Statistics Division, Administrative Office of the United States Courts [annual, 1994-date].

<http://purl.access.gpo.gov/GPO/LPS29106>

Statistics are reported by circuit for the U.S. Courts of Appeals as follows: appeals commenced, terminated, and pending (Tables B-1, B-5); and nature of suit or offense in cases arising from the U.S. District Courts (Table B-7). Statistics are reported by judicial circuit and district for criminal cases in U.S. District Courts as follows: cases commenced, terminated, and pending (Tables D, D-1); defendants commenced, terminated, and pending (Tables D, D-1); cases commenced, by offense and district (Table D-3); and defendants commenced, by offense and district (Table D-3). Statistics are reported by circuit and district for the federal probation system as follows: persons received for and removed from post-conviction supervision (Table E-1) and persons under post-conviction supervision (Table E-2). Statistics are reported by circuit and district for pretrial services in U.S. District Courts as follows: cases activated (Table H-1); interviews and types of pretrial reports (Table H-2); and pretrial services defendants received for and under supervision (Table H-7). Statistics are reported by circuit and district for grand and petit jurors in U.S. District Courts as follows: grand juror service (Table J-1) and petit juror service on days jurors were selected for trial (Table J-2).

Research Note: Reporting year ends March 31. Reports are available online back to 2001. Previously published under the title *Federal Judicial Workload Statistics* (1977–1993). Texas is in the U.S. Court of Appeals Fifth Circuit and has four districts: Eastern, Northern, Southern, and Western. This data is also reported biannually in *Statistical Tables of the Federal Judiciary* (2001–date). <http://purl.access.gpo.gov/GPO/LPS21918> Datasets for some categories are available through the Inter-university Consortium for Political and Social Research (ICPSR), Institute for Social Research, University of Michigan. <http://www.icpsr.umich.edu/icpsrweb/ICPSR/series/00072>

•**187** *State Court Caseload Statistics: An Analysis of [year] State Court Caseloads.* Williamsburg, Va.: Courts Statistics Project, National Center for State Courts [annual, 1975-date].

<http://www.ncsconline.org/D_Research/csp/CSP_Main_Page.html>

Provides state-level statistics for the following categories: reported grand total state trial court caseloads (Table 2); reported total state trial court criminal caseloads (Table 6); felony caseloads in state trial courts of general jurisdiction (Table 7); reported total state trial court juvenile caseloads (Table 8); reported grand total state appellate court caseloads (Table 11); reported total state appellate court appeal by right caseloads (Table 12); reported total state appellate court appeal by permission caseloads (Table 13); reported total state appellate court death penalty caseloads (Table 14); reported total state appellate court original proceeding/other appellate matter caseloads (Table 15); and opinions reported by state appellate courts (Table 16).

Research Note: This compilation is a joint project of the Conference of State Court Administrators, the Bureau of Justice Statistics, and the Court Statistics Project of the National Center for State Courts. Datasets are available through the Inter-university Consortium for Political and Social Research (ICPSR), Institute for Social Research, University of Michigan. <http://www.icpsr.umich.edu/icpsrweb/ICPSR/series/00080>

Court Personnel

•**188** *Census of Governments: Government Employment and Payroll.* Washington, D.C.: Governments Division, U.S. Census Bureau, U.S. Department of Commerce [quinquennial, 1957–date].

<http://purl.access.gpo.gov/GPO/LPS33151>

The Census of Governments is conducted in years ending in "2" and "7" as mandated by 13 U.S.C. § 161 (2009). The Annual Survey of Government Employment is conducted in the intervening years under the provisions of 13 U.S.C. § 182 (2009). The latter includes a sample of state and local governments, with a new sample being selected every five years (years ending in "4" and "9"). The Census Bureau website provides a Build-a-Table function, which allows users to access data at the level of state government, local government (aggregated county, municipality, township, school district, and special district), or combined state and local government. Data is presented for the government function "judicial and legal" as follows: full-time employees and pay, part-time employees and pay, total employees, total pay, and full-time equivalent.

Research Note: Editions are available online back to 1992. The government function "judicial and legal" encompasses "all court and court related activities (except probation and parole activities that are included at the 'Correction' [sic] function), court activities of sheriff's offices, prosecuting attorneys' and public defenders' offices, legal departments, and attorneys providing government-wide legal service." Datasets are available through the Inter-university Consortium for Political and Social Research (ICPSR), Institute for Social Research, University of Michigan. <http://www.icpsr.umich.edu/icpsrweb/ICPSR/series/00012>

•**189** *Justice Expenditure and Employment.* Washington, D.C.: Bureau of Justice Statistics, Office of Justice Programs, U.S. Department of Justice [annual, 1982–date].

<http://bjs.ojp.usdoj.gov/index.cfm?ty=daa>

Presents data extracted from the Census Bureau's Annual Survey of Government Finances and Annual Survey of Government Employment, which provide estimates of full-time only and full-time equivalent employment for the government function "judicial/legal." Data is reported at the level of states, large counties (with populations of 500,000 or more), and large cities (with populations of 300,000 or more). Annual March payrolls are also reported.

Research Note: Definitions are provided for the judicial/legal categories covered in the report. Prior data is reported in various publications series of the U.S. Department of Justice's Law Enforcement Assistance Administration and the Census Bureau's Governments Division. Datasets are available through the Inter-university Consortium for Political and Social Research (ICPSR), Institute for Social Research, University of Michigan. <http://www.icpsr.umich.edu/icpsrweb/ICPSR/series/00087>

•190 *Occupational Employment Statistics: Occupational Employment and Wage Estimates.* Washington, D.C.: Bureau of Labor Statistics, U.S. Department of Labor [annual, online only, 1999–date].

<http://purl.access.gpo.gov/GPO/LPS68663>

Provides employment and wage estimates for states, metropolitan areas, and nonmetropolitan areas, and includes the following occupations (Standard Occupational Classification codes noted): lawyers (23-1011); administrative law judges, adjudicators, and hearing officers (23-1021); judges, magistrate judges, and magistrates (23-1023); court reporters (23-2091); and bailiffs (33-3031).

Court Structure

191 *State Court Organization, 2004.* Washington, D.C.: Bureau of Justice Statistics, Office of Justice Programs, U.S. Department of Justice, 2006. NCJ 212351

<http://purl.access.gpo.gov/GPO/LPS22184>

While not providing statistics per se, this handbook contains 428 items of information arranged in forty-seven tables as follows: Courts and Judges (Tables 1–3); Judicial Selection and Service (Tables 4–11); The Judicial Branch: Governance, Funding, and Administration (Tables 12–21); Appellate Courts: Jurisdiction and Procedures (Tables 22–27); Trial Courts: Administration, Specialized Jurisdiction, and Procedures (Tables 28–37); The Jury (Tables 38–42); and The Sentencing Context (Tables 43–47).

Research Note: The handbook represents a collaboration between the Conference of State Court Administrators and the National Center for State Courts. Earlier editions are available.

Drug Courts

•192 *Summary of Drug Court Activity by State and County.* Washington D.C.: Drug Court Clearinghouse, Justice Programs Office, School of Public Affairs, American University [online only].

<http://www1.spa.american.edu/justice/project.php?ID=1>

The Bureau of Justice Assistance, Office of Justice Programs, U.S. Department of Justice, has operated the Drug Court Clearinghouse at American University since 1994. An interactive United States map allows users to access individual state reports, which provide county-level statistics for drug court activity, juvenile/family drug court activity, and tribal drug court activity.

Research Note: The clearinghouse compiles statistics on a continuing basis and updates the online summary reports as needed. An indication of OJP/BJA funding source for each court is provided. The reports also include a notation for each county that has a mental health court, based on information provided in *Survey of Mental Health Courts* (Criminal Justice/Mental Health Consensus Project, August 2004).

193 *Initial Process and Outcome Evaluation of Drug Courts in Texas.* Austin: Criminal Justice Policy Council, 2003.

<http://www.lbb.state.tx.us/PubSafety_CrimJustice/6_Links/Documents_Alpha_Links.htm>

Drug courts are legislatively mandated in Texas for counties with populations over 550,000 (Tex. Health & Safety Code Ann. §§ 469.001–.009 (Vernon 2010)). This report covers process and outcome evaluations of drug courts in Dallas, Jefferson, and Travis counties, which were selected on the basis of the size of their programs, years in operation, and availability of computerized data. This data includes program funding and costs; characteristics of the participating offenders; completion rates; drug testing; and recidivism rates.

Research Note: See also the council's earlier report, *Overview of Drug Courts in Texas* (2002).

194 *Problem Solving Courts.* Austin: Texas Courts Online, Office of Court Administration [online only].

<http://www.courts.state.tx.us/courts/pscourts.asp>

Provides a directory of current and planned drug courts reporting to the governor's office (county, drug court name, court name, presiding judge, population served, drug court start date, drug court coordinator/title, and contact information).

Executive Clemency

195 *Texas Secretary of State, Statutory Documents Section: An Inventory of Secretary of State Executive Clemency Records at the Texas State Archives, 1840, 1845–2006.* Austin: Texas State Library and Archives Commission.

<http://www.lib.utexas.edu/taro/tslac/30056/tsl-30056.html>

The records of executive clemency, created by the governors of the State of Texas and maintained by the Texas Secretary of State, include executive record books; clemency proclamations; indexes to clemency proclamations; applications for pardons and other forms of executive clemency; and registers of applications for pardons.

Research Note: Researchers must obtain preapproval from the archivist before accessing these documents.

Juries

•**196** *Annual Statistical Report for the Texas Judiciary.* Austin: Office of Court Administration [2005–date].

<http://www.courts.state.tx.us/pubs/annual-reports.asp>

Presents annual fiscal year data on the State of Texas court system for jury activity in district and county-level courts.

•**197** *Judicial Business of the United States Courts: Annual Report of the Director.* Washington, D.C.: Statistics Division, Office of Judges Programs, Administrative Office of the United States Courts [annual, 1994–date].

<http://purl.access.gpo.gov/GPO/LPS2715>

The Appendix (Detailed Statistical Tables) provides the following statistics for U.S. District Courts: grand juror service (Table J-1), and petit juror service on days jurors were selected for trial (Table J-2);

Research Note: Reports are available online back to 1997. Texas is in the U.S. Court of Appeals Fifth Circuit and has four districts: Eastern, Northern, Southern, and Western. This data is also reported biannually in *Statistical Tables of the Federal Judiciary* <http://purl.access.gpo.gov/GPO/LPS21918> and annually in *Federal Judicial Caseload Statistics* (see entry 186).

Juvenile Courts

•**198** *Juvenile Court Statistics* [Report]. Pittsburgh, Pa: National Center for Juvenile Justice, National Council of Juvenile and Family Court Judges [biennial, 1927–date].

<http://purl.access.gpo.gov/GPO/LPS16327>

Provides county-level statistics on juvenile courts' petitioned and nonpetitioned delinquency, status, and dependency caseloads (Appendix C).

Research Note: Published annually (by varying agencies) prior to the 2001/2002 edition. The 1984 edition was the first to contain detailed, case-level descriptions of the delinquency and status offense cases handled by U.S. juvenile courts. More detailed presentations of this data can be accessed through the *National Juvenile Court Data Archive* (see entry 199). Datasets are available through the Inter-university Consortium for Political and Social Research (ICPSR), Institute for Social Research, University of Michigan.

<http://www.icpsr.umich.edu/icpsrweb/ICPSR/series/00074>

•**199** *National Juvenile Court Data Archive.* Washington, D.C.: Office of Juvenile Justice and Delinquency Prevention, Office of Justice Programs, U.S. Department of Justice [online].

<http://ojjdp.ncjrs.org/ojstatbb/njcda/>

The Office of Juvenile Justice and Delinquency Prevention (OJJDP) established the National Juvenile Court Data Archive with the goal of providing the most detailed information available on the activities of juvenile courts in the United States. It currently contains over fifteen million automated case records, with the majority of data consisting of delinquency and status offense records, although some state-level data contains traffic and dependency cases. The records provide demographic information on the juvenile offender (e.g., age at referral, gender, race, county of residence); the offense(s) charged; the date of referral; the processing characteristics of the case (e.g., detention and manner of handling); and the case disposition.

Research Note: The archive has been maintained for the OJJDP since 1975 by the National Center for Juvenile Justice (NCJJ), which is the research division of the National Council of Juvenile and Family Court Judges. Files that contain information identifiable to a private person are made available only to qualified individuals or organizations involved in research and statistical activities. Summary county-level data for delinquency, status, and dependency cases can be obtained through *Easy Access to State and County Juvenile Court Case Counts* (1997–date). <http://www.ojjdp.ncjrs.gov/ojstatbb/ezaco/> Datasets are available through the Interuniversity Consortium for Political and Social Research (ICPSR), Institute for Social Research, University of Michigan. <http://www.icpsr.umich.edu/icpsrweb/ICPSR/series/00074>

200 Sickmund, Melissa. *Juveniles in Court* [Juvenile Offenders and Victims National Report Series Bulletin]. Washington, D.C.: Office of Juvenile Justice and Delinquency Prevention, Office of Justice Programs, U.S. Department of Justice, 2003. NCJ 195420

<http://purl.access.gpo.gov/GPO/LPS33410>

Provides state-level information for 1999 on the ways in which adult sanctions can be imposed on juveniles; the minimum age for judicial waiver to criminal court and judicial waiver offense and minimum age criteria; and the minimum age for statutory exclusion and statutory exclusion offense and minimum age criteria.

•**201** Snyder, Howard N., and Melissa Sickmund. *Juvenile Offenders and Victims: 2006 National Report.* Washington, D.C.: Office of Juvenile Justice and Delinquency Prevention, Office of Justice Programs, U.S. Department of Justice, 2006. NCJ 212906

<http://www.ojjdp.ncjrs.gov/ojstatbb/nr2006/index.html>

Chapter 4 provides data on the juvenile justice system structure and processes as follows: history and overview of the juvenile justice system; U.S. Supreme Court cases and the juvenile justice system; state definitions of juvenile court jurisdiction; juvenile justice system case processing; public access to juvenile proceedings; state provisions for trying juveniles as adults; judicial waiver, concurrent jurisdiction, and statutory exclusion; blended sentencing; and juveniles in the federal justice system. Chapter 6 provides data on juvenile offenders in court as follows: delinquency caseload, trends in delinquency cases, gender variations in delinquency cases, offense profiles by gender, racial variations in delinquency cases, age variations in delinquency cases, detention, detention variations by demographics, formal vs. informal case processing, adjudication, disposition, delinquency case processing, delinquency case processing by offense and demographics, judicial waiver, and monitoring racial disparity.

Research Note: Earlier editions are available. Not all subsections contain state-level data. This report incorporates data from some earlier specialized OJJDP reports individually authored by Sickmund and Snyder that are not otherwise included in this book.

•**202** *Statistical Briefing Book.* Washington, D.C.: Office of Juvenile Justice and Delinquency Prevention, Office of Justice Programs, U.S. Department of Justice [online only, 1993–date].

<http://purl.access.gpo.gov/GPO/LPS73143>

This website provides access to a wide array of publications, data analysis tools, and national datasets, covering the following topics: juvenile population characteristics, juveniles as victims, juveniles as offenders, juvenile justice system structure and process, law enforcement and juvenile crime, juveniles in court, juveniles on probation, juveniles in corrections, and juvenile reentry and aftercare.

Juvenile Designated Felonies

203 Rainville, Gerard A. *Juvenile Felony Defendants in Criminal Courts: Survey of 40 Counties, 1998* [Special Report]. Washington, D.C.: Bureau of Justice Statistics, Office of Justice Programs, U.S. Department of Justice, 2003. NCJ 197961

<http://purl.access.gpo.gov/GPO/LPS75618>

Presents data on juvenile defendants (number and percentage) who were charged with felonies during 1998 in the adult criminal courts of the nation's forty largest urban counties (Appendix 2).

Life Sentences

204 Nellis, Ashley, and Ryan S. King. *No Exit: The Expanding Use of Life Sentences in America.* Washington, D.C.: The Sentencing Project, 2009.

<http://www.sentencingproject.org/doc/publications/publications/inc_
noexitseptember2009.pdf>

Presents state-level data on life sentences and life sentences without parole (LWOP) as follows: life sentencing policy (Table 1); life population and life without parole population (Table 2); racial and ethnic distribution of life sentenced population (Table 3); racial and ethnic distribution of LWOP population (Table 5); juvenile life and LWOP population (Table 6); juveniles as percentage of life sentenced population (Table 7); racial and ethnic distribution of juvenile life population (Table 8); and racial and ethnic distribution of juvenile LWOP population (Table 9).

Pretrial Procedures

•205 *Judicial Business of the United States Courts: Annual Report of the Director*. Washington, D.C.: Statistics Division, Office of Judges Programs, Administrative Office of the United States Courts [1994-date].

<http://purl.access.gpo.gov/GPO/LPS2715>

The Appendix (Detailed Statistical Tables) reports the following statistics for U.S. District Courts by circuit and district: pretrial services cases activated (Table H-1); pretrial services interviews and types of pretrial services reports (Table H-2); pretrial services recommendations made for initial pretrial release (Table H-3); pretrial services recommendations made for initial pretrial release, excluding immigration cases (Table H-3A); pretrial services defendants released on bond (Table H-6); pretrial services defendants received for and under supervision (Table H-7); pretrial service defendants with conditions of release (Table H-8); pretrial services cases closed, by type of disposition (Table H-13); pretrial services release and detention (Table H-14); pretrial services release and detention, excluding immigration cases (Table H-14A).

Research Note: Reports are available online back to 1997. Texas is in the U.S. Court of Appeals Fifth Circuit and has four districts: Eastern, Northern, Southern, and Western. Some of this data is reported biannually in *Statistical Tables of the Federal Judiciary* (2001–date). <http://purl. access.gpo.gov/GPO/LPS21918> Datasets for some categories are available through the Inter-university Consortium for Political and Social Research (ICPSR), Institute for Social Research, University of Michigan.

<http://www.icpsr.umich.edu/icpsrweb/ICPSR/series/00072>

Prosecuting Attorneys

•206 *Federal Justice Statistics—Statistical Tables*. Washington, D.C.: Bureau of Justice Statistics, Office of Justice Programs, U.S. Department of Justice [annual, online only, 2005–date].

<http://purl.access.gpo.gov/GPO/LPS113898>

Reports fiscal year data from the Federal Justice Statistics Program (FJSP) and includes a United States map (along with an accompanying spreadsheet) that provides data on suspects referred to U.S. attorneys, by federal judicial district (Map 2.1).

Research Note: This publication series supersedes *Compendium of Federal Justice Statistics* (1984–2004). Texas is in the U.S. Court of Appeals Fifth Circuit and has four districts: Eastern, Northern, Southern, and Western. Datasets are available through the Inter-university Consortium for Political and Social Research (ICPSR), Institute for Social Research, University of Michigan.

<http://www.icpsr.umich.edu/icpsrweb/ICPSR/series/00073>

207 *Prosecutors in State Courts, 2005* [Bulletin]. Washington, D.C.: Bureau of Justice Statistics, Office of Justice Programs, U.S. Department of Justice, 2006. NCJ 213799

<http://purl.access.gpo.gov/GPO/LPS36819>

Reports findings from the 2005 National Survey of State Court Prosecutors (see entry 208), which are based on a nationally representative sample of 310 prosecutors' offices that try felony cases. The Appendix provides state-level statistics on the number of chief prosecutors who handle felony cases in state courts of general jurisdiction.

Research Note: Earlier editions are available.

•208 *Prosecutors' Offices Statistics.* Washington, D.C.: Bureau of Justice Statistics, Office of Justice Programs, U.S. Department of Justice [2001, online only].

<http://bjsdata.ojp.usdoj.gov/dataonline/Search/Prosecutors/index.cfm>

The National Survey of Prosecutors is a biennial series that began in 1990. It collects data on resources, policies, and practices of local prosecutors from a nationally representative sample of chief litigating prosecutors in state court systems (the 2001 survey is a census as opposed to a sample of all state court prosecutors). Judicial district profiles are available for searching by single districts or by multiple districts (within one state or by population size across one or more states). Variables include chief prosecutor (full-time or part-time, and chief prosecutor salary); number of employees (prosecutors and other staff); budget; and caseload (felony jury verdicts, felony cases closed, felony cases convicted, misdemeanor cases closed, and misdemeanor cases convicted).

Research Note: Datasets are available through the Inter-university Consortium for Political and Social Research (ICPSR), Institute for Social Research, University of Michigan. <http://www.icpsr.umich.edu/icpsrweb/ICPSR/series/00084>

Public Defenders

•209 *Annual and Expenditure Report.* Austin: Texas Task Force on Indigent Defense, Office of Court Administration [2002–date].

<http://www.courts.state.tx.us/tfid/Annual_Reports_Archives.asp>

The Texas Fair Defense Act provides that "An indigent defendant is entitled to have an attorney appointed to represent him in any adversary judicial proceeding that may result in punishment by confinement and in any other criminal proceeding if the court concludes that the interests of justice require representation" (Tex. Code Crim. Proc. Ann. art. 1.051 (Vernon 2005 & Supp. 2010)). The Texas Task Force on Indigent Defense was established by the 77th Texas Legislature to improve the delivery of indigent defense services through fiscal assistance, accountability and professional support to state, local judicial, county, and municipal officials, with the goal of promoting justice and fairness to all indigent persons accused of criminal conduct, including juvenile respondents, as provided by the laws and constitutions of the United States and Texas. It is a permanent standing committee of the Texas Judicial Council and staffed as a component of the Office of Court Administration by eight *ex officio* members and five members appointed by the governor. The annual report provides fiscal-year data on felony appointments statewide, misdemeanor appointments statewide, indigent defense expenses statewide, operating budget, and grants awarded (formula, direct disbursement, extraordinary disbursement, equalization disbursement, technical assistance, and discretionary).

210 Carmichael, Dottie, and Michael Voloudakis. *Study to Assess the Impacts of the Fair Defense Act on Texas Counties: Final Report.* College Station: Public Policy Research Institute, Texas A&M University, 2005.

<http://www.courts.state.tx.us/tfid/Resources.asp>

This report was prepared for the Task Force on Indigent Defense, Texas Office of Court Administration, and contains data on the impact of the Texas Fair Defense Act on four Texas counties (Cameron, Collin, Dallas, and Webb).

211 *The Fair Defense Report—Analysis of Indigent Defense Practices in Texas.* Austin: Texas Appleseed, 2000.

<http://www.texasappleseed.net/pdf/projects_fairDefense_fairref.pdf>

Presents data on indigent defense prior to the enactment of the Texas Fair Defense Act. Indigent defense representation was studied in a representative sample of twenty-three Texas counties in the following categories of criminal cases: non-capital adult felony and Class A and Class B misdemeanors, capital felony, cases involving mentally ill defendants, and juvenile delinquency.

212 Farole, Jr. Donald, and Lynn Langton. *County-based and Local Public Defender Offices, 2007* [Special Report]. Washington, D.C.: Bureau of Justice Statistics, Office of Justice Programs, U.S. Department of Justice, 2010. NCJ 231175

<http://bjs.ojp.usdoj.gov/index.cfm?ty=dcdetail&iid=401>

Presents aggregate data, derived from the 2007 Census of Public Defender Offices, on the public defender services in the District of Columbia and the twenty-seven states (including Texas) in which indigent defense services were funded and administered by counties or local jurisdictions.

•213 *Judicial Business of the United States Courts: Annual Report of the Director*. Washington, D.C.: Statistics Division, Office of Judges Programs, Administrative Office of the United States Courts [1994–date].

<http://purl.access.gpo.gov/GPO/LPS2715>

The Appendix (Detailed Statistical Tables) reports a summary of representations by federal defender organizations for U.S. District Courts (Table K-1).

Research Note: Reports are available online back to 1997. Texas is in the U.S. Court of Appeals Fifth Circuit and has four districts: Eastern, Northern, Southern, and Western.

Sentencing

•214 *Federal Sentencing Statistics by State, District, and Circuit.* Washington, D.C.: United States Sentencing Commission [online only, 1995–date].

<http://purl.access.gpo.gov/GPO/LPS79751>

Provides fiscal year federal sentencing statistics by state, judicial circuit, and judicial district as follows: distribution of guideline defendants sentenced by select primary offense category (Figure A); distribution of guideline defendants sentenced by primary offense category (Table 1); mode of conviction by circuit and district (Table 2); mode of conviction by primary offense category (Table 3); type of sentence imposed by primary offense category—national (Table 4); type of sentence imposed by primary offense category—district (Table 5); incarceration rate of defendants eligible for non-prison sentences by primary offense category (Table 6); average length of imprisonment by primary offense category (Table 7); comparison of sentence imposed and position relative to the guideline range (Table 8); guideline departure rate by circuit and district (Table 9); and guideline departure rate by primary offense category (Table 10).

Research Note: Published quarterly with annual cumulations. Texas is in the U.S. Court of Appeals Fifth Circuit and has four districts: Eastern, Northern, Southern, and Western. Datasets are available through the Inter-university Consortium for Political and Social Research (ICPSR), Institute for Social Research, University of Michigan.

<http://www.icpsr.umich.edu/icpsrweb/ICPSR/series/00083>

215 *National Judicial Reporting Program.* Ann Arbor: Inter-university Consortium for Political and Social Research, Institute for Social Research, University of Michigan [biennial, online only, 1986–date].
<http://www.icpsr.umich.edu/icpsrweb/ICPSR/series/00077>

This survey of felony sentences in state courts and the demographic characteristics of convicted felons is conducted biennially by the Census Bureau, U.S. Department of Commerce, for the Bureau of Justice Statistics, National Institute of Justice, U.S. Department of Justice. Data is collected from a nationally stratified cluster sample of state courts in 300 counties deemed to be representative (state courts are the source of data for approximately one-half of the sampled counties, with the remaining balance supplied by prosecutors' offices, sentencing commissions, and statistical agencies). The offenses covered are violent (murder, sexual assault, robbery, aggravated assault, and other); property (burglary, larceny, and fraud); drug (possession and trafficking); weapons; and other (which includes nonviolent offenses such as receiving stolen property and vandalism).

216 Stemen, Don, Andres Rengifo, and James Wilson. *Of Fragmentation and Ferment: The Impact of State Sentencing Policies on Incarceration Rates, 1975–2002.* New York: Vera Institute of Justice, 2005. NCJ 213003
<http://www.ncjrs.gov/pdffiles1/nij/grants/213003.pdf>

Reports data from a comprehensive survey of state-level sentencing and corrections policies implemented between 1975 and 2002, which assessed the impact of those policies on state incarceration rates. Tabular data includes state incarceration rates, 1970 and 2002, and percentage change (Table 1-1); percentage change in state incarceration rates, 1970–1985 and 1985–2002 (Table 1-2); and statutory minimum sentences for sale of 28g of powder cocaine, 1975 and 2002 (Table 1-8).

•217 *Sourcebook of Federal Sentencing Statistics.* Washington, D.C.: United States Sentencing Commission [online only, 1995–date].
<http://purl.access.gpo.gov/GPO/LPS56837>

Provides fiscal year federal sentencing statistics as follows: document submission by each circuit and district (Table 1); guideline offenders in each circuit and district (Table 2); guilty pleas and trials in each circuit and district (Table 10); comparison of sentence imposed and position relative to the guideline range by circuit (Fifth Circuit) (Table N-5); sentences relative to the guideline range by circuit and district (Table 26); types of appeal in each circuit and district (Table 55); disposition of defendant sentencing appeals in each circuit and district (Table 56); disposition of government sentencing appeals in each circuit and district (Table 56a); and type of resentencing or other modification of sentence by each circuit and district (Table 62). Appendix B provides fiscal year summaries by judicial district for federal guideline sentences, which includes demographics (average age, gender, race, ethnicity, mode of conviction, and departure status); and sentencing information by primary offense for cases involving prison (total receiving prison and prison sentence ordered); cases involving probation (total receiving probation, probation only, and probation and confinement); and cases involving fines and restitution (total cases and median dollar amount).

Research Note: Texas is in the U.S. Court of Appeals Fifth Circuit and has four districts: Eastern, Northern, Southern, and Western. Datasets are available through the Inter-university Consortium for Political and Social Research (ICPSR), Institute for Social Research, University of Michigan.

<http://www.icpsr.umich.edu/icpsrweb/ICPSR/series/00083> [Monitoring of Federal Criminal Sentences Series]

<http://www.icpsr.umich.edu/icpsrweb/ICPSR/series/00075> [Monitoring of Federal Criminal Convictions and Sentences: Appeals Data Series]

Sentencing Disparity

218 *U.S. Sentencing Commission Preliminary Crack Cocaine Retroactivity Data Report.* Washington, D.C.: U.S. Sentencing Commission [quarterly, 2008–date].

<http://www.ussc.gov/linktojp.htm>

Provides information on all cases reported to the U.S. Sentencing Commission in which the court considered a motion to reduce a sentence under 18 U.S.C. § 3582(c)(2) (2007) for an offender convicted of an offense involving crack cocaine as follows: geographical distribution of application of retroactive crack cocaine amendment by judicial district (Table 1); geographical distribution of application of retroactive crack cocaine amendment by judicial circuit (Table 2); origin of granted motion for sentence reduction due to retroactive application of crack cocaine amendment by judicial circuit (Table 4); and degree of decrease in sentence due to retroactive application of crack cocaine amendment by judicial circuit and district (Table 8).

Research Note: Texas is in the U.S. Court of Appeals Fifth Circuit and has four districts: Eastern, Northern, Southern, and Western. This sentencing disparity was addressed in the Fair Sentencing Act of 2010 (P.L. 111-220, 124 Stat. 2372). For further background, see *Unfairness in Federal Cocaine Sentencing: Is it Time to Crack the 100 to 1 Disparity?: Hearing before the Subcommittee on Crime, Terrorism, and Homeland Security of the Committee on the Judiciary, House of Representatives, One Hundred Eleventh Congress, First Session, on H.R. 1459, H.R. 1466, H.R. 265, H.R. 2178, and H.R. 18, May 21, 2009* (Washington, D.C.: G.P.O., 2009), and *Restoring Fairness to Federal Sentencing: Addressing the Crack-Powder Disparity: Hearing* *before the Subcommittee on Crime and Drugs of the Committee on the Judiciary, United States Senate, One Hundred Eleventh Congress, First Session, April 29, 2009* (Washington, D.C.: G.P.O., 2010).

<http://purl.access.gpo.gov/GPO/FDLP1873> [House]

<http://purl.access.gpo.gov/GPO/LPS126571> [Senate]

Sentencing Guideline Compliance

219 *Final Report on the Impact of* United States v. Booker *on Federal Sentencing.* Washington, D.C.: United States Sentencing Commission, 2006. <http://purl.access.gpo.gov/GPO/LPS71967>

In *United States v. Booker*, 543 U.S. 220 (2005), the Supreme Court held that the U.S. Sentencing Guidelines, where they allow judges to impose enhanced sentences beyond the statutory maximum using a determination of facts—other than a prior conviction—that were not found by the jury beyond a reasonable doubt or admitted by the defendant, violated the Sixth Amendment. It further held that although a sentencing court is required to consult and take into account guideline ranges, the court is permitted to tailor the sentence in light of other statutory concerns as well, effectively rendering the guidelines discretionary by invalidating the provisions that made them mandatory. This report provides data on the impact of *Booker* on federal sentencing as follows: position of sentences relative to the guideline range post-Booker for each federal circuit (Figure 9); rates of within-range sentences for each federal judicial circuit (Table 10); sentences relative to the guideline range for each judicial district ordered by decreasing rates of within-range sentences post-*Booker* (Table 11); sentences relative to the guideline range for each judicial district ordered by decreasing rates of overall below-range sentences post-Booker (Table 12); and sentences relative to the guideline range for each judicial district ordered by decreasing rates of guideline conformance post-*Booker* (Table 13).

Research Note: Texas is in the U.S. Court of Appeals Fifth Circuit and has four districts: Eastern, Northern, Southern, and Western. See also the related publication, *Post*-Kimbrough/ Gall *Data Report*, which analyses federal sentencing data for cases decided during the period beginning on the date of the U.S. Supreme Court decisions in *Kimbrough v. United States*, 552 U.S. 85 (2007), *Gall v. United States*, 552 U.S. 35 (2007), and afterward. <http://www.ussc. gov/USSC_Kimbrough_Gall_Report_Final_FY2008.pdf> For further background, see *United States v. Booker: One Year Later, Chaos or Status Quo? : Hearing before the Subcommittee on Crime, Terrorism, and Homeland Security of the Committee on the Judiciary, House of Representatives, One Hundred Ninth Congress, Second Session, March 16, 2006* (Washington, D.C.: G.P.O., 2006). <http://purl.access.gpo.gov/GPO/LPS74966>

Texas State Courts

•**220** *Annual Statistical Report for the Texas Judiciary.* Austin: Office of Court Administration [2005–date].

<http://www.courts.state.tx.us/pubs/annual-reports.asp>

Presents annual fiscal-year data on the State of Texas court system as follows: structure and operation (including subject matter jurisdiction, appropriations, judicial qualifications, and judicial salaries); summary of court activity for appellate, district, and county-level courts; detailed activity for the Supreme Court, Court of Criminal Appeals, and Courts of Appeals; trends in district and county-level courts (caseload trends by case type and by court type); district courts (overall activity, summary of activity by case type, summary by county, clearance rate and backlog index, ages of cases disposed, summary of jury activity, summary of death sentences and life sentences imposed, and reported criminal activity by county); county-level courts (overall activity, summary of activity by case type, summary by county, clearance rate and backlog index, ages of cases disposed, summary of jury activity, and reported civil and criminal activity by county); district and county-level juvenile activity; justice court activity; municipal court activity; and alternative dispute resolution centers.

Research Note: Statistics on court activity were previously reported, with varying levels of detail, in the following series: *Annual Report of the Texas Civil Judicial Council to the Governor and Supreme Court* (1929–1964); *Annual Report* [Texas Civil Judicial Council] (1965–1973); *Texas Judicial Council Annual Report* (1974–1978), *Texas Judicial System Annual Report of Statistical and Other Data for Calendar Year [year]* (1979–1983), and *Texas Judicial System Annual Report Fiscal Year [year]* (1984–2004). Reports are available online back to 1965. Data on juvenile courts was previously published by the Texas Youth Council in *Texas Juvenile Court Statistics for [year]: An Analysis of Juvenile Court Cases* (1952–1974).

221 Smith, Erica L., and Donald J. Farole, Jr. *Profile of Intimate Partner Violence Cases in Large Urban Counties: State Court Processing Statistics* [Special Report]. Washington, D.C.: Bureau of Justice Statistics, Office of Justice Programs, U.S. Department of Justice, 2009. NCJ 228193

<http://bjs.ojp.usdoj.gov/index.cfm?ty=pbdetail&iid=2024>

Reports the number of defendants in intimate partner violence cases in sixteen large counties (including El Paso, Tarrant, and Travis), by county, state, and charge type, May 2002 (Appendix Table 2). A case was defined as intimate partner violence if it involved an allegation of intentional physical violence committed, attempted, or threatened between spouses, ex-spouses, common-law spouses, boyfriends, or girlfriends, present or past.

•**222** *Trial Court Judicial Data Management System.* Austin: Office of Court Administration [online only, 1992–date].

<http://www.courts.state.tx.us/pubs/annual-reports.asp>

This website allows users to generate the following types of county-level reports: county court data, court data, district court data, justice court data, juvenile court data, management (i.e., cases received), and municipal court data. Depending on the individual type selected, reports are restricted to the following parameters: ages of case disposed, case activity by city, case activity by county, caseload trends, cases received, county activity summary by case type, court-ordered mental health services, death and life sentences, district activity summary by case type, judge profile, jury activity, monthly activity report, other proceedings, performance measures, probate and mental health activity, reported activity by county, reported activity summary, and reported criminal activity by county.

Research Note: Reports can be viewed in HTML, or exported to Acrobat, MS Excel, or MS Word.

Tribal Justice

223 Perry, Steven W. *Census of Tribal Justice Agencies in Indian Country, 2002.* Washington, D.C.: Bureau of Justice Statistics, Office of Justice Programs, U.S. Department of Justice, 2005. NCJ 205332

<http://www.ojp.usdoj.gov/bjs/pub/pdf/ctjaic02.pdf>

The Census of Tribal Justice Agencies, conducted in 2002, received responses from 314 federally recognized American Indian tribes in the lower forty- eight states, including the three Texas tribes (Kickapoo Traditional Tribe of Texas, Alabama-Coushatta Tribes of Texas, and Ysleta del Sur Pueblo). Information is presented in the following categories: law enforcement (Tables 3–4); federal, state, and tribal court systems (Tables 2, 5–7); corrections (Tables 8–9); and criminal history records (Tables 10–13).

Research Note: Datasets are available through the National Archive of Criminal Justice Data, Inter-university Consortium for Political and Social Research (ICPSR), Institute for Social Research, University of Michigan.

<http://dx.doi.org/10.3886/ICPSR04439>

U.S. Federal Courts

•**224** *Federal Justice Statistics Resource Center.* Washington, D.C.: Bureau of Justice Statistics, Office of Justice Programs, U.S. Department of Justice [annual, online only, 1998–date].

<http://fjsrc.urban.org/index.cfm>

The Prosecution/Courts subsection of this website provides access to statistics on defendants charged in criminal cases, defendants in criminal cases closed, and offenders sentenced, by federal judicial circuit and district. Users can generate reports utilizing a range of variables for each category.

Research Note: Reports can be viewed in HTML, or exported to Acrobat, MS Excel, or MS Word. The database is maintained by the Urban Institute through a cooperative agreement with the Bureau of Justice Statistics, Office of Justice Programs, U.S. Department of Justice. Data is derived from the Federal Justice Statistics Program (FJSP) database and reported by fiscal year. Texas is in the U.S. Court of Appeals Fifth Circuit and has four districts: Eastern, Northern, Southern, and Western. Archived datasets (1994–date) are available for downloading (preregistration is required). Datasets from earlier years are available through the National Archive of Criminal Justice Data, Inter-university Consortium for Political and Social Research (ICPSR), Institute for Social Research, University of Michigan.

<http://dx.doi.org/10.3886/ICPSR09296>

•225 *Judicial Business of the United States Courts: Annual Report of the Director*. Washington, D.C.: Statistics Division, Office of Judges Programs, Administrative Office of the United States Courts [annual, 1994–date].

<http://purl.access.gpo.gov/GPO/LPS2715>

The Appendix (Detailed Statistical Tables) contains the following statistics for U.S. Courts of Appeals by circuit and district: appeals commenced, terminated, and pending (Table B-1); sources of appeals and original proceedings commenced (Table B-3); sources of appeals in civil and criminal cases (Table B-3A); median time intervals in cases terminated after hearing or submission (Table B-4); median time intervals for merit terminations of appeals (Table B-4A); appeals terminated on the merits (Table B-5); appeals terminated by procedural judgments (Table B-5); appeals filed, terminated, and pending (Table B-6); and pro se appeals commenced and terminated (Table B-9). Also reported are the following statistics for U.S. District Courts— Criminal by circuit and district: criminal cases commenced, terminated, and pending (including transfers) for the current and previous reporting periods (Table D. Cases); criminal defendants commenced, terminated, and pending (including transfers) for the current and previous reporting periods (Table D. Defendants); criminal cases commenced, terminated, and pending (including transfers) for the current reporting period (Table D-1. Cases); criminal defendants commenced, terminated, and pending (including transfers) for the current reporting period (Table D-1. Defendants); criminal cases commenced, by major offense (Table D-3. Cases); criminal defendants commenced, by major offense (Table D-3. Defendants); median time intervals from filing to disposition for criminal defendants disposed of (Table D-6); criminal defendants disposed of, by type of disposition (Table D-7); all criminal defendants pending, by major offense (Table D-8); criminal defendants terminated, by major offense (Table D-9); median time from conviction to sentencing for criminal defendants convicted (Table D-12); felony preliminary proceedings handled by U.S. Magistrate Judges under 28 U.S.C. 636(a) (2006) (Table M-3); miscellaneous matters handled by U.S. Magistrate Judges (Table M-3A); criminal pretrial matters handled by U.S. Magistrate Judges under 28 U.S.C. 636(b) (Table M-4); reports and recommendations issued by U.S. Magistrate Judges under 28 U.S.C. 636(b) (2006) (Table M-4B); evidentiary proceedings conducted by U.S. Magistrate Judges under 28 U.S.C. 636(b) (Table M-4C); civil and criminal trials (Table T-1); lengths of civil and criminal trials resulting in verdicts or judgments (Table T-2); services provided to and received from other District Courts (Table V-1); services provided by visiting judges in appeals terminated (Table V-2); and weighted and unweighted filings per authorized judgeship (Table X-1A).

Research Note: Reports are available online back to 1997. Texas is in the U.S. Court of Appeals Fifth Circuit and has four districts: Eastern, Northern, Southern, and Western. Some of this data is reported biannually in *Statistical Tables of the Federal Judiciary* (2001–date). <http://purl. access.gpo.gov/GPO/LPS21918> Datasets for some categories are available through the Inter-university Consortium for Political and Social Research (ICPSR), Institute for Social Research, University of Michigan.

<http://www.icpsr.umich.edu/icpsrweb/ICPSR/series/00072>

Chapter 5

Adult Corrections, Parole, and Probation

Aliens

225A *Justice for Immigration's Hidden Population: Protecting the Rights of Persons with Mental Disabilities in the Immigration Court and Detention System.* Austin: Texas Appleseed, 2010.

<http://www.texasappleseed.net/

Provides data on immigrants in Texas with mental disabilities who are held in U.S. Immigration and Customs Enforcement (ICE) detention facilities, including the number of psychotropic prescriptions issued, percentage of detainee cases without counsel, detention facilities with the highest percentage of unrepresented detainees, and the number of cases adjourned because the Department of Homeland Security requested a certification of the detainee's mental competency.

226 Salant, Tanis J. *Undocumented Immigrants in U.S.–Mexico Border Counties: The Costs of Law Enforcement and Criminal Justice Services.* Tucson: Eller College of Management, School of Public Administration and Policy, University of Arizona, 2008. NCJ 223285

<http://www.bordercounties.org/>

Provides a breakdown of the costs of undocumented immigrants to law enforcement and criminal justice services in the U.S. counties bordering Mexico, which includes fifteen in Texas. County-level statistics are given for sheriff's offices, detention facilities, adult probation, and juvenile probation.

Research Note: This report was sponsored by the U.S./Mexico Border Counties Coalition. For earlier data, see Tanis J. Salant, *Illegal Immigrants in U.S.-Mexico Border Counties: Costs of Law Enforcement, Criminal Justice and Emergency Medical Services.* Tucson: Eller College of Business and Public Administration, School of Public Administration and Policy, University of Arizona, 2001. NCJ 201492

227 *Undocumented Immigrants in Texas: A Financial Analysis of the Impact to the State Budget and Economy* [Special Report]. Austin: Texas Comptroller of Public Accounts, 2006.

<http://www.window.state.tx.us/specialrpt/undocumented/>

Section V provides data on the state and local costs of incarcerating undocumented immigrants, the impact these costs have on the state budget, and federal reimbursement from the U.S. Bureau of Justice Assistance's State Criminal Alien Assistance Program (SCAAP).

Correctional Institutions

•**228** *Census of State and Federal Adult Correctional Facilities.* Ann Arbor: National Archive of Criminal Justice Data, Inter-university Consortium for Political and Social Research, Institute for Social Research, University of Michigan [quinquennial, online only, 1974–date].

<http://www.icpsr.umich.edu/icpsrweb/ICPSR/series/00067>

This census is conducted every five years by the Criminal Justice Statistics Branch, U.S. Census Bureau, U.S. Department of Commerce, for the Bureau of Justice Statistics, National Institute of Justice, U.S. Department of Justice. Data is provided for each institution on physical security, age, functions, capacity, court orders for specific conditions, one-day counts and average populations, race/ethnicity of inmates, inmate work assignments, inmate deaths, special inmate counts, assaults, and incidents caused by inmates. The census covers a wide range of federal, state, and private facilities intended for adult offenders including prisons, penitentiaries, and correctional institutions; boot camps; community corrections; prison farms; reception, diagnostic and classification centers; road camps; forestry and conservation camps; youthful offender facilities; vocational training facilities; prison hospitals; and drug and alcohol treatment facilities for prisoners. Specifically excluded are private facilities not primarily for state or federal inmates, military facilities, Immigration and Naturalization Service facilities, Bureau of Indian Affairs facilities, facilities operated by or for local governments, including those housing state prisoners, facilities operated by the U.S. Marshals Service, hospital wings and wards reserved for state prisoners, and facilities that hold only juveniles (although some of the adult facilities covered also house juvenile offenders).

Research Note: The 1990 census was the first to report data on federal institutions (the title varied prior to that edition). Summary state-level data is reported in the corresponding Bureau of Justice Statistics publication beginning with the 2005 edition (see entry 230). The ICPSR datasets contain additional 2005 information that is not reported in the BJS publication, including the following: year of original facility construction; plans to add to, close, or renovate the facility; facilities by gender of inmates authorized to house; inmates by gender under and over age eighteen; inmates by race and ethnicity; inmates by custody level; inmates by sentence status; non-U.S. citizen inmates; geriatric unit inmates; U.S. military veteran inmates; inmates in protective custody, disciplinary action, administrative segregation, death row, and other restricted population units; inmates held for federal, state, local, and tribal authorities; per diem fees charged to house inmates for other correctional authorities; employees by race and ethnicity; disciplinary/misconduct reports; major and other disturbances; assaults on staff and resulting staff deaths; assaults on other inmates; escapes from secure custody; and walkaways from community facilities.

•**229** *Correctional Populations in the United States.* Washington, D.C.: Bureau of Justice Statistics, Office of Justice Programs, U.S. Department of Justice [annual, 1985–1998, 2009–date].

<http://bjs.ojp.usdoj.gov/index.cfm?ty=pbse&sid=5>

Provides state-level data on prisoners under state or federal jurisdiction, by sentence length (total and by gender); incarceration rates for prisoners under state or federal jurisdiction or in state or federal custody, by sentence length; prisoners housed in jails because of crowded state facilities, by gender; prisoners under state or federal jurisdiction, by race (total, by gender, and by Hispanic origin and gender); sentenced prisoners admitted to state or federal jurisdiction, by type of admission; sentenced prisoners released from state or federal jurisdiction, by type of release; sentenced male/female prisoners admitted to state or federal jurisdiction, by type of admission; sentenced male/female prisoners released from state or federal jurisdiction, by type of release; sentenced prisoners released conditionally or unconditionally from state or federal jurisdiction, by type of release (total and by gender); sentenced prisoners admitted to state or federal jurisdiction for violation of parole or other conditional release, by gender and status of sentence; deaths among sentenced prisoners under state or federal jurisdiction, by gender and cause of death; and prisoners in custody of state or federal correctional authorities, by sentence length (total and by gender).

Research Note: Provides only national-level summary data beginning with the 2009 edition. Statistics were previously reported in various U.S. Department of Justice publication series including *Capital Punishment* (1971–1984); *Prisoners in State and Federal Prisons and Reformatories* (1926–1946); *National Prisoner Statistics: Prisoners in State and Federal Institutions* (1950–1963); *National Prisoner Statistics: Prisoners in State and Federal Institutions for Adult Felons* (1964–1970); and *Prisoners in State and Federal Institutions on December 31, [year]* (1971–1984).

•230 Stephan, James J. *Census of State and Federal Correctional Facilities*, 2005 [National Prisoner Statistics Program]. Washington, D.C.: Bureau of Justice Statistics, Office of Justice Programs, U.S. Department of Justice, 2008. NCJ 222182

<http://bjs.ojp.usdoj.gov/index.cfm?ty=dcdetail&iid=255>

Reports the results of the Census of State and Federal Adult Correctional Facilities, which is conducted approximately every five years by the Criminal Justice Statistics Branch, U.S. Census Bureau, U.S. Department of Commerce, for the Bureau of Justice Statistics, National Institute of Justice, U.S. Department of Justice. This survey included adult correctional facilities operating under state or federal authority as of December 30, 2005 (midyear 2000 data from the previous survey is also reported for selected categories). The census also included private and local facilities operating under contract to house inmates for federal or state correctional authorities. The Appendix Tables report the following state-level data: number of correctional facilities and inmates under state or federal authority, population change, and number of inmates per 100,000 U.S. residents (Table 1); number of correctional facilities under state or federal authority, by type (Table 2); number of correctional facilities under state or federal authority, by facility size (Table 3); design and rated capacities of correctional facilities under state or federal authority (Table 4); number of correctional facilities under state or federal authority, by facility security level (Table 5); number of correctional facilities under state or federal authority, under court order or consent decree (Table 6); number of correctional facilities under state or federal authority under court order or consent decree to limit population, by facility size (Table 7); number of private correctional facilities under contract to state or federal authorities and average daily population (Table 8); number of private correctional facilities under contract to state or federal authorities, by facility size (Table 9); number of inmates in correctional facilities under state or federal authority, by gender and type of facility (Table 10); number of inmates in correctional facilities under state or federal authority, by facility security level (Table 11); all employees and correctional officers in correctional facilities under state or federal authority, by gender (Table 12); number of employees in correctional facilities under state or federal authority, by occupational category (Table 13); number of inmates, employees, and inmate-to-staff ratios in correctional facilities under state or federal authority (Table 14); number of inmates, employees, and inmate-to-staff ratios in correctional facilities under state or federal authority, by type of facility (Table 15); number of correctional facilities under state or federal authority that provided work programs and number of inmates with work assignments (Table 16); number of correctional facilities under state or federal authority that provided work release and number of inmates participating in work release (Table 17); number of facilities under state or federal authority that provided educational programs to inmates (Table 18); number of facilities under state or federal authority that provided counseling programs to inmates (Table 19).

Research Note: Although earlier editions are available (published under slightly varying titles prior to 1990), this is the first to report state-level data. The word "Adult" is omitted from the title of the print report. Datasets are available, which contain additional information not reported in this publication (see entry 228), through the National Archive of Criminal Justice Data, Inter-university Consortium for Political and Social Research (ICPSR), Institute for Social Research, University of Michigan.

<http://dx.doi.org/10.3886/ICPSR24642>

Correctional Personnel

231 *2008 Salary Survey Fact Sheet.* Austin, Tex.: Community Justice Assistance Division, Texas Department of Criminal Justice [2008]. CJAD09002

<http://www.tdcj.state.tx.us/publications/cjad/publications-cjad-salary-turnover-survey.htm>

232 *2008 Turnover Survey Fact Sheet.* Austin, Tex.: Community Justice Assistance Division, Texas Department of Criminal Justice, [2008]. CJAD09001 <http://www.tdcj.state.tx.us/publications/cjad/publications-cjad-salary-turnover-survey.htm>

The Community Justice Assistance Division of the Texas Department of Criminal Justice worked with Texas Community Supervision and Corrections Departments (CSCDs) to gather and analyze demographic, salary, education, and job duty data for all probation officers and direct care staff employed by a CSCD on December 31, 2007. These two fact sheets present the results of that analysis.

•233 *Census of Governments: Government Employment and Payroll.* Washington, D.C.: Governments Division, U.S. Census Bureau, U.S. Department of Commerce [quinquennial, 1957–date].
<http://purl.access.gpo.gov/GPO/LPS33151>

The Census of Governments is conducted in years ending in "2" and "7" as mandated by 13 U.S.C. § 161 (2009). The Annual Survey of Government Employment is conducted in the intervening years under the provisions of 13 U.S.C. § 182 (2009). The latter includes a sample of state and local governments, with a new sample being selected every five years (years ending in "4" and "9"). The Census Bureau website provides a Build-a-Table function, which allows users to access data at the levels of state government, local government (aggregated county, municipality, township, school district, and special district), or combined state and local government. Data is presented for the government function "corrections" as follows: full-time employees and pay, part-time employees and pay, total employees, total pay, and full-time equivalent.

Research Note: Editions are available online back to 1992. The government function "corrections" encompasses "activities pertaining to the confinement and correction of adults and minors convicted of criminal offenses. Pardon, probation, and parole activities are also included here." Datasets are available through the Inter-university Consortium for Political and Social Research (ICPSR), Institute for Social Research, University of Michigan. <http://www.icpsr.umich.edu/icpsrweb/ICPSR/series/00012>

•234 *Justice Expenditure and Employment.* Washington, D.C.: Bureau of Justice Statistics, Office of Justice Programs, U.S. Department of Justice [annual, 1982–date].
<http://bjs.ojp.usdoj.gov/index.cfm?ty=daa>

Presents data extracted from the Census Bureau's Annual Survey of Government Finances and Annual Survey of Government Employment, which provide estimates of full-time only and full-time equivalent employment for the government function "corrections." Data is reported at the level of states, large counties (with populations of 500,000 or more), and large cities (with populations of 300,000 or more). Annual March payrolls are also reported.

Research Note: Definitions are provided for the corrections categories covered in the report. Prior data is reported in various publications series of the U.S. Department of Justice's Law Enforcement Assistance Administration and the Census Bureau's Governments Division. Datasets are available through the Inter-university Consortium for Political and Social Research (ICPSR), Institute for Social Research, University of Michigan. <http://www.icpsr.umich.edu/icpsrweb/ICPSR/series/00087>

•**235** *Occupational Employment Statistics: Occupational Employment and Wage Estimates.* Washington, D.C.: Bureau of Labor Statistics, U.S. Department of Labor [annual, online only, 1999–date].

<http://purl.access.gpo.gov/GPO/LPS68663>

Provides employment and wage estimates for states, metropolitan areas, and nonmetropolitan areas, and includes the following occupations (Standard Occupational Classification codes noted): first-line supervisors/managers of correctional officers (33-1011); correctional officers and jailers (33-3012); and probation officers and correctional treatment specialists (21-1092).

Corrections Costs

•**236** *Criminal Justice Uniform Cost Report, Fiscal Years [year–year].* Austin: Legislative Budget Board [online only, 2003–date].

<http://www.lbb.state.tx.us/PubSafety_CrimJustice/PubSafety_CrimJustice.htm>

This report utilizes agency budgets and reported expenditures to calculate uniform costs per day (with certain specified exclusions) for the following: Texas Department of Criminal Justice (TDCJ) Correctional Institutions Division—State-Operated Facilities; TDCJ Correctional Institutions Division—Programs in Correctional Institutions; TDCJ Correctional Institutions Division—Privately Operated Facilities; TDCJ Correctional Institutions Division—State-Operated Facilities versus Privately Operated Facilities; TDCJ Parole Division; TDCJ Community Justice Assistance Division; and TDCJ Community Justice Assistance Division—Programs within Community Supervision. Expenditures of the Texas Board of Pardons and Paroles and the Texas Correctional Office on Offenders with Medical or Mental Impairments are reported separately.

Research Note: Earlier data can be found in reports published by the Criminal Justice Policy Council (under varying titles).

237 Stephan, James J. *State Prison Expenditures, 2001*. Washington, D.C.: Bureau of Justice Statistics, Office of Justice Programs, U.S. Department of Justice, 2004. NCJ 202949

<www.ojp.usdoj.gov/bjs/pub/pdf/spe01.pdf>

Reports state-level prison expenditures for FY2001 (total, operating, and capital), based on corrections data extracted from each state's responses to the U.S. Census Bureau's Annual Survey of Government Finances (Table 1). Categories were standardized across jurisdictions and the reported figures were verified with state budget officials. Also lists state-level prison operating expenses for salaries, wages and benefits, and other operating costs (Table 3), and state-level prison capital expenses for construction and equipment (Table 4).

Research Note: Earlier editions are available.

Criminal Justice System Planning

238 *Biennial Report to the Governor and the . . . Texas Legislature*. Austin: Criminal Justice Policy Council [1999–2003].

<http://www.lbb.state.tx.us/PubSafety_CrimJustice/6_Links/Documents_ Alpha_Links.htm>

This report, subtitled "The Big Picture in Adult and Juvenile Justice Issues," was legislatively mandated and required the CJPC to submit to the governor and legislature "a plan detailing the actions necessary to promote an effective and cohesive criminal justice system." It contains statistics on adult and juvenile crime and arrest rates.

Research Note: The council disbanded in 2003 after the governor's line-item veto of its legislative appropriation.

239 *House Committee on Corrections, Texas House of Representatives Interim Report, [year]: A Report to the House of Representatives . . . Texas Legislature*. Austin: House Committee on Corrections [biennial, 1987–date].

<http://www.house.state.tx.us/committees/reports/welcome.htm>

This report summarizes the work undertaken by the Texas House Committee on Corrections regarding the Interim Study Charges it receives from the Speaker of the House of Representatives. These charges involve policy, procedural, regulatory, and budgetary issues relating to agencies and programs under the committee's jurisdiction, which include adult and juvenile corrections, parole, and probation. The report contains selected statistics as well as recommendations for consideration by the succeeding legislature.

Research Note: Published under slightly varying titles.

240 *Interim Report to the . . . Legislature.* Austin: Senate Committee on Criminal Justice [biennial, 1996–date].

<http://www.senate.state.tx.us/75r/senate/commit/c590/c590.htm>

This report summarizes the work undertaken by the Texas Senate Committee on Criminal Justice regarding the Interim Charges it receives from the Lieutenant Governor of the State of Texas. These charges involve policy, procedural, regulatory, and budgetary issues relating to agencies and programs under the committee's jurisdiction, which include adult and juvenile corrections, parole, and probation; law enforcement; criminal law and procedure; and victims of crimes. The report contains minutes of the committee's public hearings on these charges, selected statistics, and recommendations for consideration by the succeeding legislature.

Research Note: Published under slightly varying titles.

241 *Justice Reinvestment in Texas: Assessing the Impact of the 2007 Justice Reinvestment Initiative.* New York: Justice Center, Council of State Governments, 2009.

<http://justicereinvestment.org/states/texas/pubmaps-tx>

The Council of State Governments prepared a series of policy briefs in 2007 for the 80th Texas Legislature, which analyzed the reasons behind the growth of the State's prison population and increased recidivism rates. They also reviewed aspects of two possible justice reinvestment scenarios in which policymakers enact policies to address the projected shortfall of over 17,000 prison beds in Texas by 2012. This follow-up report assesses the extent to which the legislative policies enacted in 2007 were implemented and outlines correctional trends and projections for the future.

Drug-abusing Inmates

242 *Arrestee Drug Abuse Monitoring (ADAM) Program/Drug Use Forecasting (DUF) Series.* Ann Arbor: Inter-university Consortium for Political and Social Research, Institute for Social Research, University of Michigan [annual, online only, 1998–2003].

<http://www.icpsr.umich.edu/icpsrweb/ICPSR/series/00110>

Contains data from the National Institute of Justice's Arrestee Drug Abuse Monitoring (ADAM) Program/Drug Use Forecasting (DUF) series, which was designed to determine the extent and correlates of illicit drug use in the population of booked arrestees in local areas through quarterly data collected in metropolitan areas in the United States. These areas varied by collection period, but included Dallas, Houston, Laredo, and San Antonio. An expanded adult data collection instrument was introduced in 2000. Data for adult males (probability-based sampling) is presented in Part 1; data for adult females in Part 2.

Research Note: ADAM represented a major redesign of the Drug Use Forecasting (DUF) system, the NIJ's multi-site drug-monitoring program (1988–1997). The NIJ restricts this data from general dissemination and users must secure preapproval from the ICPRS. The NIJ published annual reports (under varying titles) on the DUF and ADAM programs (1990–2003). Beginning in 2007, the ADAM II program began data collection under the auspices of the Office of National Drug Control Policy, Executive Office of the President. It continues the original ADAM methodology, but is restricted to adult male arrestees in ten U.S. counties (none in Texas). Selected data from ADAM and ADAM II is reported in *National Drug Control Strategy: Data Supplement.* <http://purl.access.gpo.gov/GPO/LPS6500>

243 Kerber, Lisa, and Rand Harris. *Substance Use Among Female Inmates: Texas Department of Criminal Justice—Institutional Division, 1998.* Austin: Texas Commission on Alcohol and Drug Abuse, 2001.

<http://www.dshs.state.tx.us/sa/research/criminaljustice/Female_Prison.pdf>

Reports the results of a survey of 658 female inmates newly admitted to the two Texas Department of Criminal Justice—Institutional Division (TDCJ-ID) intake facilities from May to November 1998. Statistics are presented on the prevalence of substance use (licit and illicit) and comparisons with non-incarcerated females in Texas (1996); treatment needs and options; factors relating to substance abuse and dependence (e.g., family background, childhood neglect and abuse; violence and victimization during adulthood; mental health; physical health; peer relations and partner characteristics; reproductive history and children; and gambling); criminal behavior; and comparisons with male TDCJ-ID inmates (1998). The appendices provide statistics on the prevalence and recency of substance use and crime among survey population, by age, in the following categories: female, female African-American, female Anglo, and female Hispanic.

Research Note: Earlier editions are available.

244 Kerber, Lisa. *Substance Use Among Female Inmates: Texas Department of Criminal Justice—State Jail Division, 1998.* Austin: Texas Commission on Alcohol and Drug Abuse, 2001.

<http://www.dshs.state.tx.us/sa/research/criminaljustice/female_inmates1998.pdf>

Reports the results of a survey of 542 female inmates newly admitted to the two Texas Department of Criminal Justice—State Jail Division intake facilities from February 1998 to January 1999. Statistics are presented on the prevalence of substance use (licit and illicit) and comparisons with non-incarcerated females in Texas (1996) and TDCJ-ID female inmates (1998); treatment needs and options; factors relating to substance abuse and dependence (e.g., family background, childhood neglect and abuse; violence and victimization during adulthood; mental health; physical health; peer relations and partner characteristics; reproductive history and children; and gambling); criminal behavior; and comparisons with Texas Department of Criminal Justice—State Jail Division male inmates (1998). The appendices provide statistics on the prevalence and recency of substance use and crime among survey population, by age, in the following categories: female, female African-American, female Anglo, and female Hispanic.

245 Kerber, Lisa. *Substance Use Among Male Inmates: Texas Department of Criminal Justice—Institutional Division, 1998.* Austin: Texas Commission on Alcohol and Drug Abuse, 2000.

<http://www.dshs.state.tx.us/sa/research/criminaljustice/Substance_Abuse98.pdf>

Reports the results of a survey of 792 male inmates newly admitted to the four Texas Department of Criminal Justice—Institutional Division (TDCJ-ID) intake facilities from January to July 1998. Statistics are presented on the prevalence of substance use (licit and illicit) and comparisons with non-incarcerated males in Texas (1996); treatment needs and options; factors relating to substance abuse and dependence (e.g., family background; childhood neglect and abuse; violence and victimization during adulthood; mental health; physical health; peer relations and partner characteristics; children; and gambling); drinking and driving; and criminal behavior. The appendices provide statistics on the prevalence and recency of substance use and crime among the survey population, by age, in the following categories: male, male African-American, male Anglo, and male Hispanic.

Research Note: Earlier editions are available.

246 Kerber, Lisa. *Substance Use Among Male Inmates: Texas Department of Criminal Justice—State Jail Division, 1998.* Austin: Texas Commission on Alcohol and Drug Abuse, 2001.

<http://www.dshs.state.tx.us/sa/research/criminaljustice/MensState.pdf>

Reports the results of a survey of 498 male inmates newly admitted to the six Texas Department of Criminal Justice—State Jail Division intake facilities from January to July 1998. Statistics are presented on the prevalence of substance use (licit and illicit) and comparisons with non-incarcerated males in Texas (1996) and male TDJC-ID inmates (1998); treatment needs and options; factors relating to substance abuse and dependence (e.g., family background; childhood neglect and abuse; violence and victimization during adulthood; mental health; physical health; peer relations and partner characteristics; children; and gambling); and criminal behavior. The appendices provide statistics on the prevalence and recency of substance use and crime among the survey population, by age, in the following categories: male, male African-American, male Anglo, and male Hispanic.

247 *Substance Abuse Treatment in Adult and Juvenile Correctional Facilities: Findings from the Uniform Facility Data Set 1997 Survey of Correctional Facilities.* [DASIS Series]. Rockville, Md.: Office of Applied Studies, Substance Abuse and Mental Health Services Administration, U.S. Department of Health and Human Services, 2000.

<http://oas.samhsa.gov/UFDS/CorrectionalFacilities97/index.htm>

This survey of 7,243 federal prisons, state prisons, jails, and juvenile facilities reports the percent of responding facilities that provide substance abuse treatment, by state and facility type (Appendix A).

Research Note: Datasets are available through the Substance Abuse and Mental Health Data Archive, Inter-university Consortium for Political and Social Research (ICPSR), Institute for Social Research, University of Michigan. <http://dx.doi.org/10.3886/ICPSR02995>

248 Von Sternberg, Kirk, and Joseph P. Carbonari. *Evaluation of the "New Choices" Substance Abuse Program in the Harris County Jail, Houston, Texas—PROJECT CARE Final Report.* Houston, Tex.: Change Assessment Research, University of Houston, 2000. NCJ 182364

<http://www.ncjrs.gov/pdffiles1/nij/grants/182364.pdf>

Presents data relating to Project CARE (Change Assessment Research Evaluation), which was an evaluation of the "New Choices" substance abuse treatment program in the Harris County Jail (Houston, Texas).

Ex-offender Employment

249 *Project RIO Strategic Plan, Fiscal Years [year–year].* Austin: Texas Workforce Commission [biennial].

<http://www.twc.state.tx.us/svcs/rio.html>

Project RIO is administered by the Texas Workforce Commission in collaboration with local Workforce Development Boards, the Texas Department of Criminal Justice, the Windham School District, and the Texas Youth Commission. The project is designed to coordinate offenders' pre- and post-release education, training, and employment, with the overall goal of reducing recidivism. The project's strategic plan, which is prepared for the Legislative Budget Board and the Governor's Office of Budget and Planning, contains statistics on intake, obtained employment, and release.

Ex-offender Rights

250 Porter, Nicole D. *Expanding the Vote: State Felony Disenfranchisement Reform, 1997–2010.* New York: The Sentencing Project, 2010.
<http://www.sentencingproject.org/doc/publications/publications/vr_ ExpandingtheVoteFinalAddendum.pdf

Presents state-level data on disenfranchisement policies, i.e., those that restrict voting rights for individuals with felony convictions. The number and rates for total disenfranchisement and African-American disenfranchisement are reported for Texas.

Research Note: This report updates *Losing the Vote: The Impact of Felony Disenfranchisement Laws in the United States* (1998), issued jointly by the Sentencing Project and Human Rights Watch, and the earlier 2008 edition of this report authored by Ryan S. King.

Federal Bureau of Prisons

251 *Expenditures Related to Hurricane Rita, Roof Repair at the Federal Correctional Complex, Beaumont, Texas.* Washington, D.C.: Evaluation and Inspections Division, Office of the Inspector General, U.S. Department of Justice, 2006. I-2006-034
<http://www.usdoj.gov/oig/reports/BOP/a0634/final.pdf>

An audit report on repairs to the Federal Correctional Complex (FCC), Beaumont, Texas, in the aftermath of Hurricane Rita in 2005.

252 *The Federal Bureau of Prisons' Drug Interdiction Activities.* Washington, D.C.: Evaluation and Inspections Division, Office of the Inspector General, U.S. Department of Justice, 2003. I-2003-002
<http://www.usdoj.gov/oig/reports/BOP/e0302/final.pdf>

Appendix IV provides data on positive drug test rates by institution security level (high, medium, low, minimum, and administrative). Appendix VI provides data on the rate and number of drug misconduct charges by institution security level.

•253 *State of the Bureau.* Washington, D.C.: Federal Bureau of Prisons, U.S. Department of Justice [annual, 1991–date].
<http://purl.access.gpo.gov/GPO/LPS8545>

The bureau's annual report provides data on inmate and staff totals for federal correctional institutions at all five security levels.

254 Villanueva, Chandra Kring. *Mothers, Infants and Imprisonment: A National Look at Prison Nurseries and Community-Based Alternatives.* New

York: Institute on Women and Criminal Justice, Women's Prison Association, 2009.

<http://wpaonline.org/resources/publications.htm>

Provides profiles of Federal Bureau of Prisons contract facilities that provide Mother and Infant Nurturing Together (MINT) programs, including Volunteers of America, Fort Worth, which was the original MINT location (Appendix IV).

•**255** *Weekly Population Report.* Washington, D.C.: Federal Bureau of Prisons, U.S. Department of Justice [weekly, online only].

<http://purl.access.gpo.gov/GPO/LPS2060>

Provides a weekly total of all federal inmates along with separate tables for Federal Bureau of Prisons facilities, privately managed secure facilities, and CCM (Community Corrections Management) offices.

Female Inmates

256 Frost, Natasha, Judith Greene, and Kevin Pranis. *The Punitiveness Report—Hard Hit: The Growth in Imprisonment of Women, 1977–2004.* New York: Institute on Women and Criminal Justice, Women's Prison Association, 2004.

<http://wpaonline.org/institute/hardhit/reporthome.htm>

Part II contains state rankings and individual state reports that provide statistics on female imprisonment, female imprisonment rates, and male to female imprisonment ratios.

Imprisonment

257 Mauer, Marc, and Ryan S. King. *Uneven Justice: State Rates of Incarceration by Race and Ethnicity.* Washington, D.C.: The Sentencing Project, 2007.

<http://www.sentencingproject.org/doc/publications/rd_
stateratesofincbyraceandethnicity.pdf>

Utilizing data from *Prison and Jail Inmates at Midyear 2005,* state rankings for prison and jail incarceration rates per 100,000 population are presented as follows: black incarceration rate (Table 3); white incarceration rate (Table 4); black-to-white ratio incarceration rate (Table 6); Hispanic incarceration rate (Table 7); and Hispanic-to-white ratio incarceration rate (Table 8).

Inmate Fatalities

•**258** Mumola, Christopher J. *Medical Causes of Death in State Prisons, 2001–2004* [Data Brief]. Washington, D.C.: Bureau of Justice Statistics, Office of Justice Programs, U.S. Department of Justice, 2007. NCJ 216340

<http://bjs.ojp.usdoj.gov/index.cfm?ty=dcdetail&iid=243>

In order to implement the mandates of the Death in Custody Reporting Act of 2000 (P.L. 106-297, 114 Stat. 1045), the Bureau of Justice Statistics established a nationwide data collection program that includes inmate death records from state prison authorities beginning in 2001 (see entry 266).

259 Mumola, Christopher J. *Suicide and Homicide in State Prisons and Local Jails* [Special Report]. Washington, D.C.: Bureau of Justice Statistics, Office of Justice Programs, U.S. Department of Justice, 2005. NCJ 210036

<http://bjs.ojp.usdoj.gov/index.cfm?ty=dcdetail&iid=243>

In order to comply with the mandates of the Death in Custody Reporting Act of 2000 (P.L. 106-297, 114 Stat. 1045), the Bureau of Justice Statistics established a nationwide data collection program that includes inmate death records from local jail jurisdictions (beginning in 2000) and state prison authorities (beginning in 2001). This report provides data from the early years of the program as follows: number of prisoner deaths, suicides, and homicides, and mortality rates, per 100,000 prisoners in custody, from state prison jurisdictions, 2001–2002 (Table 1), and number of inmate deaths and suicides, and mortality rates per 100,000 inmates, from the fifty largest jail jurisdictions, 2000–2002 (Table 2).

Research Note: Datasets are available through the Inter-university Consortium for Political and Social Research (ICPSR), Institute for Social Research, University of Michigan. <http://www.icpsr.umich.edu/icpsrweb/ICPSR/series/00225>

•**260** Mumola, Christopher J., and Margaret E. Noonan. *Deaths in Custody Statistical Tables: Local Jail Deaths.* Washington, D.C.: Bureau of Justice Statistics, Office of Justice Programs, U.S. Department of Justice [annual, online only, 2000–date].

<http://bjs.ojp.usdoj.gov/content/dcrp/dictabs.cfm>

In order to comply with the mandates of the Death in Custody Reporting Act of 2000 (P.L. 106-297, 114 Stat. 1045), the Bureau of Justice Statistics established a nationwide data collection program that includes inmate death records from local jail jurisdictions (2000–date) and from state prison authorities (2001–date). The Local Jail Deaths Statistical Tables report the number of local jail inmate deaths, by the fifty largest jail jurisdictions, and mortality rate per 100,000 local jail inmates, by the fifty largest jail jurisdictions. Cases of death reported include illness, AIDS, suicide, drug/alcohol intoxication, accident, homicide, and other/unknown.

Research Note: Datasets are available through the Inter-university Consortium for Political and Social Research (ICPSR), Institute for Social Research, University of Michigan. <http://www.icpsr.umich.edu/icpsrweb/ICPSR/series/00225>

•261 Mumola, Christopher J., and Margaret E. Noonan. *Deaths in Custody Statistical Tables: State Prison Deaths*. Washington, D.C.: Bureau of Justice Statistics, Office of Justice Programs, U.S. Department of Justice [annual, online only, 2001–date].

<http://bjs.ojp.usdoj.gov/content/dcrp/dictabs.cfm>

In order to comply with the mandates of the Death in Custody Reporting Act of 2000 (P.L. 106-297, 114 Stat. 1045), the Bureau of Justice Statistics established a nationwide data collection program that includes inmate death records from local jail jurisdictions (2000–date) and from state prison authorities (2001–date). The State Prison Deaths Statistical Tables report the number of state prisoner deaths, by state; mortality rate per 100,000 state prisoners, by state; number of state prisoner deaths, by cause of death and state; and average annual mortality rate, per 100,000 state prisoners, by cause of death and state. Causes of death reported include illness, AIDS , suicide, homicide, drug/alcohol intoxication, accident, and other/unknown.

Research Note: Executions are excluded from causes of death. Datasets are available through the Inter-university Consortium for Political and Social Research (ICPSR), Institute for Social Research, University of Michigan. <http://www.icpsr.umich.edu/icpsrweb/ICPSR/series/00225>

•261A Noonan, Margaret. *Mortality in Local Jails, 2000–2007* [Special Report]. Washington, D.C.: Bureau of Justice Statistics, Office of Justice Programs, U.S. Department of Justice, 2010. NCJ 222988

<http://bjs.ojp.usdoj.gov/index.cfm?ty=dcdetail&iid=243>

In order to comply with the mandates of the Death in Custody Reporting Act of 2000 (P.L. 106-297, 114 Stat. 1045), the Bureau of Justice Statistics established a nationwide data collection program that includes inmate death records from local jail jurisdictions (2000–date) and from state prison authorities (2001–date). This report provides jail inmate mortality rate per 100,000 inmates, by the fifty largest jail jurisdictions and ten selected cause of death, 2000–2007 (Appendix Table 5).

Research Note: Datasets are available through the Inter-university Consortium for Political and Social Research (ICPSR), Institute for Social Research, University of Michigan. <http://www.icpsr.umich.edu/icpsrweb/ICPSR/series/00225>

Inmate Health

262 *An Audit Report on the Cost of the State's Correctional Managed Health Care* [SAO Report]. Austin: State Auditor's Office, 2006. 07-003

<http://www.sao.state.tx.us/reports/main/07-003.html>

This audit focused on the methodologies employed by the University of Texas Medical Branch at Galveston and the Texas Tech University Health Sciences Center to allocate the overhead costs associated with providing inmate health care from September 2004 through February 2006 under their contracts with the Correctional Managed Health Care Committee. These contracts were managed by the Correctional Managed Care Department at the Medical Branch and by the Correctional Managed Health Care Department at the Health Sciences Center.

Research Note: See also the earlier SAO reports, and *An Audit Report on Managed Health Care at the Texas Department of Criminal Justice* (1998), and *An Audit Report on Management of Correctional Managed Health Care Contracts* (2004).

263 Beck, Allen J., and Laura M. Maruschak. *Hepatitis Testing and Treatment in State Prisons* [Special Report]. Washington, D.C.: Bureau of Justice Statistics, Office of Justice Programs, U.S. Department of Justice, 2004 [corr. reprint]. NCJ 199173C

<http://purl.access.gpo.gov/GPO/LPS56449>

Reports data from the 2000 Census of State and Federal Adult Correctional Facilities (covering July 1, 1999, through June 30, 2000) for states testing 500 or more inmates for hepatitis C (Table 3), and facilities treating 50 or more inmates for hepatitis C (Table 4).

•264 *HIV in Prisons* [Bulletin]. Washington, D.C.: Bureau of Justice Statistics, Office of Justice Programs, U.S. Department of Justice [1993–date].

<http://purl.access.gpo.gov/GPO/LPS20824>

The appendices report year-end data on inmates in custody of state and federal prison authorities as follows: inmates in custody of state or federal prison authorities and reported to be HIV positive or to have confirmed AIDS, by jurisdiction (Appendix Table 1); inmates in custody of state and federal prison authorities reported to be HIV positive or to have confirmed AIDS, by jurisdiction and gender (Appendix Table 2); inmates in custody of state or federal prison authorities and reported to have confirmed AIDS, by jurisdiction (Appendix Table 3); AIDS-related deaths among state prison inmates reported to the Deaths in Custody Reporting Program (Appendix Table 4); circumstances under which inmates were tested for the antibody to HIV, by jurisdiction (Appendix Table 5).

Research Note: The 2006 edition was released in electronic format only. Previously published in alternating years with the related BJS publication *HIV in Prisons and Jails*. For earlier data, see Theodore M. Hammett, *Aids in Correctional Facilities: Issues and Options*, 1st–3rd eds. (Washington, D.C.: Office of Communication and Research Utilization, National Institute of Justice, U.S. Department of Justice, 1986–1988), and the annual updates (1986–1997).

265 "Methicillin-Resistant *Staphylococcus aureus* Infections in Correctional Facilities—Georgia, California, and Texas, 2001–2003." *Morbidity and Mortality Weekly Report* (*MMWR*), 52, no. 41 (October 17, 2003), 992–996.
<http://www.cdc.gov/mmwr/PDF/wk/mm5241.pdf>

Reports the incidence of *S. aureus* infections that were methicillin-resistant in Texas Department of Criminal Justice facilities during the surveillance period from January 1996–July 2002.

•266 Mumola, Christopher J. *Medical Causes of Death in State Prisons, 2001–2004* [Data Brief]. Washington, D.C.: Bureau of Justice Statistics, Office of Justice Programs, U.S. Department of Justice, 2007. NCJ 216340
<http://bjs.ojp.usdoj.gov/index.cfm?ty=dcdetail&iid=243>

In order to implement the mandates of the Death in Custody Reporting Act of 2000 (P.L. 106-297, 114 Stat. 1045), the Bureau of Justice Statistics established a nationwide data collection program that includes inmate death records from state prison authorities beginning in 2001. This publication reports the following statistics from that program for 2001–2004: average annual mortality rate of state prison inmates, per 100,000 inmates, from leading causes of illness deaths, by state (Appendix Table 9) and average annual mortality rate from leading causes of illness deaths, per 100,000 state prison inmates, among the states (Appendix Table 10). Causes of death reported include heart disease, cancer, liver disease, AIDS, and respiratory disease.

Research Note: Appendix Tables are available in the online edition only. Datasets are available through the Inter-university Consortium for Political and Social Research (ICPSR), Institute for Social Research, University of Michigan.

<http://www.icpsr.umich.edu/icpsrweb/ICPSR/series/00225>

•267 Mumola, Christopher J., and Margaret E. Noonan. *Deaths in Custody Statistical Tables: State Prison Deaths*. Washington, D.C.: Bureau of Justice Statistics, Office of Justice Programs, U.S. Department of Justice [annual, online only, 2001–date].
<http://bjs.ojp.usdoj.gov/content/dcrp/dictabs.cfm>

In order to comply with the mandates of the Death in Custody Reporting Act of 2000 (P.L. 106-297, 114 Stat. 1045), the Bureau of Justice Statistics established a nationwide data collection program that includes inmate death records from local jail jurisdictions (2000–date) and from state prison authorities (2001–date). The State Prison Deaths Statistical Tables report the number of state prisoner deaths, by cause of death and state (Table 12); and average annual mortality rate, per 100,000 state prisoners, by cause of death and state (Table 13). Causes of death reported include illness and AIDS.

Research Note: Datasets are available through the Inter-university Consortium for Political and Social Research (ICPSR), Institute for Social Research, University of Michigan. <http://www.icpsr.umich.edu/icpsrweb/ICPSR/series/00225>

•267A Noonan, Margaret. *Mortality in Local Jails, 2000–2007* [Special Report]. Washington, D.C.: Bureau of Justice Statistics, Office of Justice Programs, U.S. Department of Justice, 2010. NCJ 222988

<http://bjs.ojp.usdoj.gov/index.cfm?ty=dcdetail&iid=243>

In order to comply with the mandates of the Death in Custody Reporting Act of 2000 (P.L. 106-297, 114 Stat. 1045), the Bureau of Justice Statistics established a nationwide data collection program that includes inmate death records from local jail jurisdictions (2000–date) and from state prison authorities (2001–date). This report provides jail inmate mortality rate per 100,000 inmates, by the fifty largest jail jurisdictions and selected cause of death, 2000–2007 (Appendix Table 5). Causes of death reported include heart disease , AIDS, cancer, liver disease, and all other illnesses.

Research Note: Datasets are available through the Inter-university Consortium for Political and Social Research (ICPSR), Institute for Social Research, University of Michigan. <http://www.icpsr.umich.edu/icpsrweb/ICPSR/series/00225>

268 *Reported Tuberculosis in the United States.* Atlanta, Ga.: Division of Tuberculosis Elimination, National Center for HIV, STD, and TB Prevention, Coordinating Center for Infectious Diseases, Centers for Disease Control and Prevention, U.S. Department of Health and Human Services [annual].

<http://purl.access.gpo.gov/GPO/LPS20186>

One table in each report is devoted to state-level statistics for tuberculosis cases and percentages by residence in correctional facilities for persons age fifteen and over.

269 *Statistical Information on HIV/AIDS.* Huntsville: Health Services Division, Texas Department of Criminal Justice [annual, online only, 1996–date].

<http://www.tdcj.state.tx.us/health/health-aids-stats.htm>

Provides statistics on the incidence of HIV/AIDS in the inmate population of the Texas Department of Criminal Justice (average offender population, number of tests, number of positive tests, HIV population, and AIDS population) and totals (by gender) for CDC Clinical Classifications.

270 *Syphilis/Sexually Transmitted Diseases (STD's)*. Huntsville: Health Services Division, Texas Department of Criminal Justice [annual, 2001–date].

<http://www.tdcj.state.tx.us/health/health-syphilus.htm#SYPHILIS%20 TREATMENT>

Provides statistics on syphilis treatment (male, female, and total) in the inmate population of the Texas Department of Criminal Justice.

271 *Texas HIV/STD Surveillance Report: Annual Report.* Austin: TB/HIV/ STD Epidemiology and Surveillance Branch, Texas Department of State Health Services [annual, 2000–date].

<http://www.dshs.state.tx.us/hivstd/stats/default.shtm#surveillance>

Provides data for inmates held in Texas Department of Criminal Justice (TDCJ) facilities diagnosed with HIV (non-AIDS) and AIDS (cases and rates), and TDCJ inmates living with HIV/AIDS for the reporting year and the previous year.

272 *Tuberculosis Program Statistics.* Huntsville: Health Services Division, Texas Department of Criminal Justice [annual, 2000–date].

<http://www.tdcj.state.tx.us/health/health-tb.htm#Statistics>

Provides statistics on active tuberculosis cases in the inmate population of the Texas Department of Criminal Justice and the case rate per 100,000 population.

273 *Tuberculosis Statistics.* Austin: Infectious Disease Control Unit, Texas Department of State Health Services [online].

<http://www.dshs.state.tx.us/idcu/disease/tb/statistics/default.asp>

Provides statistics for the most recent five years on tuberculosis cases and rates for inmates held in Texas Department of Criminal Justice facilities. Data is presented on the percentage of tuberculosis cases with risk factors, ages eighteen years and up, and the number of reported cases and percentages by race/ethnicity.

274 *United States Marshals Service's Prisoner Medical Care* [Audit Report]. [Washington, D.C.]: Audit Division, Office of the Inspector General, U.S. Department of Justice, 2004. 04-14

<http://www.usdoj.gov/oig/reports/USMS/a0414/final.pdf>

An audit of the U.S. Marshals Service's (USMS) management of medical care of prisoners in its custody—who were housed in local jails, contract facilities, and U.S. Bureau of Prisons facilities—from FY 2000 through FY 2003. It contains data for the Southern and Western districts of Texas as follows: pre-authorization of outside medical procedures (p. 8); prisoner outside medical treatment procured in violation of the Federal Acquisition Regulation (FAR) (p. 13); administrative costs associated with management of outside medical care (p. 20); summary of USMS district jail inspections (p. 28); conditions of confinement reviews (p. 31); documentation of personal contract guard qualifications in district files (p. 43); and contract guard training (p. 45).

Inmate Lawsuits

275 Scalia, John. *Prisoner Petitions Filed in U.S. District Courts, 2000, with Trends, 1980–2000* [Special Report]. Washington, D.C.: Bureau of Justice Statistics, Office of Justice Programs, U.S. Department of Justice, 2002. NCJ 189430

<http://bjs.ojp.usdoj.gov/index.cfm?ty=pbdetail&iid=882>

Provides statistics on petitions filed by federal and state inmates in U.S. district court, by type of petition and state or jurisdiction (Table 2).

Research Note: Earlier editions are available.

Inmate Records

276 *Review of the United States Marshals Service's Prisoner Tracking System.* [Washington, D.C.]: Audit Division, Office of the Inspector General, U.S. Department of Justice, 2004.

<http://www.usdoj.gov/oig/reports/USMS/a0429/final.pdf>

A review of the U.S. Marshals Service's Prisoner Tracking System (PTS) as implemented in eight district offices, including the Southern District of Texas (S/TX) in Houston. Data is provided on the number of invalid accounts, prisoner file folder completeness, accuracy of output reports, deficiencies found pertaining to system administrator training and expertise, and emergency procedures deficiencies.

Inmate Statistics

•**277** *National Corrections Reporting Program.* Ann Arbor: Inter-university Consortium for Political and Social Research, Institute for Social Research, University of Michigan [annual, 1983–date].

<http://www.icpsr.umich.edu/icpsrweb/ICPSR/series/00038>

The National Corrections Reporting Program (NCRP) was established in 1983 through the merger of the National Prisoner Statistics (NPS) program and the Uniform Parole Reports (UPR). The program is managed by the

Criminal Justice Statistics Branch, U.S. Census Bureau, U.S. Department of Commerce, who compiles, assembles, and prepares calendar-year statistics for analysis and dissemination by the Bureau of Justice Statistics, Office of Justice Programs, U.S. Department of Justice. County-level data is gathered on prisoners entering and leaving the custody or supervision of state and federal authorities as follows: admitted to prison (Part 1); released from prison (Part 2); or released from parole (Part 3). The data includes offender demographics as well as variables such as incarceration history, current offenses, and total time served.

Research Note: Statistics from this program are reported in a number of BJS series, including *Correctional Populations in the United State; Prisoners in . . . ; Prison and Jail Inmates at Midyear; and Probation and Parole in the United States*. CD-ROM editions are available from the National Criminal Justice Reference Service (2000–date). Although it does not contain state-level data, another important series is the *Survey of Inmates of State and Federal Correctional Facilities*, which is conducted every five to six years by the Criminal Justice Statistics Branch, U.S. Census Bureau, U.S. Department of Commerce, for the Bureau of Justice Statistics, National Institute of Justice, U.S. Department of Justice. It is a sample survey of inmates held in prisons (both state and federally owned and operated).and provides nationally representative data on current offenses and sentences; criminal history; family background and personal characteristics; prior drug and alcohol use and treatment programs; gun possession and use; and prison activities, programs, and services.

<http://www.icpsr.umich.edu/icpsrweb/ICPSR/series/00070>

278 *One in 31: The Long Reach of American Corrections.* Washington, D.C.: Pew Center on the States, Pew Charitable Trusts, 2009.

<http://www.pewcenteronthestates.org/report_detail.aspx?id=49382>

The Appendix Tables provide state-level statistics (based on federal sources and the Pew Public Safety Performance Project) as follows: state and national correctional spending (Table A-2); state correctional populations, year-end 2007 (Table A-3); adult incarceration rates (jail and prison) (Table A-4); adult community supervision rates (probation and parole) (Table A-5); and adult correctional control rates (jail, prison, probation, and parole) (Table A-6).

Research Note: The methodological and jurisdictional notes provide background on the data presented in the tables. This report is a follow-up to *One in 100: Behind Bars in America 2008* (Washington, DC: Pew Center on the States, Pew Charitable Trusts, 2008). <http://www.pewcenteronthestates.org/report_detail.aspx?id=35904>

•279 *Prison Inmates at Midyear—Statistical Tables.* Washington, D.C.: Bureau of Justice Statistics, Office of Justice Programs, U.S. Department of Justice [annual, 2007–date].

<http://bjs.ojp.usdoj.gov/index.cfm?ty=pbse&sid=38>

Reports midyear statistics from the National Prisoner Statistics (NPS) Program, Annual Survey of Jails (ASJ), and Federal Justice Statistics Program (FJSP), as follows: prisoners under the jurisdiction of state or federal correctional authorities, by jurisdiction; male prisoners under the jurisdiction of state or federal correctional authorities, by jurisdiction; female prisoners under the jurisdiction of state or federal correctional authorities, by jurisdiction; sentenced prisoners under the jurisdiction of state or federal correctional authorities, by jurisdiction; sentenced male prisoners under the jurisdiction of state or federal correctional authorities, by jurisdiction; sentenced female prisoners under the jurisdiction of state or federal correctional authorities, by jurisdiction; imprisonment rates of sentenced prisoners under jurisdiction of state and federal correctional authorities, by gender, region, and jurisdiction; number of state and federal prisoners in private facilities, by jurisdiction; number of state and federal prisoners in local jails, by jurisdiction; reported number of non-U.S. citizens held in state or federal prisons, by gender, region, and jurisdiction; and reported number of inmates under age eighteen held in state prisons, by gender, region, and jurisdiction.

Research Note: Beginning with the 2008 edition, this report is available online only in the form of data tables on the BJS website ("Statistical Tables" was added to the title beginning with that edition). Previously published under the title *Prison and Jail Inmates at Midyear* (1995–2006). <http://purl.access.gpo.gov/GPO/LPS3695>

•280 *Prisoners in [year]* [Bulletin]. Washington, D.C.: Bureau of Justice Statistics, Office of Justice Programs, U.S. Department of Justice [annual, 1980–date].

<http://purl.access.gpo.gov/GPO/LPS2497>

Reports year-end state-level statistics from the National Prisoner Statistics (NPS) Program, Annual Survey of Jails (ASJ), and Federal Justice Statistics Program (FJSP), as follows: prisoners under the jurisdiction of state or federal prisons or in the custody of state or federal prisons or local jails; prisoners under the jurisdiction of state or federal correctional authorities, by jurisdiction; male prisoners under the jurisdiction of state or federal correctional authorities, by jurisdiction; female prisoners under the jurisdiction of state or federal correctional authorities, by jurisdiction; sentenced prisoners under the jurisdiction of state or federal correctional authorities, by jurisdiction; number of sentenced male prisoners under the jurisdiction of state and federal correctional authorities; sentenced male prisoners under the jurisdiction of state or federal correctional authorities, by jurisdiction; sentenced female prisoners under the jurisdiction of state or federal correctional authorities, by jurisdiction; imprisonment rates of sentenced prisoners under jurisdiction of state and federal correctional authorities, by gender and jurisdiction; number of sentenced prisoners admitted to and released from state or federal jurisdiction, by jurisdiction; number of sentenced prisoners admitted and released from state or federal jurisdiction, by type; number of state and federal prisoners in private facilities, by jurisdiction; number of state and federal prisoners in local jail facilities, by jurisdiction; and reported state and federal prison capacities.

Research Note: No edition for 1995 was published. For midyear statistics, see *Prison Inmates at Midyear—Statistical Tables* (entry 279). For earlier data, see *Historical Statistics on Prisoners in State and Federal Institutions, Yearend 1925–1986* (Ann Arbor: National Archive of Criminal Justice Data, Inter-university Consortium for Political and Social Research, Institute for Social Research, University of Michigan, 1989). <http://dx.doi.org/10.3886/ICPSR08912>

Inmate Suicide

281 Mumola, Christopher J. *Suicide and Homicide in State Prisons and Local Jails* [Special Report]. Washington, D.C.: Bureau of Justice Statistics, Office of Justice Programs, U.S. Department of Justice, 2005. NCJ 210036

<http://purl.access.gpo.gov/GPO/LPS68364>

In order to implement the mandates of the Death in Custody Reporting Act of 2000 (P.L. 106-297, 114 Stat. 1045), the Bureau of Justice Statistics implemented a nationwide data collection program that includes inmate death records from local jail jurisdictions (beginning in 2000), and from state prison authorities (beginning in 2001). This report provides data from the early years of the program as follows: number of prisoner deaths, suicides, and homicides, and mortality rates, per 100,000 prisoners in custody, state prison jurisdictions, 2001–2002 (Table 1), and number of inmate deaths and suicides, and mortality rates per 100,000 inmates, the fifty largest jail jurisdictions, 2000–2002 (Table 2).

Research Note: Datasets are available through the Inter-university Consortium for Political and Social Research (ICPSR), Institute for Social Research, University of Michigan. <http://www.icpsr.umich.edu/icpsrweb/ICPSR/series/00225>

•**282** Mumola, Christopher J. and Margaret E. Noonan. *Deaths in Custody Statistical Tables: State Prison Deaths*. Washington, D.C.: Bureau of Justice Statistics, Office of Justice Programs, U.S. Department of Justice [annual, on-line only, 2001–date].

<http://bjs.ojp.usdoj.gov/content/dcrp/dictabs.cfm>

In order to comply with the mandates of the Death in Custody Reporting Act of 2000 (P.L. 106-297, 114 Stat. 1045), the Bureau of Justice Statistics established a nationwide data collection program that includes inmate death records from local jail jurisdictions (2000–date) and from state prison authorities (2001–date). The State Prison Deaths Statistical Tables report the number of state prisoner deaths, by cause of death and state (Table 12); and average annual mortality rate, per 100,000 state prisoners, by cause of death and state (Table 13). Causes of death reported include suicide.

Research Note: Datasets are available through the Inter-university Consortium for Political and Social Research (ICPSR), Institute for Social Research, University of Michigan. <http://www.icpsr.umich.edu/icpsrweb/ICPSR/series/00225>

•**282A** Noonan, Margaret. *Mortality in Local Jails, 2000–2007* [Special Report]. Washington, D.C.: Bureau of Justice Statistics, Office of Justice Programs, U.S. Department of Justice, 2010. NCJ 222988

<http://bjs.ojp.usdoj.gov/index.cfm?ty=dcdetail&iid=243>

In order to comply with the mandates of the Death in Custody Reporting Act of 2000 (P.L. 106-297, 114 Stat. 1045), the Bureau of Justice Statistics established a nationwide data collection program that includes inmate death records from local jail jurisdictions (2000–date) and from state prison authorities (2001–date). This report provides jail inmate mortality rate per 100,000 inmates, by the fifty largest jail jurisdictions and selected cause of death, 2000–2007 (Appendix Table 5). Causes of death reported include suicide.

Research Note: Datasets are available through the Inter-university Consortium for Political and Social Research (ICPSR), Institute for Social Research, University of Michigan. <http://www.icpsr.umich.edu/icpsrweb/ICPSR/series/00225>

Jails

•**283** *Annual Survey of Jails—Jurisdiction-Level Data.* Ann Arbor: Inter-university Consortium for Political and Social Research, Institute for Social Research, University of Michigan [online only, 1982–date].

<http://www.icpsr.umich.edu/icpsrweb/ICPSR/series/00007>

This survey is conducted annually by the Criminal Justice Statistics Branch, U.S. Census Bureau, U.S. Department of Commerce, for the Bureau of Justice Statistics, National Institute of Justice, U.S. Department of Justice, except every fifth year when the National Jail Census is produced (see entry 288). This is a sample survey—based on information from the most recent National Jail Census—conducted to estimate baseline characteristics of locally administered jails and the inmates they house. It includes data on admissions and releases; growth in the number of jail facilities and changes in their rated capacities and level of occupancy (including overcrowding issues); juveniles housed in adult facilities; growth in the population of offenders under community supervision; changes in community-supervision methods; and the number of inmates being held by specific federal authorities (e.g., the U.S. Marshals Service, U.S. Bureau of Prisons, U.S. Immigration and Customs Enforcement, and the Bureau of Indian Affairs). Since 1995 separate counts have been obtained for the total number lof offenders under jail supervision, held in jail facilities, and supervised outside jail facilities.

Research Note: The survey was called the *National Survey of Jails: Jurisdiction-Level and Jail-Level Data* prior to 1987.

•284 *Correctional Populations in the United States.* Washington, D.C.: Bureau of Justice Statistics, Office of Justice Programs, U.S. Department of Justice [annual, 1985–1998, 2009–date].

<http://bjs.ojp.usdoj.gov/index.cfm?ty=pbse&sid=5>

Provides data on the number of inmates held, average daily population, and rated capacity of the twenty-five largest local jail jurisdictions (which includes Harris, Dallas, Tarrant, and Bexar counties in Texas).

Research Note: See entry 229 for background on this publication series.

285 *Historical Criminal Justice Statistics: Adult Offender Characteristics.* Austin: Legislative Budget Board [annual, online only, 2004–date].
<http://www.lbb.state.tx.us/PubSafety_CrimJustice/PubSafety_CrimJustice.htm>

Provides historical fiscal year statistics on offenders in Texas state jail facilities (on-hand population, admissions, and releases) by age, race, gender, sentence length, offense type, citizenship, and offense category.

•286 *Jail Inmates at Midyear—Statistical Tables.* Washington, D.C.: Bureau of Justice Statistics, Office of Justice Programs, U.S. Department of Justice [annual, 2007–date].

<http://bjs.ojp.usdoj.gov/index.cfm?ty=pbse&sid=38>

Reports midyear data from the Annual Survey of Jails (ASJ) on the nation's fifty largest local jail jurisdictions as follows: number of inmates held, average daily population, and rated capacity.

Research Note: Beginning with the 2008 edition, this report is available online only in the form of data tables on the BJS website ("Statistical Tables" was added to the title beginning with that edition). Previously published under the title *Prison and Jail Inmates at Midyear* (1995–2006). <http://purl.access.gpo.gov/GPO/LPS3695>

287 Kellar, Mark. *Texas County Jails, 2001: A Status Report.* [The Woodlands, Tex.: Kellar & Associates; Austin: Texas Commission on Jail Standards, 2001.]

<http://www.tcjs.state.tx.us/docs/Final%20DraftTJSbu.pdf>

Reports the results of a mail survey of 145 Texas county jails conducted on behalf of the Texas Commission on Jail Standards. The survey's 116 questions covered correctional philosophy, human resource issues, jail operations, and administrative issues.

•288 *National Jail Census Series.* Ann Arbor: Inter-university Consortium for Political and Social Research, Institute for Social Research, University of Michigan [quinquennial, online only, 1970–date].
<http://www.icpsr.umich.edu/icpsrweb/ICPSR/series/00068>

The quinquennial National Jail Census (NJC) is conducted by the Criminal Justice Statistics Branch, U.S. Census Bureau, U.S. Department of Commerce, for the Bureau of Justice Statistics, National Institute of Justice, U.S. Department of Justice. In 2005 the NJC was broken out into two collections in order to reduce respondent burden and improve data quality and timeliness. The Census of Jail Inmates (CJI) collects data on each surveyed facility's supervised populations, inmate counts and movements, and persons supervised in the community. The Census of Jail Facilities (CJF) collects data on each surveyed facility's staffing levels, programming, and facility policies. The initial CJI conducted under this two-part scenario collected data as of June 30, 2005; the initial CJF collected data as of March 31, 2006. Together they enumerated 2,960 locally administered adult confinement facilities that held inmates beyond arraignment (a period normally exceeding seventy-two hours) and were staffed by municipal or county employees (including privately operated jails under contract to local governments and regional jails operated for two or more jail authorities). Also enumerated were a small number of facilities maintained by the U.S. Bureau of Prisons that functioned as jails, although other federal- and state-administered facilities were excluded, as were temporary holding or lockup facilities.

Research Note: The BJS has reported selected data from earlier censuses in several series, including *Census of Jails* and *Census of Local Jails.* Although it does not contain state-level data, another important series is the *Survey of Inmates in Local Jails,* which is conducted every five to six years by the Criminal Justice Statistics Branch, U.S. Census Bureau, U.S. Department of Commerce, for the Bureau of Justice Statistics, National Institute of Justice, U.S. Department of Justice. It is a sample survey of inmates housed in adult and juvenile jail facilities and provides nationally representative data on persons held prior to trial and on those convicted offenders serving sentences in local jails or awaiting transfer to prison, including individual characteristics of jail inmates; current offenses, sentences, and time served; criminal histories; jail activities, conditions and programs; prior drug and alcohol use and treatment; medical and mental health conditions; and health care services provided while in jail. <http://www.icpsr. umich.edu/icpsrweb/ICPSR/series/00069>

•289 *Reports.* Austin: Texas Commission on Jail Standards [monthly].
<http://www.tcjs.state.tx.us/index.php?linkID=320>

The Texas Commission on Jail Standards serves as the regulatory agency for all county jails and privately operated municipal jails in the state (Tex. Gov't Code Ann. §§ 511.001–.017 (Vernon 2004 & Supp. 2010)). Its mission is to assist local governments in providing safe, secure, and suitable local jail facilities through the provision of the following services: the establishment of reasonable minimum standards for the construction and operation of jails; the monitoring and enforcement of compliance with adopted standards through on-site inspections; review and comment on all jail construction documents; and the provision of consultation, training, and technical assistance on efficient, effective, and economical means of jail construction and management. The Commission issues monthly reports covering jail populations, county jail population summaries, county jail incarceration rates, historical county jail populations by offense type, counties housing local inmates elsewhere, and planning and construction.

290 *Self-evaluation Report to the Sunset Advisory Commission*. Austin: Texas Commission on Jail Standards, 2007.

<http://www.sunset.state.tx.us/81streports/tcjs/ser.pdf>

The Texas Sunset Act requires the automatic termination of designated State agencies twelve years after review unless the legislature extends the life of the agency by statute (Tex. Gov't Code Ann. §§ 325.001–.024 (Vernon 2005)). The Sunset Advisory Commission assists the legislature in making these determinations by evaluating the operations of agencies scheduled for termination. As a part of the review process, each agency submits a Self-Evaluation Report (SER) to the commission. This report provides statistics on fiscal matters (appropriations, revenues, expenditures, and federal aid); personnel; complaints against the agency received, investigated, and resolved; and key performance measures.

Research Note: Earlier editions are available. See also the report of the commission's decisions regarding this review. <http://www.sunset.state.tx.us/81streports/tcjs/tcjs_dec.pdf>

291 *The State Jail System Today: An Update.* Austin: Criminal Justice Policy Council, 2000.

<http://www.lbb.state.tx.us/PubSafety_CrimJustice/6_Links/Documents_Alpha_Links.htm>

A profile of state jail felons, including those under community supervision and those serving time as inmates in state or county jails, as of August 31, 1999.

Research Note: Earlier editions are available.

Offender Mental Health Services

292 Beck, Allen J., and Laura M. Maruschak. *Mental Health Treatment in State Prisons, 2000* [Special Report]. Washington, D.C.: Bureau of Justice Statistics, Office of Justice Programs, U.S. Department of Justice, 2001. NCJ 188215

<http://purl.access.gpo.gov/GPO/LPS19685>

Reports data from the Census of State and Federal Adult Correctional Facilities on mental health screening and treatment in state correctional facilities (Appendix Table A); inmates receiving mental health treatment in state correctional facilities (Appendix Table B); and the thirty-five largest state correctional facilities providing mental health therapy/treatment (Appendix Table C).

•**293** *The Biennial Report of the Texas Correctional Office on Offenders with Medical and Mental Impairments.* Austin: The Office [2005–date].

<http://www.tdcj.state.tx.us/publications/publications-home.
htm#TCOOMMI>

The Texas Council on Offenders with Mental Impairments (TCOMI) was established by the 70th Texas Legislature to address policy issues, programs, and initiatives involving the care and treatment of adult and juvenile offenders with special needs, specifically mental illness, mental retardation, and developmental disabilities. Its role was subsequently expanded to include elderly offenders and offenders with serious medical conditions and physical disabilities. The 78th Legislature changed its name to the Texas Correctional Office on Offenders with Medical and Mental Impairments (TCOOMMI) and reorganized the functions of the Council to an advisory committee reporting to the Texas Board of Criminal Justice. The biennial report is prepared and submitted in accordance with Tex. Health & Safety Code Ann. § 614.009 (Vernon 2010). It provides data on the Office's three major programs: Community-Based Programs, which include the jail diversion and mental health/criminal justice initiative; Continuity of Care (COC); and Medically Recommended Intensive Supervision (MRIS).

Research Note: The first report covers FY2003 and FY2004. Earlier reports were published under the title *The Biennial Report of the Texas Council on Offenders with Mental Impairments.*

294 *Overview of the Enhanced Mental Health Services Initiative.* Austin: Criminal Justice Policy Council, 2002.

<http://www.lbb.state.tx.us/PubSafety_CrimJustice/6_Links/Documents_
Alpha_Links.htm>

The 77th Texas Legislature appropriated new funding for an Enhanced Mental Health Services Initiative to provide additional specialized services and supervision to mentally ill adult and juvenile offenders, with the overall goal of reducing recidivism. The funding was earmarked for the Texas Council on Offenders with Mental Impairments (since renamed the Texas Correctional Office on Offenders with Medical and Mental Impairments), the Texas Juvenile Probation Commission, and the Community Assistance Division of the Texas Department of Criminal Justice. This report provides data on specialized caseloads and case management for mentally ill offenders eligible for service under this initiative.

Research Note: See also the council's three earlier reports published in 2000: *Mentally Ill Offenders and County Jails: Survey Results and Policy Issues*; *The Public Mental Health System in Texas and Its Relation to Criminal Justice; and Intervention for Mentally Ill Offenders: Planning and Policy Issues to Consider.*

Parole

•295 *Annual Report.* Austin: Texas Board of Pardons and Paroles [1948–date]. <http://www.tdcj.state.tx.us/bpp/publications/publications.html>

The Texas Board of Pardons and Paroles is comprised of seven members appointed by the governor with the advice and consent of the Texas Senate (Tex. Gov. Code Ann. §§ 508.001–.324 (Vernon 2004 & Supp. 2010)). It is responsible for determining which eligible offenders are to be released on parole, the conditions of their release, and the disposition of those who violate their conditions of release. It also makes executive clemency recommendations to the governor, which comprise reprieve, pardon, and commutation of sentence. This report provides statistics as follows: summary of board parole activity (approvals, considerations, types, rates, and votes); hearings activity; executive clemency activity; parole supervision dynamics (population under active supervision, ten largest counties for offenders under active supervision, Super Intensive Supervision Program (SISP), and residential release facilities); and agency budget and expenditures. The appendixes provide data on parole considerations and approval rates by offense type; parole considerations by board members and parole commissioners; parole considerations and approval rates by guideline level; parole approval types; parole considerations for offenders serving consecutive sentences; Discretionary Mandatory Supervision (DMS) considerations by board members and parole commissioners; DMS considerations and approval rates by offense type; Medically Recommended Intensive Supervision (MRIS) considerations by board members and parole commissioners; MRIS parole panel considerations; special review cases considered by parole panel; allegations presented for administrative decisions; decisions to send the offender to an ISF (Intermediate Sanction Facility) or SAFPF (Substance Abuse Felony Punishment Facility); decisions to continue supervision or place in normal review; offenders revoked by grounds for revocation; and population on SISP.

Research Note: Data is reported by fiscal year. Published under slightly varying titles. Reports are available online back to 2001.

296 *An Audit Report on Selected Parole Functions at the Department of Criminal Justice and the Board of Pardons and Paroles* [SAO Report]. Austin: State Auditor's Office, 2008. 08-036

<http://www.sao.state.tx.us/reports/main/08-036.html>

The objectives of this audit were to (1) determine whether the Texas Department of Criminal Justice and the Texas Board of Pardons and Paroles were in compliance with applicable laws and agency policies in identifying and addressing violations of conditions of parole or mandatory supervision, including the use of progressive sanctions and the revocations of offenders' parole and mandatory supervision, and (2) review the implementation and performance of the TDCJ's Offender Information Management System (OIMS) and the utilization of this system by the two agencies.

297 Bonczar, Thomas P. *Characteristics of State Parole Supervising Agencies, 2006* [Special Report]. Washington, D.C.: Bureau of Justice Statistics, Office of Justice Programs, U.S. Department of Justice, 2008 (rev. 2009). NCJ 222180

<http://purl.access.gpo.gov/GPO/LPS122946>

Reports midyear 2006 state-level data from the Census of State Parole Supervising Agencies as follows: characteristics of adult parole supervising agencies (Table 2); adult parole supervising agency staff, by type (Table 15); and adult parole supervising agency staff, by gender (Table 16).

Research Note: The report also provides a comparison of the 2006 Census of State Parole Supervising Agency and 2006 Annual Parole Survey data collections (Table 14). A technical supplement, which includes Tables 14–16, was added to the report in March 2009.

•298 *Correctional Populations in the United States.* Washington, D.C.: Bureau of Justice Statistics, Office of Justice Programs, U.S. Department of Justice [annual, 1985–1998, 2009–date].

<http://bjs.ojp.usdoj.gov/index.cfm?ty=pbse&sid=5>

Provides state-level data on the number of adults on parole (total and by status of supervision); adults entering parole, by type of sentence; adults leaving parole, by type of discharge; adults on parole, by gender and Hispanic origin; adults on parole, by race; adults on parole, by sentence length; adults on parole under intensive supervision, under electronic monitoring, or in a boot camp; adults on parole, by type of release; and deaths of adults on parole, by cause of death.

Research Note: See entry 229 for background on this publication series.

•299 *Federal Justice Statistics—Statistical Tables*. Washington, D.C.: Bureau of Justice Statistics, Office of Justice Programs, U.S. Department of Justice [annual, online only, 2005–date].

<http://purl.access.gpo.gov/GPO/LPS113898>

Reports fiscal year data from the Federal Justice Statistics Program (FJSP) and includes a United States map (along with an accompanying spreadsheet) that provides data on defendants under federal supervision, by federal judicial district (Map 7.1).

Research Note: This publication series supersedes *Compendium of Federal Justice Statistics* (1984–2004). Texas is in the U.S. Court of Appeals Fifth Circuit and has four districts: Eastern, Northern, Southern, and Western. Datasets are available through the Inter-university Consortium for Political and Social Research (ICPSR), Institute for Social Research, University of Michigan. <http://www.icpsr.umich.edu/icpsrweb/ICPSR/series/00073>

300 Hughes, Timothy A., Doris James Wilson, and Allen J. Beck. *Trends in State Parole, 1990–2000* [Special Report]. Washington, D.C.: Bureau of Justice Statistics, Office of Justice Programs, U.S. Department of Justice, 2001. NCJ 184735.

<http://purl.access.gpo.gov/GPO/LPS19680>

Provides state-level data on the number of adults on parole, year-end 1990, 1995, and 2000 (Table 2); time served, maximum sentence, and percent of sentence served for Part 1 violent offenders, 1993, 1996, and 1999 (Table 6); percent successful among state parole discharges, 1990, 1995, and 1999 (Table 15); and percent parole violators among admissions to state prison, 1990 and 1999 (Table 19).

301 *Overview of Special Needs Parole Policy and Recommendations for Improvement*. Austin: Criminal Justice Policy Council, 2000.

<http://www.lbb.state.tx.us/PubSafety_CrimJustice/6_Links/Documents_Alpha_Links.htm>

Reports data on cases referred to the Special Needs Parole program, which provides for early parole review for certain non-aggravated offenders who have a medical condition that requires round-the-clock skilled nursing care.

•302 *Probation and Parole in the United States* [Bulletin]. Washington, D.C.: Bureau of Justice Statistics, Office of Justice Programs, U.S. Department of Justice [annual, 1998–date].

<http://purl.access.gpo.gov/GPO/LPS24505>

The Appendix Tables report state-level statistics from the Annual Parole Survey as follows: adults under community supervision; adults on parole; adults entering parole, by type of sentence; adults exiting parole, by type of exit; adults on parole, by gender; adults on parole, by race and Hispanic origin; adults on parole, by status of supervision; adults on parole, by maximum sentence to incarceration; adults on parole, by most serious offense; adults on parole, by type of release from prison; and adults on parole tracked by a Global Positioning System (GPS), also on probation, or incarcerated.

Research Note: The 2007 edition was issued in electronic format only. Previously published under the title *Probation and Parole Populations* (1994–1997). See also entry 321. Datasets are available through the Inter-university Consortium for Political and Social Research (ICPSR), Institute for Social Research, University of Michigan. <http://www.icpsr.umich.edu/icpsrweb/ICPSR/series/00038>

303 Travis, Jeremy, and Sarah Lawrence. *Beyond the Prison Gates: The State of Parole in America* [Research Report]. Washington, D.C.: Justice Policy Center, Urban Institute, 2002.

<http://www.urban.org/UploadedPDF/310583_Beyond_prison_gates.pdf>

Presents state-level statistics as follows: percentage of released prisoners who begin parole as a result of a parole board decision, 1998 (Fig. 3); percentage of state prison releases that are unconditional, 1998 (Fig. 5); percentage change in parole population, 1990 to 2000 (Fig. 8); distribution of populations across states, 2000 (Fig. 9); ratio of prisoners to parolees, 2000 (Fig. 11); percentage of parole discharges that were successful, 1999 (Fig. 14); and percentage of prison admissions that are parole violators, 1999 (Fig. 17).

Pre-release Programs

304 *Initial Process and Outcome Evaluation of the InnerChange Freedom Initiative: The Faith-Based Prison Program in TDCJ.* Austin: Criminal Justice Policy Council, 2003.

<http://www.lbb.state.tx.us/PubSafety_CrimJustice/6_Links/Documents_Alpha_Links.htm>

The InnerChange Freedom Initiative is a faith-based pre-release program operated by Prison Fellowship Ministries through a contract with the Texas Department of Criminal Justice. It is a component of the TDCJ's tier of rehabilitation programs and based at the Carol S. Vance Unit in Richmond. This report provides data on the initiative's selection processes and criteria, completion rates, and recidivism rates.

Research Note: See also the council's earlier report *Overview of the InnerChange Freedom Initiative: The Faith-Based Prison Program within the Texas Department of Criminal Justice* (2002) and *The InnerChange Freedom Initiative: A Preliminary Evaluation of a Faith-Based Prison Program*, by Byron R. Johnson and David B. Larson. Philadelphia, Pa.: Center for Research on Religion and Urban Civil Society, School of Arts and Sciences, University of Pennsylvania, 2003.

Prisoner Sexual Assault

305 Austin, James, Tony Fabelo, Angela Gunter, and Ken McGinnis. *Sexual Violence in the Texas Prison System.* Washington, D.C.: The JFA Institute, 2006. NCJ 215774

<http://www.ncjrs.gov/pdffiles1/nij/grants/215774.pdf>

Provides data on approximately 2,000 officially reported sexual assaults that occurred in Texas Department of Criminal Justice (TDCJ) units between January 1, 2002, and August 31, 2005, including number and rates of alleged prisoner on prisoner sexual assaults (1993–2005); TDCJ incidents by case resolution status; TDCJ sexual assault allegations classified by BJA definition; time lapse from incident occur date to incident report date; whether a rape kit or forensic exam was performed; reasons a rape kit or forensic exam was not performed; whether the medical exam revealed injuries to the victim or assailant; characteristics of the victims and assailants (e.g., demographics, custody class, gang affiliation, etc.); offense category of victims, assailants, and all other TDCJ inmates on hand; average time served for victims, assailants, and all other TDCJ inmates on hand; top ten TDCJ units where sexual assaults were alleged to have occurred; top ten TDCJ units by incidence rate where sexual assaults were alleged to have occurred; all TDCJ units where sexual assault allegations were sustained; and top ten TDCJ units by major use of force (MUF) rate where sexual assault allegations were made.

•**306** Beck, Allen J., et al. *Sexual Victimization in Prisons and Jails Reported by Inmates, 2008–09* [National Inmate Survey]. Washington, D.C.: Bureau of Justice Statistics, Office of Justice Programs, U.S. Department of Justice, 2010. NCJ 231169

<http://bjs.ojp.usdoj.gov/index.cfm?ty=dcdetail&iid=278>

The Prison Rape Elimination Act of 2003 (P.L. 108-79, 117 Stat. 972) requires the Bureau of Justice Statistics to conduct a comprehensive annual statistical review and analysis of the incidence and effects of prison rape in correctional facilities. The overall program is called the National Prison Rape Statistics Program (NPRSP) and comprises several data collections. The BJS conducted the second National Inmate Survey (NIS-2) between October 2008 and December 2009. It was administered to 81,566 inmates age eighteen and older held in 167 state and federal prisons, 286 jails, and ten special confinement facilities operated by Immigration and Customs Enforcement (ICE), the U.S. military, and correctional authorities in Indian country. The survey was restricted to adult confinement facilities, including prisons, penitentiaries, prison hospitals, prison farms, boot camps, and centers for reception, classification, or alcohol and drug treatment (excluding community-based facilities, such as halfway houses, group homes, and work release centers). Unlike the Bureau's Survey of Sexual Violence (SSV), which is based on administrative records (see entry 307), the NIS is based on self-administered, anonymous surveys completed by the inmates themselves. The Appendix Tables contain facility-level data as follows: characteristics of state and federal prisons and prevalence of sexual victimization (Table 1); percent of prison inmates reporting sexual victimization, by type of incident (Table 2); percent of prison inmates reporting sexual victimization, by level of coercion (Table 3); percent of prison inmates reporting nonconsensual sexual acts and abusive sexual contacts (Table 4); characteristics of jails and prevalence of sexual victimization (Table 5); percent of jail inmates reporting victimization, by type of incident (Table 6); percent of jail inmates reporting sexual victimization, by level of coercion (Table 7); percent of jail inmates reporting nonconsensual sexual acts and abusive sexual contacts (Table 8); and characteristics of special correctional facilities and prevalence of sexual victimization (Table 9).

Research Note: The NIS will be conducted annually as funding permits. NIS-1 was conducted between April and August 2007 and published under the titles *Sexual Victimization in State and Federal Prisons Reported by Inmates* (NCJ 219414) and *Sexual Victimization in Local Jails Reported by Inmates* (NCJ 221946).

•307 *Sexual Victimization Reported by Adult Correctional Authorities* [Special Report]. Washington, D.C.: Bureau of Justice Statistics, Office of Justice Programs, U.S. Department of Justice [annual, 2004–date].
<http://purl.access.gpo.gov/GPO/LPS122044>

This annual data collection is mandated by the Prison Rape Elimination Act of 2003 (see entry 306). The Survey of Sexual Violence (SSV) is based on administrative records and includes federal and state prison systems, state-operated juvenile facilities, and facilities in the United States operated by the U.S. military. In addition, a representative sample is drawn from local jails, jails in Indian country, facilities operated by the Bureau of Immigration and Customs Enforcement (ICE), privately operated adult prisons and jails, and privately or locally operated juvenile facilities. The Appendix Tables contain state- and facility-level data as follows: allegations of inmate-on-inmate sexual victimization reported by state or federal prison authorities, by type; allegations of staff-on-inmate sexual victimization reported by state or federal prison authorities, by type; allegations of inmate-on-inmate sexual victimization reported by local jail authorities, by type; local jail authorities with no reported allegations of inmate-on-inmate sexual victimization; allegations of staff-on-inmate sexual victimization reported by local jail authorities, by type; local jail authorities with no reported allegations of staff-on-inmate sexual victimization; allegations of inmate-on-inmate sexual victimization reported in private prisons and jails; private prison and jail authorities with no reported allegations of inmate-on-inmate sexual victimization; allegations of staff-on-inmate sexual victimization reported in private prisons and jails, by type; private prison and jail authorities with no reported allegations of staff-on-inmate sexual victimization; allegations of inmate-on-inmate sexual victimization reported in other correctional facilities, by type; allegations of staff-on-inmate sexual victimization reported in other correctional facilities, by type.

308 *Texas Update: Texas State Prisons Plagued by Sexual Abuse.* Los Angeles, Calif.: Stop Prisoner Rape, 2008.

<http://www.justdetention.org/pdf/TexasUpdate.pdf>

This report is based on approximately 180 letters received directly from TDCJ inmates between 2004 and 2008.

Research Note: The organization Stop Prisoner Rape was renamed Just Detention International in 2008.

309 Zweig, Janine M., and John Blackmore. *Strategies to Prevent Prison Rape by Changing the Correctional Culture* [Research for Practice]. Washington, D.C.: National Institute of Justice, Office of Justice Programs, U.S. Department of Justice, 2008. NCJ 222843

<http://purl.access.gpo.gov/GPO/LPS105430>

Presents research conducted collaboratively between the Urban Institute and the Association of State Correctional Administrators. Exhibit 2 enumerates the topics covered in prison sexual violence education curricula for inmates in each of the eleven case study states (including Texas).

Prisoner Transport

310 *The United States Marshals Service's Management of the Justice Prisoner and Alien Transportation System* [Audit Report]. [Washington, D.C.]: Audit Division, Office of the Inspector General, U.S. Department of Justice, 2006.

<http://www.usdoj.gov/oig/reports/USMS/a0701/final.pdf>

Appendix IV of this audit of the U.S. Marshals Service's management of the Justice Prisoner and Alien Transportation System (JPATS) contains statistics on non-federal prisoner movements by state or territory of requestor for FY2004 and FY2005.

Private Prisons

311 *CCA Facility Locations.* Nashville, Tenn: Corrections Corporation of America, [online only].

<http://www.correctionscorp.com/facilities/>

Corrections Corporation of America develops and manages private correctional and detention facilities in Texas for the Federal Bureau of Prisons, U.S. Immigration and Customs Enforcement, U.S. Marshals Service, and Texas Department of Criminal Justice. This website provides the following information on their facilities: facility type (gender, total beds, and security level), year CCA management started, customer base, programs offered, and accreditation.

•**312** *Contracted Facilities*. Huntsville: Private Facility Contract Monitoring/Oversight Division, Texas Department of Criminal Justice [online only].

<http://www.tdcj.state.tx.us/private_facilities/private_facilities_unit_list.htm>

Provides a list of contracted TDCJ facilities with information on the contractor and number of beds. These include correctional facilities, Lockhart Work program, state jail facilities, DWI Program/SAFPF, intermediate sanction facilities, pre-parole transfer facilities, county jail work release program, halfway house facilities, and substance abuse (residential) facilities. A list is also provided of Substance Abuse Felony Punishment Facilities (SAFPF)/In-Prison Therapeutic Community (IPTC) contracted slots.

313 *Correctional Facilities*. Centerville, Utah: Management & Training Corporation [online only].

<http://www.mtctrains.com/corrections/facilities.php>

Management & Training Corporation develops and manages correctional and detention facilities in Texas for the Texas Department of Criminal Justice, Federal Bureau of Prisons, U.S. Immigration and Customs Enforcement, and U.S. Marshals Service. This website provides the following information on their facilities: contracting agency, security level, rated capacity, background, rehabilitation programs, and accreditation.

314 *Global Facilities*. Boca Raton, Fla.: The GEO Group, Inc. [online only].

<http://www.thegeogroupinc.com/locations.asp>

The GEO Group, Inc., develops and manages private correctional and detention facilities in Texas for the Federal Bureau of Prisons, U.S. Immigration and Customs Enforcement, U.S. Marshals Service, Texas Department of Criminal Justice, and individual city and county governments. This website provides the following information on their facilities: contractee, contract award, type and design, capacity, date opened, services/work, and accreditation.

Research Note: Called the Wackenhut Corrections Corporation prior to November 2003.

Probation

315 *Community Supervision in Texas: Statistical Trends in Community Supervision.* Updated and revised by Jen Todhunter. Austin: Community Justice Assistance Division, Texas Department of Criminal Justice, 2003.

<http://www.tdcj.state.tx.us/publications/cjad/publications-cjad-statistical-trends.htm>

The Appendix provides county-level data (1993–2002) as follows: CSCD (Community Supervision and Corrections Department) direct offender population (August 31); CSCD percent of statewide direct offender population (August 31); CSCD direct, indirect, and pretrial offender population (August 31); CSCD percentage of statewide direct, indirect, and pretrial offender population (August 31); revocations to TDCJ-ID (Texas Department of Criminal Justice-Institutional Division) and state jail; revocations to TDCJ-ID; revocations to state jail; and misdemeanant revocations to county jail.

•**316** *Correctional Populations in the United States.* Washington, D.C.: Bureau of Justice Statistics, Office of Justice Programs, U.S. Department of Justice [annual, 1985–1998, 2009–date].

<http://bjs.ojp.usdoj.gov/index.cfm?ty=pbse&sid=5>

Provides state-level data on adult probation as follows: total entries and exits, by status of probation, by status of supervision, entering by type of sentence, leaving by type of discharge, by gender and Hispanic origin, by race, by severity of offense, under intensive supervision, under electronic monitoring, in a boot camp, or incarcerated, and by selected offenses.

Research Note: See entry 229 for background on this publication series.

•**317** *Federal Justice Statistics—Statistical Tables.* Washington, D.C.: Bureau of Justice Statistics, Office of Justice Programs, U.S. Department of Justice [annual, online only, 2005–date].

<http://purl.access.gpo.gov/GPO/LPS113898>

Reports fiscal year data from the Federal Justice Statistics Program (FJSP) and includes a United States map (along with an accompanying spreadsheet) that provides data on defendants under federal supervision, by federal judicial district (Map 7.1).

Research Note: This publication series supersedes *Compendium of Federal Justice Statistics* (1984–2004). Texas is in the U.S. Court of Appeals Fifth Circuit and has four districts: Eastern, Northern, Southern, and Western. Datasets are available through the Inter-university Consortium for Political and Social Research (ICPSR), Institute for Social Research, University of Michigan. <http://www.icpsr.umich.edu/icpsrweb/ICPSR/series/00073>

318 Kim, Bitna, Jurg Gerber, and Dan R. Beto. "Collaboration between Law Enforcement and Community Corrections Agencies." *TELEMASP Bulletin* [Texas Law Enforcement Management and Administrative Statistics Program] 14, no. 1 (January/February 2007): 1–12.

<http://www.lemitonline.org/telemasp/>

Presents the results of a survey of 231 Texas law enforcement agencies. It reports the percentage of respondents with informal partnerships with community corrections agencies (Table 1); with informal "enhanced supervision" partnerships with community corrections agencies (Table 2); with "specialized enforcement" partnerships with community corrections agencies (Table 3); that view existing partnerships positively (Table 4); with partnerships with adult probation (Table 5); with partnerships with adult parole departments (Table 6); and with juvenile probation departments (Table 7).

•319 *Judicial Business of the United States Courts: Annual Report of the Director*. Washington, D.C.: Statistics Division, Office of Judges Programs, Administrative Office of the United States Courts, [annual, 1994–date].

<http://purl.access.gpo.gov/GPO/LPS2715>

The Appendix (Detailed Statistical Tables) provides the following statistics for the U.S. District Courts—Federal Probation System: received for and removed from post-conviction supervision (Table E-1); under post-conviction supervision (Table E-2); and under post-conviction supervision, by offense (Table E-3).

Research Note: Reports are available online back to 1997. Texas is in the U.S. Court of Appeals Fifth Circuit and has four districts: Eastern, Northern, Southern, and Western. The data in Tables E-1 and E-2 is also reported annually in *Federal Judicial Caseload Statistics* (see entry 186) and biannually in *Statistical Tables of the Federal Judiciary*. <http://purl.access.gpo.gov/GPO/LPS21918>

320 *Probation and Parole Directory*. Alexandria, Va.: American Correctional Association [biennial, 1981–date].

Provides the following state-level data for community supervision and corrections department offices: fiscal information, beginning salary ranges, personnel, and client caseload.

Research Note: This data is not provided for every listed department.

•321 *Probation and Parole in the United States* [Bulletin]. Washington, D.C.: Bureau of Justice Statistics, Office of Justice Programs, U.S. Department of Justice [annual, 1998–date].

<http://purl.access.gpo.gov/GPO/LPS24505>

The Appendix Tables report state-level statistics from the Annual Probation Survey as follows: adults under community supervision; adults on probation;

adults entering probation, by type of sentence; adults exiting probation, by type of exit; adults on probation, by gender; adults on probation, by race and Hispanic origin; adults on probation, by status of supervision; adults on probation, by type of offense; adults on probation, by most serious offense; adults on probation tracked by a Global Positioning System (GPS), also on parole, or incarcerated.

Research Note: The 2007 edition was issued in electronic format only. Previously published under the title *Probation and Parole Populations* (1994–1997). See also entry 302. Datasets are available through the Inter-university Consortium for Political and Social Research (ICPSR), Institute for Social Research, University of Michigan. <http://www.icpsr.umich.edu/icpsrweb/ICPSR/series/00038>

322 *Report to the Governor and the Legislative Budget Board on Monitoring of Community Supervision Diversion Funds.* Huntsville: Community Justice Assistance Division, Texas Department of Criminal Justice [annual].
<http://cjadweb.tdcj.state.tx.us/Research/EvaluationCriteria/evalcriteriamenu.aspx>

In 2005, the Texas Legislature appropriated funds to the Texas Department of Criminal Justice to provide prison diversions through probation and community-based programs. (Item A.1.2 (Strategy) through Item A.1.4 (Strategy), page V-10, Chapter 1369, Acts of the 79th Legislature, Regular Session, 2005, the General Appropriations Act). This report is compiled and published in accordance with Rider 79, page V-25, Chapter 1369, Acts of the 79th Legislature, Regular Session, 2005, the General Appropriations Act, which states,

> From funds appropriated above, the Texas Department of Criminal Justice (TDCJ) shall develop a specific accountability system for tracking community supervision funds targeted at making a positive impact on the criminal justice system. In addition to implementing the recommendations made by the State Auditor's Office in the September 2004 report (Report No. 05-002) to the Texas Department of Criminal Justice to increase the accuracy and completeness of information used to allocate funds for adult probation services and to improve the monitoring agreements made with the community supervision and corrections departments (CSCDs), the agency shall implement a monitoring system so that the use of funds appropriated in Strategies A.1.2, A.1.3, and A.1.4. can be specifically identified. The agency shall produce, on an annual basis, detailed monitoring, tracking, utilization, and effectiveness information on the above mentioned funds. This information shall include information on the impact of any new initiatives. Examples include, but are not limited to, number of offenders served, number of residential beds funded, number of community supervision

officers hired, and caseload sizes. The agency shall provide documentation regarding the methodology used to distribute the funds. In addition to any other requests for information, the agency shall report the above information for the previous fiscal year to the Legislative Budget Board and the Governor's Office by December 1st of each year.

Research Note: The website provides results for the most recent quarter, and percent change as compared to a FY2005 baseline, statewide and by CSCD for the following categories: felony placements, average CCF (Community Correctional Facility) population, average CSOs (Community Supervision Officer), felony revocations to TDCJ, felony technical revocations, felony revocation rate (percent), and felony early discharges.

323 *The Substance Abuse Felony Punishment Program: Evaluation and Recommendations.* Austin: Criminal Justice Policy Council, 2001.

<http://www.lbb.state.tx.us/PubSafety_CrimJustice/6_Links/Documents_Alpha_Links.htm>

A legislatively mandated evaluation of the effectiveness of the Substance Abuse Felony Punishment Program, which is the largest, most intensive, and most costly substance abuse treatment program the state provides for felony probationers.

324 *Texas Community-Based Substance Abuse Treatment Programs* [Report to Senate Criminal Justice Interim Committee]. [Huntsville]: Judicial Advisory Council, Community Supervision and Corrections Departments, Texas Department of Criminal Justice, 2002.

<http://www.tdcj.state.tx.us/publications/cjad/publications-cjad-lr-tx-comm-sub-abuse-treat.htm>

Provides statistics on Community-based Substance Abuse Treatment Programs (residential and non-residential): type, capacity, total served, and cost. Also provides recidivism rates for successful graduates and unsuccessful discharges from DIVERT Court programs.

325 *Texas Community Supervision Revocation Project: A Comparison of Revoked Felons During September 2005 and September 2007.* Austin: Legislative Budget Board, 2008.

<http://www.lbb.state.tx.us/PubSafety_CrimJustice/PubSafety_CrimJustice.htm>

This report relates to the community supervision diversion funds appropriated by the 79th Texas Legislature (see entry 322). In order to evaluate the impact of the additional community supervision funding, this report established a baseline profile of revocations prior to the implementation of new and expanded programs and initiatives funded through these appropriations. The baseline was established to serve as a comparison for revocation profiles in the future after the programs have been fully implemented. The Legislative Budget Board, in coordination with the Community Justice Assistance Division of the Texas Department of Criminal Justice, conducted an interim research project wherein five Community Supervision and Corrections Departments (CSCD) were selected as data collection sites: Bexar, Dallas, Harris, Tarrant, and Travis counties (which accounted for forty-four percent of all statewide felony community supervision revocations in 2005). Data was collected for all verified felony community supervision revocations that occurred during September 2005 in the selected CSCDs. This report compares information on revoked felons in the selected CSCDs during September 2007 with September 2005 cohort.

326 *Texas Residential Programs Community Corrections Facilities* [Report to House Corrections Interim Committee]. [Huntsville]: Judicial Advisory Council, Community Supervision and Corrections Departments, Texas Department of Criminal Justice, 2002.

<http://www.tdcj.state.tx.us/publications/cjad/publications-cjad-lr-tx-res-pgms.htm>

Provides an overview of Community Corrections Facilities, which include Court Residential Treatment Centers, Substance Abuse Treatment Facilities, Restitution Centers, Local Boot Camps, and Intermediate Sanction Facilities. It contains data on program duties, capacities, number served, waiting times, resident profiles, funding, operational costs, staffing, technical revocation rates, and long-term recidivism rates.

Recidivism

327 Langan, Patrick A., and David J. Levin. *Recidivism of Prisoners Released in 1994* [Special Report]. Washington, D.C.: Bureau of Justice Statistics, Office of Justice Programs, U.S. Department of Justice, 2002. NCJ 193427

<http://purl.access.gpo.gov/GPO/LPS33477>

A study of the rearrest, reconviction, and reincarceration of 272,111 former inmates who were tracked for three years following their discharge in 1994 from prisons in fifteen states (including Texas). Table 7 presents the number of out-of-state rearrest charges against prisoners released in fourteen of these states (including Texas), by state where rearrested.

Research Note: Earlier editions are available. Datasets are available through the National Archive of Criminal Justice Data, Inter-university Consortium for Political and Social Research (ICPSR), Institute for Social Research, University of Michigan.

<http://dx.doi.org/10.3886/ICPSR03355>

328 *The Second Biennial Report on the Performance of the Texas Department of Criminal Justice Rehabilitation Tier Programs.* Austin: Criminal Justice Policy Council, 2003.

<http://www.lbb.state.tx.us/PubSafety_CrimJustice/6_Links/Documents_Alpha_Links.htm>

This legislatively mandated report measures the effectiveness of the Texas Department of Criminal Justice's rehabilitation tier programs in reducing recidivism.

Research Note: Earlier editions are available.

•329 *Statewide Criminal Justice Recidivism and Revocation Rates.* Austin: Legislative Budget Board [biennial, online only, 2005–date].

<http://www.lbb.state.tx.us/PubSafety_CrimJustice/PubSafety_CrimJustice.htm>

Provides rates of felony community supervision revocations, Substance Abuse Felony Punishment Facility (SAFPF) reincarcerations, state jail reincarcerations, state jail rearrests, prison reincarcerations, prison rearrests, active parole revocations, and Intermediate Sanction Facility (ISF) reincarcerations. Appendix A provides a comparison of three-year recidivism rates by state; Appendix B provides a comparison of Texas recidivists.

Research Note: Reports were previously published by the Criminal Justice Policy Council (under varying titles).

Religious Freedom

330 *Enforcing Religious Freedom in Prison.* Washington, D.C.: U.S. Commission on Civil Rights, 2008.

<http://purl.access.gpo.gov/GPO/LPS107906>

Provides state-level statistics on prisoner plaintiff cases filed in federal court pursuant to the provisions of the Religious Land Use and Institutionalized Persons Act of 2000 (P.L. 106-274, 114 Stat. 803) as follows: number of cases by year, 2001–2006 (Table D.4), and total number cases by plaintiff's religious tradition, 2001–2006 (Table D.5). Statistics are also provided for the magnitude, trend, nature, and percentage of religious grievances granted at the FCI La Tuna (Federal Correctional Institution), Anthony, Texas, FY1997–FY2007 (Table C.1c); and the magnitude, trend, and nature of religious grievances at the TDCJ Stiles Unit, Beaumont, Texas, FY2003–FY2007 (Table C.2g).

Social Reintegration

331 *After Prison: Roadblocks to Reentry: A Report on State Legal Barriers Facing People with Criminal Records*. New York: Legal Action Center, 2004 (rev. 2009). NCJ 205269

<http://lac.org/roadblocks-to-reentry/>

Provides "report cards" that grade and rank each state on the prevalence of legal barriers facing ex-convicts in the areas of employment, public assistance, access to records, voting, public housing, parenting, and drivers' licenses.

332 La Vigne, Nancy G., Lisa E. Brooks, and Tracey L. Shollenberger. *Returning Home: Exploring the Challenges and Successes of Recently Released Texas Prisoners* [Policy Brief]. Washington, D.C.: Justice Policy Center, Urban Institute, 2007.

<http://www.urban.org/publications/311471.html>

Compares state prison and state jail offenders released in 2004 to Houston area communities in terms of their participation in pre-release educational and job training programs, employment, substance use, and supervision and recidivism.

333 La Vigne, Nancy G., Lisa E. Brooks, and Tracey L. Shollenberger. *Women on the Outside: Understanding the Experiences of Female Prisoners Returning to Houston, Texas* [Research Report]. Washington, D.C.: Justice Policy Center, Urban Institute, 2009.

<http://www.urban.org/publications/411902.html>

Presents the results from a representative sample of 142 women who were released from Texas prisons and state jails in 2005 and interviewed shortly before their release and subsequent return to the Houston area, and two times following their release—once at two to four months after release, and a second time at eight to ten months after release. Topics covered include post-release housing arrangements; employment levels; which family member they are closest to now; what services, programs, or support they would find useful now; self-reported physical health conditions; criminal activity; and parole supervision.

334 La Vigne, Nancy G., and Vera Kachnowski. *Texas Prisoners' Reflections on Returning Home*. Washington, D.C.: Justice Policy Center, Urban Institute, 2005. NCJ 213605

<http://www.urban.org/publications/311247.html>

Reports results from a survey of 676 male and female prisoners shortly before their release from Texas prisons and state jails and subsequent return to the Houston area. Topics covered include the respondents' criminal, substance abuse, and employment histories; current health problems; in-prison programming experiences; relationships with family members; and expectations for release.

335 La Vigne, Nancy G., Tracey L. Shollenberger, and Sara Debus. *One Year Out: Tracking the Experiences of Male Prisoners Returning to Houston, Texas* [Research Report]. Washington, D.C.: Justice Policy Center, Urban Institute, 2009.

<http://www.urban.org/publications/411911.html>

Reports the results of a study of 210 men who were interviewed shortly before their release from Texas prisons and state jails and subsequent return to the Houston area, and two times following their release—once at two to four months after release, and a second time at eight to ten months after release. Topics covered include conviction offense, in-prison programming, housing on first night out, impressions of neighborhood, most important factor in staying out, frequent illegal drug use, participation in substance abuse treatment, sources of income, chronic physical health conditions and treatment, mental health conditions and treatment, programs most needed in the community, and supervision conditions for those on supervision.

336 Shollenberger, Tracey L. *When Relatives Return: Interviews with Family Members of Returning Prisoners in Houston, Texas* [Research Report]. Washington, D.C.: Justice Policy Center, Urban Institute, 2009.

<http://www.urban.org/publications/411903.html>

Presents the results of interviews with family members of 427 men and women who were recently released from Texas state correctional facilities and subsequently returned to the Houston area. Topics covered include obstacles to keeping in touch during prison (family members' view); types of support provided by family; difficulty providing emotional support by gender; difficulties faced by returning parents (family members' view); parents' involvement with minor children by gender (family members' view); and effect of parents' return on minor children (family members' view).

337 Watson, Jamie, et al. *A Portrait of Prisoner Reentry in Texas* [Research Report]. Washington, D.C.: Justice Policy Center, Urban Institute, 2004. NCJ 205538

<http://www.urban.org/publications/410972.html>

This report is part of a larger Urban Institute initiative called *Returning Home: Understanding the Challenges of Prisoner Reentry.* It provides a detailed analysis of prisoners released from Texas Department of Criminal Justice facilities in 2001, including the characteristics and geographic distribution of returning prisoners, pre-release preparation and processes, post-release supervision, and the social and economic climates of the communities that are home to the largest numbers of returning prisoners.

Supervised Release

•**338** *Federal Justice Statistics—Statistical Tables*. Washington, D.C.: Bureau of Justice Statistics, Office of Justice Programs, U.S. Department of Justice [annual, online only, 2005–date].

<http://purl.access.gpo.gov/GPO/LPS113898>

Reports fiscal year data from the Federal Justice Statistics Program (FJSP) and includes a United States map (along with an accompanying spreadsheet) that provides data on offenders under federal supervision, by federal judicial district (Map 7.1).

Research Note: This publication series supersedes *Compendium of Federal Justice Statistics* (1984–2004). Offenders under supervision include those on probation, supervised release, and parole. Texas is in the U.S. Court of Appeals Fifth Circuit and has four districts: Eastern, Northern, Southern, and Western. Datasets are available through the Inter-university Consortium for Political and Social Research (ICPSR), Institute for Social Research, University of Michigan.

<http://www.icpsr.umich.edu/icpsrweb/ICPSR/series/00073>

Texas Department of Criminal Justice

•**339** *Adult and Juvenile Correctional Population Projections: Fiscal Years [year–year]*. Austin: Legislative Budget Board, [annual, online only, 2004–date].

<http://www.lbb.state.tx.us/PubSafety_CrimJustice/PubSafety_CrimJustice.htm>

Provides correctional population projections for the forthcoming six fiscal years in order to serve as a basis for the biennial legislative appropriations requests of the Texas Department of Criminal Justice. It contains data on the Texas crime rate, adult incarceration actual and projected populations, adult incarceration projected population, active adult parole supervision actual and projected populations, adult felony community supervision actual and projected populations, adult misdemeanor community supervision actual and projected populations, and qualitative review findings.

Research Note: Projections were previously published by the Criminal Justice Policy Council (under varying titles).

340 *Agency Strategic Plan for the Fiscal Years [year–year].* Huntsville: Texas Department of Criminal Justice [biennial, 1992–date].

<http://www.tdcj.state.tx.us/publications/publications-home.htm>

Provides statistics on offenders (inmate population characteristics and projections, educational and rehabilitation programs, community supervision, supervision following release, and time served upon release); TDCJ workforce (demographics and turnover); and fiscal matters.

Research Note: Published under slightly varying titles.

341 *Annual Report.* Huntsville: Manufacturing and Logistics Division, Texas Department of Criminal Justice [2003–date].

<http://www.tci.tdcj.state.tx.us>

Provides statistics on Texas Correctional Industries, Prison Industry Enhancement (PIE) Certification Program, and Work Against Recidivism (WAR) program.

342 *Annual Review.* Huntsville: Texas Department of Criminal Justice, 2001–date.

<http://www.tdcj.state.tx.us/publications/publications-home.htm>

Although primarily a narrative report, the review contains selected statistics pertaining to departmental finances, facilities, operations, personnel, and programs.

Research Note: Some editions have individual titles. Previously published under the title *Annual Report* (1990–2000).

343 *An Audit Report on the Department of Criminal Justice's Oversight of Selected Providers That Deliver Residential Services and Substance Abuse Treatment Programs* [SAO Report]. Austin: State Auditor's Office, 2010. 10-025

<http://www.sao.state.tx.us/Reports/report.cfm/report/10-025>

The Department of Criminal Justice has assigned its Private Facilities Contract Monitoring and Oversight Division the responsibility for assessing the contract compliance of its private facility providers that deliver residential services and substance abuse treatment programs through the operation of secure correctional facilities, halfway houses, work release programs, and substance abuse treatment programs. The Texas Board of Criminal Justice granted the division independent status in May 2007. The goal of this audit was to evaluate the division's contract administration and monitoring processes.

344 *An Audit Report on Selected Rehabilitation Programs at the Department of Criminal Justice* [SAO Report]. Austin: State Auditor's Office, 2007. 07-026

<http://www.sao.state.tx.us/reports/main/07-026.html>

This audit focused on the following TDCJ rehabilitation programs designed to reduce recidivism: Sex Offender Treatment Program, Sex Offender Education Program, Pre-Release Substance Abuse Program, Pre-Release Therapeutic Community program, and InnerChange Freedom Initiative program. The objectives of the audit were to determine if TDCJ collects and maintains sufficient data for measuring the effectiveness of these programs; determine the outcomes for participants in selected programs; for the selected programs, determine whether there is a documented selection process for program participation and that the selection of participants is consistent with that process; and identify rehabilitation programs in other states that have demonstrated a high level of success.

345 *An Audit Report on the Department of Criminal Justice's Complaint Resolution and Investigation Functions* [SAO Report]. Austin: State Auditor's Office, 2008. 09-004

<http://www.sao.state.tx.us/reports/main/09-004.html>

The objectives of this audit were to determine (1) whether TDCJ was in compliance with policies and procedures and best practices governing the screening, investigation, and resolution of allegations of criminal behavior, serious policy violations, and serious offender and employee grievances, and (2) whether the Office of the Inspector General, Office of the Ombudsman, Offender Grievance Program, Human Resources Division, and other areas of TDCJ effectively coordinate their activities to resolve complaints and allegations of criminal behavior, serious policy violations, and serious offender and employee grievances. The report presents results from surveys of 1,641 inmates at seven TDCJ units and 673 TDCJ employees.

•346 *Current Correctional Population Indicators: Adult and Juvenile Correctional Populations Monthly Report*. Austin: Legislative Budget Board, [monthly, online only, 2004–date].

<http://www.lbb.state.tx.us/PubSafety_CrimJustice/PubSafety_CrimJustice.htm>

This continuously updated monthly report presents data on the Texas Department of Criminal Justice as follows: capacity and correctional populations (total population, bed capacity, contract beds, operating capacity, and available operating capacity) and community supervision—felony and misdemeanor—populations (offenders under direct supervision, supervision placements, successful/unsuccessful supervision terminations, and average active parole supervision population).

347 *Directory: Adult and Juvenile Correctional Departments, Institutions, Agencies, and Probation and Parole Authorities* [cover title]. Alexandria, Va.: American Correctional Association [annual, 2001–date].

Provides profiles of adult facilities, adult detention, and adult contract facilities in Texas including the year opened, security level, capacity, average daily population, inmate gender, and total staff.

Research Note: Published under slightly varying titles prior to 2001. See also the ACA's *National Jail and Adult Detention Directory*.

348 *Historical Criminal Justice Statistics: Adult Offender Characteristics.* Austin: Legislative Budget Board, [online only, 2004–date].

<http://www.lbb.state.tx.us/PubSafety_CrimJustice/PubSafety_CrimJustice.htm>

Provides historical fiscal year statistics on offenders in TDCJ facilities (on-hand population, admissions, and releases) by age, gender, race, citizenship, offense type, sentence length, release eligibility, and offense category.

349 *In-Depth Analysis of Correctional Populations in the Texas Department of Criminal Justice to Guide Policy Reviews.* Austin: Criminal Justice Policy Council, 2003.

<http://www.lbb.state.tx.us/PubSafety_CrimJustice/6_Links/Documents_Alpha_Links.htm>

This report on correctional subpopulations (as of August 31, 2002) was prepared for the 78th Texas Legislature at the behest of Senator John Whitmire, Chairman, Senate Criminal Justice Committee. It reports characteristics of the TDCJ prison population (adult, female, elderly, youthful offender, country of citizenship, and drug offenders by amount of drug and prior history). It also provides data on parole (violations, revocations, and considerations/approvals by lowest parole guideline levels); offenders with INS detainers; and probation revocations.

Research Note: For earlier statistics, see the council's *Sourcebook of Texas Adult Justice Population Statistics 1988–1998*.

350 *Offender Access to Courts, Counsel and Public Officials: Fiscal Year [year] Statistics.* Huntsville: Offender Access to Courts, Counsel and Public Officials Department, Administrative Review and Risk Management Division, Texas Department of Criminal Justice [annual, online only].

<http://www.tdcj.state.tx.us/publications/admin-rvw/publications-admin-rvw-access-to-courts.htm>

Reports statistics for the most recent fiscal year on TDCJ offender visits to law library sessions, items of legal research material delivered, notary signatures provided, offender/offender legal visits conducted, attorney/offender phone calls conducted, court teleconference inquiries via phone conducted, court teleconference inquiries via video conference conducted, attorney visits conducted, attorney representative visits conducted, court forms issued, court certificates of impoverishment issued, Acknowledgement of Paternity applications processed, and telephone calls/emails processed by the Access to Courts administrative office (e.g. judicial, attorneys, law enforcement, TDCJ officials, etc.).

351 *Operating Budget for Fiscal Year [year] Submitted to the Governor's Office of Budget, Planning and Policy and the Legislative Budget Board by the Texas Board of Criminal Justice.* Austin: Texas Board of Criminal Justice [annual.]

<http://www.tdcj.state.tx.us/publications/publications-home.htm#Business>

Provides the following data on the TDCJ operating budget as extracted from the Automated Budget and Evaluation System of Texas (ABEST): summary of budget by strategy, summary of budget by method of finance, summary of budget by object of expense, summary of objective outcomes, strategy level detail, sub-strategy detail. sub-strategy summary, capital budget project schedule, federal funds supporting schedule, federal funds tracking schedule, estimated revenue collections supporting schedule, and Homeland Security funding schedule, Part B: natural or man-made disasters.

Research Note: The Texas Board of Criminal Justice, a nine-member panel appointed by the governor, establishes the rules and policies that guide the Texas Department of Criminal Justice.

352 *Report to the Texas Sunset Commission: Self Evaluation Report.* Huntsville: Texas Department of Criminal Justice, 2005.

<http://www.sunset.state.tx.us/80threports/tdcj/ser.pdf>

The Texas Sunset Act requires the automatic termination of designated State agencies twelve years after review unless the legislature extends the life of the agency by statute (Tex. Gov't Code Ann. §§ 325.001–.024 (Vernon 2005)). The Sunset Advisory Commission assists the legislature in making these determinations by evaluating the operations of agencies scheduled for termination. As a part of the review process, each agency submits a Self-Evaluation Report (SER) to the commission. This report provides statistics on the fiscal matters (appropriations, revenues, expenditures, and federal aid); personnel; inmate populations; community supervision; parole; special programs and services (e.g., offenders with mental impairments, substance abuse treatment, and sex offender treatment); and key performance measures.

Research Note: Earlier editions are available. See also the report of the commission's decisions regarding this review, as well as their decisions regarding their reviews of the Texas Board of Pardons and Paroles and the Correctional Managed Health Care Committee. <http://www.sunset.state.tx.us/80threports/tdcj/tdcj_dec.pdf>

353 *Risk Management Statistics.* Huntsville: Administrative Review and Risk Management Division, Texas Department of Criminal Justice [online].

<http://www.tdcj.state.tx.us/adminrvw/adminrvw-risk-mgt-stats.htm>

A continuously updated website that provides statistics for the most recent thirteen months on TDCJ injuries: employees (including the percent that resulted in an accepted workers' compensation claims); offenders (including percent of offender population reporting injuries); and recreational/non-occupational injuries.

•354 *Statistical Report.* Huntsville: Executive Services, Texas Department of Criminal Justice, 1990–date.

<http://www.tdcj.state.tx.us/publications/publications-home.htm>

Provides fiscal year statistics covering the following: demographic highlights; on hand, i.e., incarcerated population (demographics, offense of record, county of conviction, 3G offense versus non-3G offense and receive type, and sentence length, approval status and eligibility); receives and admissions (total receives and admissions, new receives, and parole revocations, including mandatory supervision and discretionary mandatory supervision); and releases and departures (total releases and departures, discharges, releases to community supervision, and releases to parole supervision, including mandatory supervision and discretionary mandatory supervision).

Research Note: Previously published by the Texas Department of Corrections under the title *Annual Statistical Report.* For an enumeration of 3G offenses, see Tex. Code Crim. Proc. Ann. art. 42.12 § 3(g) (Vernon 2006 & Supp. 2010).

355 *Texas Department of Criminal Justice: An Inventory of Records at the Texas State Archives, 1849–2004.* Austin: Texas State Library and Archives Commission.

<http://www.lib.utexas.edu/taro/tslac/20127/tsl-20127.html>

The files in this archive contain statistical reports on various aspects of the TDCJ, including employees, inmate populations, and escapes.

356 *Texas Department of Criminal Justice Fiscal Year [year] Operating Budget and Fiscal Years [year–year] Legislative Appropriations Request as Pre-*

pared for the Texas Board of Criminal Justice. Austin: Legislative Budget Board; Governor's Office of Budget, Planning and Policy [biennial].

<http://www.tdcj.state.tx.us/publications/publications-home.htm>

Provides a detailed summary of the TDCJ's current fiscal year operating budget as well as its Legislative Appropriations Request (LAR) for the forthcoming biennium. The report also includes justifications for exceptional item requests—construction and operating—that require additional State resources.

•**357** *Unit Directory.* Huntsville: Texas Department of Criminal Justice [online only].

<http://www.tdcj.state.tx.us/stat/unitdirectory/all.htm>

Contains current profiles of all TDCJ units (prisons, private prisons, state jails, private state jails, transfer facilities, pre-release, psychiatric, mentally retarded offender program, and substance abuse felony punishment facilities); contract leased beds; and parole confinement facilities. It contains data on the date the unit was established or on line; number of employees (total, security, non-security, Windham education, and contract medical and psychiatric); offender population and gender; maximum capacity; and approximate acreage.

Time Served in Corrections

358 *Goal Met: Violent Offenders in Texas are Serving a Higher Percentage of Their Prison Sentences.* Austin: Criminal Justice Policy Council, 2000.

<http://www.lbb.state.tx.us/PubSafety_CrimJustice/6_Links/Documents_Alpha_Links.htm>

Compares time served (in years), percentage of sentence served, and parole approval rates for aggravated versus non-aggravated violent offenders.

359 Turner, Susan, Terry Fain, Peter W. Greenwood, Elsa Y. Chen, and James R. Chiesa. *National Evaluation of the Violent Offender Incarceration/Truth-in-Sentencing Incentive Grant Program* [Final Report]. Santa Monica, Calif.: RAND, 2001. NCJ 191201

<http://www.ncjrs.gov/pdffiles1/nij/grants/191201.pdf>

This report evaluates the implementation and impact of the Violent Offender Incarceration and Truth-in-Sentencing (VOI/TIS) incentive grants authorized by the Violent Crime Control and Law Enforcement Act of 1994 (P.L. 103-322, 108 Stat. 1796), as amended, which individual states are to use to increase the capacity of their correctional systems to confine serious and violent offenders, and thereby reduce early release opportunities for these inmates. The report contains the following state-level data: TIS and VOI funding,

FY1996–1999 totals (Table 5.3); states receiving TIS dollars, FY1996–1999 (Table 6.1); violent crime correlation with truth-in-sentencing (Table 6.2); reasons that states did or did not seek TIS funding grants (Table 6.3); low-crime states received more VOI/TIS dollars per violent crime (Table 6.4); uses of VOI/TIS funds through December 31, 1999 (Table 7.1); increase in prison capacity funded by VOT/TIS (Table 7.4); and TIS and VOI funding FY1996–FY1999 (Tables E1–E4). Graphs provide comparative data for TIS states, non-TIS states, Texas, and all states, 1986–1997, as follows: index crime rates (Fig. 9.1), violent crime rates (Fig. 9.3), property crime rates (Fig. 9.4), felony incarcerations per 1,000 violent crimes (Fig. 9.7), percentage of prison admissions for violent crimes (Fig. 9.9), percentage of prison admissions for property crimes (Fig. 9.10); percentage of prison admissions for drug crimes (Fig. 9.11); sentence length for released prisoners, all offenses (Fig. 9.13); sentence length for released prisoners, violent offenses (Fig. 9.14); sentence length for released prisoners, property offenses (Fig. 9.15); sentence length for released prisoners, drug offenses (Fig. 9.16); time served for all offenses (Fig. 9.20); time served for violent offenses (Fig. 9.21); time served for property offenses (Fig. 9.22); time served for drug offenses (Fig. 9.23); percentage of sentence served for all offenses (Fig. 9.27); percentage of sentence served for violent offenses (Fig. 9.28); percentage of sentence served for property offenses (Fig. 9.29); percentage of sentence served for drug offenses (Fig. 9.30); corrections expenditures as a percentage of general expenditures (Fig. 9.31); corrections expenditures per 1,000 persons (1992 dollars) (Fig. 9.33); and correctional institution construction expenditures per 1,000 persons (1992 dollars) (Fig. 9.35). Graphs provide comparative data for TIS states ≥ 170, TIS states < 170, non-TIS states ≥ 170, non-TIS states < 170, and Texas, 1986–1997, as follows: time served for violent crime, by TIS and number of beds added (Fig. 10.1); and percentage of sentence served for violent crime, by TIS and number of beds added (Fig. 10.2).

Research Note: Datasets are available through the National Archive of Criminal Justice Data, Inter-university Consortium for Political and Social Research (ICPSR), Institute for Social Research, University of Michigan. <http://dx.doi.org/10.3886/ICPSR03336>

360 Turner, Susan, Laura J. Hickman, Judith Greene, and Terry Fain. *Changing Prison Management: Strategies in Response to VOI/TIS Legislation.* Santa Monica, Calif.: RAND, 2001. NCJ 198622

<http://www.ncjrs.gov/pdffiles1/nij/grants/198622.pdf>

This report evaluates the implementation and impact of the Violent Offender Incarceration and Truth-in-Sentencing (VOI/TIS) incentive grants authorized by the Violent Crime Control and Law Enforcement Act of 1994 (P.L. 103-322, 108 Stat. 1796), as amended (see entry 359). Table 6.5 provides data on state expenditures of VOI/TIS funds through December 31,

1999 (beds constructed, under construction, leased, and total). Graphs present comparative data for TIS states, non-TIS states, Texas, and all states, as follows: percentage of prisoners with sentences of twenty years or more (1986–1999) (Fig. 6.1); percentage of offenders aged fifty and older (on January 1, 1989–1999) (Fig. 6.3); inmates with tuberculosis at intake (1996–1999) (Fig. 6.4); percentage of inmates at high/close custody level (1988–1999) (Fig. 6.5); average total cost per inmate per day (1987–1999) (Fig. 6.6); number of inmate misconduct reports, per inmate (1992–1999) (Fig. 6.8); inmate assaults on staff, per 1,000 inmates (1990–1999) (Fig. 6.9); inmate assaults on other inmates, per 1,000 inmates (1995–1999) (Fig. 6.10); grievances filed, per 1,000 inmates (1996–1999) (Fig. 6.11); percentage of correctional officer turnover (1990–1999) (Fig. 6.12); hours of initial correctional officer training required (1986–1999) (Fig. 6.13); inmates who tested positive for HIV, per 1,000 inmates (1988–1999) (Fig. 6.14); and percentage of inmates assigned to full-time or part-time academic or vocational training (1990–1999) (Fig. 6.15). Graphs present comparative sentencing statistics for structured sentencing states, indeterminate sentencing states, Texas, and all states (1986–1999), for the following: percentage of prisoners with sentences of twenty years or more, by structured sentencing (Fig. 6.2); and prison population as a percentage of rated prison capacity, by structured sentencing (Fig. 6.7).

Windham School District

•**361** *Annual Performance Report.* Huntsville: Windham School District [annual].

<http://www.windhamschooldistrict.org/>

Provides statistics on Windham School District as follows: total program participants; Literacy program; Life Skills program; Career and Technology Education; GEDs awarded; vocational certificates issued and industry certificates awarded; student performance results; degrees and certificates awarded; continuing education program, including Project RIO (Re-Integration of Offenders); and finances (revenues, expenditures, cost per participant, cost per contact hour, and estimated income).

•**362** *Windham School District Evaluation Report.* Austin: Legislative Budget Board [annual, 2007–date].

<http://www.lbb.state.tx.us/PubSafety_CrimJustice/PubSafety_CrimJustice.htm>

Legislation passed by the 79th Texas Legislature mandated that the Windham School District (WSD)—in consultation with the Legislative Budget Board—conduct an annual evaluation and analysis of the training services it provides for offenders confined or imprisoned in Texas Department of Criminal Justice (TDCJ) facilities and submit this report to the Legislature and the governor's office (Tex. Educ. Code Ann. § 19.0041 (Vernon 2006)). The report provides data on employment upon release, occupation, and earnings, according to whether they received Career and Technology Education (CTE) vocational training during their incarceration.

Research Note: See also the reports of the Criminal Justice Policy Council: *An Overview of the Windham School District* (2000); *Educational Achievement of Inmates in the Windham School District* (2000); *Impact of Educational Achievement of Inmates in the Windham School District on Post-Release Employment* (2000); *Impact of Educational Achievement of Inmates in the Windham School District on Recidivism* (2000); and the report submitted to the Texas Comptroller of Public Accounts by MGT of America, Inc.: *Texas Performance Review: Management and Performance Review of the Texas Prison Education System* [Cover title: *A Performance Review: Schools Behind Bars: Windham School System and Other Prison Education Programs*] (1992).

Wrongful Incarceration

363 [Compensation to Persons Wrongfully Imprisoned.] Austin: Judiciary Section, Texas Comptroller of Public Accounts [1999–date].

A person is entitled to compensation from the State of Texas for wrongful imprisonment if the person has served in whole or in part a sentence in prison under Texas State law and the person (a) has received a full pardon on the basis of innocence for the crime for which the person was sentenced; or (b) has been granted relief on the basis of actual innocence of the crime for which the person was sentenced. If a deceased person would be entitled to compensation under these provisions if living, including a person who received a posthumous pardon, the person's heirs, legal representatives, and estate are entitled to lump-sum compensation (Tex. Civ. Prac. & Rem. Code Ann. §§ 103.001–.154 (Vernon 2005)). Compensation payments to claimants are made by the Judiciary Section of the Texas Comptroller of Public Accounts, which disburses legislative appropriations under the authority of Tex. Gov't Code Ann. § 403.074(g) (Vernon 2005). Data is provided as follows: claimant, date filed, and total award amount.

Research Note: Although this information is unpublished, it is provided to researchers upon request.

Chapter 6

Juvenile Corrections, Parole, and Probation

Family Intervention Programs

364 *Annual Report and Data Book.* Austin: Texas Department of Family and Protective Services [annual, 2004–date].

<http://www.dfps.state.tx.us/About/Data_Books_and_Annual_Reports/default.asp>

The Prevention and Early Intervention chapter contains statistics for the most recent five fiscal years on the number of youth served through the Services to At-Risk Youth (STAR) program (see entry 365).

Research Note: Editions are available online back to 1997. The *Annual Report* and the *Data Book* were combined into a single publication beginning with the 2009 edition. Previous editions were published under the title *Legislative Data Book* (1992–1999). The agency was called the Texas Department of Protective and Regulatory Services prior to 2004.

365 *Services to At-Risk Youth (STAR) Program Evaluation.* Austin: Criminal Justice Policy Council, 2003.

<http://www.lbb.state.tx.us/PubSafety_CrimJustice/6_Links/Documents_Alpha_Links.htm>

The Services to At-Risk Youth (STAR) program is administered by the Prevention and Early Intervention Division of the Texas Department of Family and Protective Services (at the time of this report called the Prevention and Regulatory Services Division of the Texas Department of Protective and Regulatory Services). Youth up to age seventeen who are runaways, delinquent, truant, or involved in family conflict are referred to the program, which contracts with local community agencies to provide family crisis intervention counseling, short-term emergency residential care, and individual and family counseling. The report provides data on program costs and coverage, as well as participant characteristics, referrals, and outcomes.

Female Juvenile Delinquents

366 *Female Juvenile Offenders: Services in Texas.* Austin: Texas Juvenile Probation Commission, 2002.

<http://www.tjpc.state.tx.us/publications/Reports/RPTOTH200203.pdf>

Presents data on the needs (emotional, physical, behavioral, and self-enhancement) of female offenders referred to Texas juvenile probation departments and the services available to meet those needs.

Juvenile Correctional Education

367 *Juvenile Justice Alternative Education Programs: Performance Assessment Report School Year [year–year].* Austin: Texas Juvenile Probation Commission, [annual].

<http://www.tjpc.state.tx.us/publications/default.htm>

Juvenile Justice Alternative Education Programs (JJAEP) are mandated by Tex. Educ. Code Ann. §§ 37.011–.012 (2006). They are designed as separate educational settings to ensure safe and productive classrooms through the removal of dangerous and/or disruptive students while addressing and resolving the issue of expelled youth receiving no educational services during the period of expulsion. This report provides data on JJAEP as follows: student population; entries (by placement type, age, gender, race, grade level, educational classification, and special education primary disability); students identified as at-risk; percentage of students by economic indicator; mandatory/discretionary expulsion student entries by expulsion offense category; students referred to juvenile probation departments; disposition by placement type; supervision at entry for expelled students; average length of stay by county; exit reasons; student capacity by county; student entries by program format; programmatic components; staffing; programs providing services to non-expelled youth; conditions to exit program; transportation method; TAKS results; ITBS/ITED scores; attendance rates by county and placement type; disciplinary referrals; six month/one year re-contact rate by county and offense type; and cost per day by county (by size of program, model type, and operation design). The appendixes provide additional county-level data.

Research Note: Reports prior to 2006–2007 were published jointly with the Texas Education Agency.

Juvenile Correctional Population Projections

•368 *Adult and Juvenile Correctional Population Projections: Fiscal Years [year–year].* Austin: Legislative Budget Board [annual, online only, 2004–date].
<http://www.lbb.state.tx.us/PubSafety_CrimJustice/PubSafety_CrimJustice.htm>

Provides correctional population projections for the forthcoming six fiscal years in order to serve as a basis for the biennial legislative appropriations requests of the Texas Juvenile Probation Commission and the Texas Youth Commission It contains data on the Texas crime rate, juvenile arrests and juvenile arrest rate, juvenile residential actual and projected populations, juvenile residential projected population, juvenile probation supervision actual and projected populations, and qualitative review findings.

Research Note: Projections were previously published by the Criminal Justice Policy Council (under varying titles).

Juvenile Drug Abusers

369 *Arrestee Drug Abuse Monitoring (ADAM) Program/Drug Use Forecasting (DUF) Series.* Ann Arbor, Mich.: Inter-university Consortium for Political and Social Research Institute for Social Research, University of Michigan [annual, online only, 1998–2003].

<http://www.icpsr.umich.edu/icpsrweb/ICPSR/series/00110>

Contains data from the National Institute of Justice's Arrestee Drug Abuse Monitoring (ADAM) Program/Drug Use Forecasting (DUF) Series, which was designed to determine the extent and correlates of illicit drug use in the population of booked arrestees in local areas through quarterly data collected in metropolitan areas in the United States. These areas varied by collection period, but included Dallas, Houston, Laredo, and San Antonio. Part 3 presents data for juveniles.

Research Note: Data for arrestees in juvenile detention facilities was compiled using the same instrument previously utilized in the NIJ's Drug Use Forecasting (DUF) system. The NIJ restricts this data from general dissemination and users must secure preapproval from the ICPRS. The collection of juvenile data was discontinued in the second quarter of 2002. The NIJ published annual reports (under varying titles) on the DUF and ADAM programs (1990–2003). Beginning in 2007, the ADAM II program began data collection under the auspices of the Office of National Drug Control Policy, Executive Office of the President. It continues the original ADAM methodology, but is restricted to adult male arrestees in ten U.S. counties (none in Texas). Data from ADAM and ADAM II is also reported in *National Drug Control Strategy: Data Supplement.* <http://purl.access.gpo.gov/GPO/LPS6500>

Juvenile Inmate Fatalities

•**370** Mumola, Christopher J., and Margaret E. Noonan. *Deaths in Custody Statistical Tables: State Juvenile Correctional Facility Deaths.* Washington, D.C.: Bureau of Justice Statistics, Office of Justice Programs, U.S. Department of Justice [annual, online only, 2002–date].

<http://bjs.ojp.usdoj.gov/content/dcrp/juvenileindex.cfm>

In order to implement the mandates of the Death in Custody Reporting Act of 2000 (P.L. 106-297, 114 Stat. 1045), the Bureau of Justice Statistics established a nationwide data collection program that includes juvenile death records from state juvenile correctional administrators. This report contains state-level data on the number of deaths in state juvenile correctional facilities.

Research Note: Datasets are available through the Inter-university Consortium for Political and Social Research (ICPSR), Institute for Social Research, University of Michigan. <http://www.icpsr.umich.edu/icpsrweb/ICPSR/series/00225>

Juvenile Inmate Statistics

•371 *Census of Juveniles in Residential Placement Databook.* Washington, D.C.: Office of Juvenile Justice and Delinquency Prevention, Office of Justice Programs, U.S. Department of Justice [biennial, online only, 1997–date].

<http://ojjdp.ncjrs.gov/ojstatbb/cjrp/default.asp>

The Census of Juveniles in Residential Placement (CJRP) is conducted in odd-numbered years by the Criminal Justice Statistics Branch, Census Bureau, U.S. Department of Commerce, for the Office of Juvenile Justice and Delinquency Prevention, Office of Justice Programs, U.S. Department of Justice. It alternates with the Juvenile Residential Facility Census (JRFC), which is conducted in even-numbered years (see entry 372). The databook allows users to access state-level profiles covering the following: age on census date by sex, age on census date by race/ethnicity, age on census date by sex and race/ethnicity, detailed offense profile; detailed offense profile by sex, detailed offense profile by placement status, detailed offense profile in public and private facilities, offense profile by race/ethnicity, offense profile of committed residents by sex and race/ethnicity, and offense profile of detained residents by sex and race/ethnicity.

Research Note: This census replaces the earlier Juvenile Detention, Correctional, and Shelter Facility Census, which had been conducted since midyear 1971 and published under the title *Children in Custody* (1971–1991). Annual surveys were previously conducted by the Children's Bureau, which later became part of the U.S. Department of Health and Human Services, and published under the title *Statistics on Public Institutions for Delinquent Children* (1945–1967).

•372 *Juvenile Residential Facility Census: Selected Findings* [Juvenile Offenders and Victims National Report Series]. Washington, D.C.: Office of Juvenile Justice and Delinquency Prevention, Office of Justice Programs, U.S. Department of Justice, [biennial, 2000–date].

<http://purl.access.gpo.gov/GPO/LPS107204>

The Juvenile Residential Facility Census (JRFC) is conducted in even-numbered years by the Criminal Justice Statistics Branch, Census Bureau, U.S. Department of Commerce, for the Office of Juvenile Justice and Delinquency Prevention, Office of Justice Programs, U.S. Department of Justice. It alternates with the Census of Juveniles in Residential Placement (CJRP), which is conducted in odd-numbered years (see entry 371). State-level data is presented for the number of public and private juvenile facilities, and the number of juvenile offenders held in public and private facilities. In addition, it contains state-level data on the number of facilities under, at, or over capacity, and the percentage of juvenile offenders in facilities at or over capacity.

Research Note: See entry 371 for sources of earlier data.

373 Sickmund, Melissa. *Juveniles in Corrections* [Juvenile Offenders and Victims National Report Series Bulletin]. Washington, D.C.: Office of Juvenile Justice and Delinquency Prevention, Office of Justice Programs, U.S. Department of Justice, 2004. NCJ 202885

<http://purl.access.gpo.gov/GPO/LPS50569>

Reports state-level data from the 1999 Census of Juveniles in Residential Placement, including juvenile offenders in residential placement (number and rate); percentage of juvenile offenders by offense category; racial/ethnic profile of juvenile offenders in residential placement; minority proportion of juveniles in residential placement; juvenile custody rate (per 100,000) by ethnic category; juvenile female custody population (number and proportion); and offenders sentenced to death from 1973 through 2000 for under-18 crimes.

Juvenile Justice System

374 *Biennial Report to the Governor and the . . . Texas Legislature.* Austin: Criminal Justice Policy Council [1999–2003].

<http://www.lbb.state.tx.us/PubSafety_CrimJustice/6_Links/Documents_Alpha_Links.htm>

This report, subtitled "The Big Picture in Adult and Juvenile Justice Issues," was legislatively mandated and required the CJPC to submit to the governor and legislature "a plan detailing the actions necessary to promote an effective and cohesive criminal justice system." It contains statistics on adult and juvenile crime and arrest rates.

Research Note: The council disbanded in 2003 after the governor's line-item veto of its legislative appropriation.

375 *House Committee on Corrections, Texas House of Representatives Interim Report, [year]: A Report to the House of Representatives . . . Texas Legislature.* Austin: House Committee on Corrections [biennial, 1987–date].

<http://www.house.state.tx.us/committees/reports/welcome.htm>

This report summarizes the work undertaken by the Texas House Committee on Corrections regarding the Interim Study Charges it receives from the Speaker of the House of Representatives. These charges involve policy, procedural, regulatory, and budgetary issues relating to agencies and programs under the committee's jurisdiction, which include adult and juvenile corrections, parole, and probation. The report contains selected statistics as well as recommendations for consideration by the succeeding legislature.

Research Note: Published under slightly varying titles. See also the interim reports of the House Juvenile Justice and Family Issues Committee (the committee was eliminated following the 80th Texas Legislature).

376 *Interim Report to the . . . Legislature.* Austin: Senate Committee on Criminal Justice [biennial, 1996–date].

<http://www.senate.state.tx.us/75r/senate/commit/c590/c590.htm>

This report summarizes the work undertaken by the Texas Senate Committee on Criminal Justice regarding the Interim Charges it receives from the Lieutenant Governor of the State of Texas. These charges involve policy, procedural, regulatory, and budgetary issues relating to agencies and programs under the committee's jurisdiction, which include adult and juvenile corrections, parole, and probation; law enforcement; criminal law and procedure; and victims of crime. The report contains minutes of the committee's public hearings on these charges, selected statistics, and recommendations for consideration by the succeeding legislature.

Research Note: Published under slightly varying titles.

377 *An Overview of Texas Juvenile Justice Population Trends and Dynamics: An Update.* Austin: Criminal Justice Policy Council, 2003.

<http://www.lbb.state.tx.us/PubSafety_CrimJustice/6_Links/Documents_Alpha_Links.htm>

Presents statistics (1991–2001) for juvenile arrests, cases disposed to deferred prosecution and adjudicated probation, commitments to the Texas Youth Commission, and juveniles certified to stand trial in adult court.

Research Note: Earlier editions are available.

378 Snyder, Howard N., and Melissa Sickmund. *Juvenile Offenders and Victims: 2006 National Report.* Washington, D.C.: Office of Juvenile Justice and Delinquency Prevention, Office of Justice Programs, U.S. Department of Justice, 2006. NCJ 212906

<http://www.ojjdp.ncjrs.gov/ojstatbb/nr2006/index.html>

Chapter 7 provides data on juvenile offenders on correctional facilities as follows: juvenile custody population; offense trends in private and public facilities; offender trends in juvenile facilities; detained and committed populations; state custody rates; offense profiles of the custody population by state; offense profiles of detained and committed offenders by state; gender variations in the custody population; racial variations in the custody population; racial variations in custody rates by state; length of stay for juveniles in custody; types of facilities; facility security features; security arrangements for juveniles in custody; facility size; crowding in juvenile custody facilities; screening for substance abuse, mental health, and suicide risk; deaths in custody facilities; sexual violence in custody facilities; youth reentry population; recidivism and the youth custody population; juveniles in jails; juveniles in prisons; and the death penalty.

Research Note: Earlier editions are available. Not all subsections contain state-level data. This report incorporates data from some earlier specialized OJJDP reports individually authored by Sickmund and Snyder that are not otherwise included in this book.

•379 *Statistical Briefing Book.* Washington, D.C.: Office of Juvenile Justice and Delinquency Prevention, Office of Justice Programs, U.S. Department of Justice [online only, 1993–date].

<http://purl.access.gpo.gov/GPO/LPS73143>

This website provides access to a wide array of publications, data analysis tools, and national datasets, covering juvenile population characteristics; juveniles as victims; juveniles as offenders; juvenile justice system structure and process; law enforcement and juvenile crime; juveniles in court; juveniles on probation; juveniles in corrections; and juvenile reentry and aftercare.

Juvenile Mental Health Services

380 *Overview of the Enhanced Mental Health Services Initiative.* Austin: Criminal Justice Policy Council, 2002.

<http://www.lbb.state.tx.us/PubSafety_CrimJustice/6_Links/Documents_ Alpha_Links.htm>

The 77th Texas Legislature appropriated funding for a new Enhanced Mental Health Services Initiative, which was designed to provide additional specialized services and supervision to mentally ill adult and juvenile offenders with the goal of reducing recidivism. The funding was earmarked for the Texas Council on Offenders with Mental Impairments (since renamed the Texas Correctional Office on Offenders with Medical and Mental Impairments), the Texas Juvenile Probation Commission, and the Community Assistance Division of the Texas Department of Criminal Justice. This report provides data on specialized caseloads and case management for mentally ill offenders eligible for services under this initiative.

Research Note: See also the council's three reports published in 2000: *Mentally Ill Offenders and County Jails: Survey Resul Re-offense Rates in FY '05, by Home Contacts per Week & Total Contacts per Week and Policy Issues*; *The Public Mental Health System in Texas and Its Relation to Criminal Justice; and Intervention for Mentally Ill Offenders: Planning and Policy Issues to Consider.*

381 *Overview of the Special Needs Diversionary Program for Mentally Ill Juvenile Offenders, FY 2007* Austin: Texas Juvenile Probation Commission, 2008.

<http://www.criminaljusticecoalition.org/juvenile_justice/mental_health>

Provides an overview of mental health treatment and specialized supervision of juvenile offenders in the Special Needs Diversionary Program (SNDP), as provided under the Enhanced Mental Health Services Initiative (see entry 380). The following data is for FY2007 unless noted: percentage of juvenile offenders under supervision who ever had a recorded mental health contact and the gap in services, FY2001–FY2006 (Table 1); percentage of juvenile offenders under supervision who ever had a recorded mental health contact among juveniles in detention, placement, sent to TYC, or certified as an adult, FY2006 (Table 2); juveniles served in SNDP, FY2002–FY2007 (Table 3); age, ethnicity, and gender of SNDP participants (Table 4); supervision status of SNDP participants at program start (Table 5); primary DSM IV diagnosis of SNDP participants (Table 6); Global Assessment of Functioning (GAF) scores of SNDP participants (Table 7); average SNDP caseloads (Table 8); number of home visits and total visits per week (Table 9); mental health services provided to juveniles while in SNDP (Table 10); probation services provided to juveniles while in SNDP (Table 11); probation aftercare services provided to juveniles discharged (Table 12); mental health aftercare services provided to juveniles discharged (Table 13); program outcomes of SNDP juveniles discharged (Table 14); juveniles sent to TYC within one and two years of starting SNDP, FY2002–FY2006 (Table 16); re-offense rates for juveniles starting SNDP in FY2005, by DSM IV diagnosis (Table 17); and re-offense rates in FY2005, by home contacts per week and total contacts per week (Table 18).

Research Note: See also Jennifer Schwank, Erin Espinosa, and Vonzo Tolbert, *Mental Health and Juvenile Justice in Texas* (Austin: Texas Juvenile Probation Commission, 2003), which provides data on the prevalence and types of mental health disorders—including substance abuse—of juvenile offenders in Texas and the treatment programs provided through the SNDP (screenings, enrollments, costs, and outcomes).

<http://www.tjpc.state.tx.us/publications/Reports/RPTOTH200302.pdf>

Juvenile Probation

382 *An Audit Report on Monitoring and Enforcement Functions at the Juvenile Probation Commission* [SAO Report]. Austin: State Auditor's Office, 2007. 07-047

<http://www.sao.state.tx.us/reports/main/07-047.html>

The objective of this audit was to determine whether the TJPC had taken corrective action on significant issues in monitoring and enforcement identified in the earlier SAO audit, *An Audit Report on the Juvenile Probation Commission* (2002). Auditors also reviewed and reported findings for employee personnel files, including criminal history checks of employees; juvenile grievances; and investigations of abuse, neglect, and exploitation allegations at the juvenile probation departments in Bexar, Harris, Hays, and McLennan counties.

383 *Coordinated Strategic Plan: Fiscal Years [year–year]*. Austin: Texas Juvenile Probation Commission; Texas Youth Commission [biennial, 1995–date].

<http://www.tjpc.state.tx.us/publications/default.htm> [current edition]

<http://www.tyc.state.tx.us/archive/> [archived editions]

This plan for juvenile justice in Texas is developed jointly by the Texas Juvenile Probation Commission and the Texas Youth Commission in accordance with the provisions of Tex. Hum. Res. Code Ann. §§ 61.0911, 141.0471 (Vernon 2001 & Supp. 2010), and is intended to serve as a guide, but not as a substitute for, the strategic plans developed individually by the two agencies. It contains data on legislative appropriations, juvenile probation referrals, and recidivism.

Research Note: Past editions of the *Coordinated Strategic Plan* are available online in the TYC Archives. Current and past editions of the TJPC *Strategic Plan* are available on the commission's website and contain data on personnel, legislative appropriations, supervised populations, key performance measures, and projections for outcomes.

•384 *Criminal Justice Uniform Cost Report, Fiscal Years [year–year]*. Austin: Legislative Budget Board [online only, 2003–date].

<http://www.lbb.state.tx.us/PubSafety_CrimJustice/PubSafety_CrimJustice.htm>

This report utilizes agency budgets and reported expenditures to calculate uniform costs per day (with certain specified exclusions) for the Texas Juvenile Probation Commission.

Research Note: Earlier data can be found in reports published by the Criminal Justice Policy Council (under varying titles).

•385 *Current Correctional Population Indicators: Adult and Juvenile Correctional Populations Monthly Report*. Austin: Legislative Budget Board [monthly, online only, 2004–date].

<http://www.lbb.state.tx.us/PubSafety_CrimJustice/PubSafety_CrimJustice.htm>

This continuously updated monthly report presents data on Texas Juvenile Probation Commission populations as follows: adjudicated probation, deferred prosecution, supervision prior to court proceedings, and total supervision.

386 *Probation and Parole Directory.* Alexandria, Va.: American Correctional Association [biennial, 1981–date].

Provides the following data for Texas county juvenile probation departments: fiscal information, beginning salary ranges, personnel, and client caseload.

Research Note: This data is not provided for every listed department.

387 *The Recycling of Juvenile Offenders: A Pre-Reform Baseline.* Austin: Criminal Justice Policy Council, 2000.

<http://www.lbb.state.tx.us/PubSafety_CrimJustice/6_Links/Documents_Alpha_Links.htm>

The Progressive Sanction Guidelines, which became effective in January 1996, comprise a legislatively mandated sentencing policy that provides seven levels of increasingly severe disposition for juvenile offenders referred to local juvenile probation departments based on the individual's offense and prior history (Tex. Fam. Code Ann. §§ 59.001–.015 (Vernon 2008)). This report laid the groundwork for post-reform evaluation of the guidelines through establishing the pre-reform baseline subsequent contact rate for 14,853 juveniles who were disposed in 1994 and then tracked for the following two years. Fourteen juvenile probation departments in twenty counties were included in the study.

Research Note: Acts of the 78th Legislature, Regular Session, 2003, Ch. 479, § 2 amended the Texas Family Code (Chap. 59) heading by substituting "Model" for "Guidelines." See also the council's follow-up reports: *The Impact of Progressive Sanction Guidelines: Trends Since 1995*; *An In-Depth Analysis of the Use of Progressive Sanction Guidelines in 1999*; *Profile of Referrals to Selected Juvenile Probation Departments in Texas*; *The Impact of Juvenile Justice Reforms on Recycling of Juvenile Offenders*; *The Recycling of Juvenile Offenders in Selected Texas Counties*; and *Progressive Sanction Guidelines in 2001*.

388 *Self-evaluation Report: A Report for the Sunset Advisory Commission.* Austin: Texas Juvenile Probation Commission, 2007.

<http://www.sunset.state.tx.us/81streports/tjpc/ser.pdf>

The Texas Sunset Act requires the automatic termination of designated State agencies twelve years after review unless the legislature extends the life of the agency by statute (Tex. Gov't Code Ann. §§ 325.001–.024 (Vernon 2005)). The Sunset Advisory Commission assists the legislature in making these determinations by evaluating the operations of agencies scheduled for termination. As a part of the review process, each agency submits a Self-Evaluation Report (SER) to the commission. This report provides statistics on fiscal matters (appropriations, revenues, expenditures, and federal aid); customer satisfaction; key performance measures; personnel; funding distribution by county (mandatory and discretionary); allegations and investigations of abuse, neglect, or exploitation involving certified officers and registered facilities; and regulated juvenile probation departments.

Research Note: Earlier editions are available. See also the report of the commission's decisions regarding this review. <http://www.sunset.state.tx.us/81streports/tyc/tyc_dec.pdf>

389 *Social Factors of Adjudicated Juvenile Offenders in Texas.* Austin: Criminal Justice Policy Council, 2002.

<http://www.lbb.state.tx.us/PubSafety_CrimJustice/6_Links/Documents_Alpha_Links.htm>

Presents statistics on social factors involved in a sample of 1,595 referrals to juvenile probation departments in nine urban and mid-size counties that resulted in formal dispositions in court during the first six months of 1999. In the report social factors refer to "the social circumstances and risk factors in a juvenile's life that may relate to juvenile delinquency."

•390 *The State of Juvenile Probation Activity in Texas: Statistical and Other Data on the Juvenile Justice System in Texas for Calendar Year [year].* Austin: Texas Juvenile Probation Commission [2000–date].

<http://www.tjpc.state.tx.us/publications/default.htm#reports>

The Texas Juvenile Probation Commission was established in 1981. Its mandate is to ensure access to juvenile probation services statewide by supporting and overseeing the 166 juvenile probation departments that serve all counties in Texas. This report provides county-level statistics on juvenile referral activity, juvenile disposition and supervision activity, and juvenile secure detention and residential placement activity.

Research Note: Reports are available online back to 1997. Previously published under the titles *Texas Juvenile Probation Statistical Report: Statistical and Other Data on the Juvenile Justice System in Texas for Calendar Years 1980–1981, Abbreviate; Texas Juvenile Probation Statistical Report: Statistical and Other Data on the Juvenile Justice System in Texas for Calendar Year [year]* (1982–1998); and *Texas Juvenile Probation Statistical Activity Report: Statistical and Other Data on the Juvenile Justice System in Texas for Calendar Year 1999.* Earlier data was reported by the Texas Youth Council (1952–1974) and the Texas Judicial Council (1975–1979).

391 *Victim Offender Mediation Programs in Texas.* Austin: Texas Juvenile Probation Commission, 2009.

<http://www.tjpc.state.tx.us/publications/reports/RPTOTH200901.pdf>

Provides statistics on victim offender mediation (VOM) programs established within individual Texas juvenile probation departments (Appendix 1).

Prisoner Sexual Assault

•**392** *Sexual Victimization in Juvenile Facilities Reported by Youth* [Special Report]. Washington, D.C.: Bureau of Justice Statistics, Office of Justice Programs, U.S. Department of Justice [annual, 2008–date].
<http://bjs.ojp.usdoj.gov/index.cfm?ty=dcdetail&iid=321>

The Prison Rape Elimination Act of 2003 (P.L. 108-79, 117 Stat. 972) requires the Bureau of Justice Statistics to conduct a comprehensive annual statistical review and analysis of the incidence and effects of prison rape in correctional facilities. The overall program is called the National Prison Rape Statistics Program (NPRSP) and comprises several data collections. This publication reports the results of the annual National Survey of Youth in Custody (NSYC). It includes state-owned or operated juvenile facilities, and locally or privately operated juvenile facilities, which held adjudicated youths for at least ninety days. Unlike the bureau's Survey of Sexual Violence (SSV), which is based on administrative records (see entry 392), the NSYC is based on self-administered, anonymous surveys completed by the juvenile inmates themselves. Facility-level data is reported as follows: characteristics of the participating juvenile facilities (Appendix Table 1); percentage of youth reporting sexual victimization (Appendix Table 2); percentage of youth reporting sexual victimization by another youth, by type of incident (Appendix Table 3); percentage of youth reporting staff sexual misconduct, by type of incident (Appendix Table 4); and percentage of youth reporting staff sexual misconduct excluding touching, by use of force (Appendix Table 5).

•**393** *Sexual Violence Reported by Juvenile Correctional Authorities* [Special Report]. Washington, D.C.: Bureau of Justice Statistics, Office of Justice Programs, U.S. Department of Justice [annual, 2005–date].
<http://bjs.ojp.usdoj.gov/index.cfm?ty=dcdetail&iid=406>

The Prison Rape Elimination Act of 2003 (P.L. 108-79, 117 Stat. 972) requires the Bureau of Justice Statistics to conduct a comprehensive annual statistical review and analysis of the incidence and effects of prison rape in correctional facilities. The overall program is called the National Prison Rape Statistics Program (NPRSP) and comprises several data collections. The publication reports the results of the annual Survey of Sexual Violence (SSV), which is based on administrative records from all state-operated juvenile systems and a representative sample drawn from locally and privately operated facilities. Facility-level data is reported as follows: allegations of youth-on-youth sexual violence reported by state juvenile systems, by type (Appendix Table 1a); allegations of youth-on-youth sexual violence reported by locally operated juvenile facilities, by type (Appendix Table 2a); allegations of staff sexual misconduct with youth reported in locally operated juvenile facilities, by type (Appendix Table 2b); allegations of youth-on-youth sexual violence reported in privately operated juvenile facilities, by type (Appendix Table 3a); allegations of staff sexual misconduct with youth reported in privately operated juvenile facilities, by type (Appendix Table 3b); locally operated juvenile facilities with no reported allegations of youth-on-youth sexual violence, by jurisdiction (Appendix Tables 4a–b); locally operated juvenile facilities with no reported allegations of staff sexual misconduct with youth, by jurisdiction (Appendix Tables 4c–d); privately operated juvenile facilities with no reported allegations of youth-on-youth sexual violence, by jurisdiction (Appendix Tables 5a–b); and privately operated juvenile facilities with no reported allegations of staff sexual misconduct with youth, by jurisdiction (Appendix Tables 5c–d).

Recidivism

•394 *Statewide Criminal Justice Recidivism and Revocation Rates.* Austin: Legislative Budget Board [biennial, online only, 2005–date].
<http://www.lbb.state.tx.us/PubSafety_CrimJustice/PubSafety_CrimJustice.htm>

Provides recidivism rates as computed by the Texas Juvenile Probation Commission and by the Texas Youth Commission.

Texas Youth Commission

395 *Agency Strategic Plan for Fiscal Years [year–year].* Austin: Texas Youth Commission [biennial].
<http://www.tyc.state.tx.us/about/index.html> [current edition]
<http://www.tyc.state.tx.us/archive/> [archived editions]

Contains statistics for either the last nine calendar years or last ten fiscal years for referrals to juvenile probation for delinquent acts; homicide referrals to juvenile probation; delinquent referrals to juvenile probation by type; new commitments; commitments as a percentage of referrals; new violent offender commitments; percentage of new commitments with violent classifying offense; new commitment percentages by ethnicity; percentage of new female commitments; correctional programs and parole daily population (ADP), federal funds, and appropriations. Projections for the forthcoming six fiscal years are provided for new commitments and average daily population (ADP). Data is also reported for TYC workforce by gender, age, and tenure; employment utilization by minorities and females; job categories; and turnover, turnover by tenure, and projected turnover.

•396 *Annual Report.* Austin: Texas Youth Commission [online only].

<http://www.tyc.state.tx.us/about/annual_index.html> [current edition]

<http://www.tyc.state.tx.us/archive/> [archived editions]

Beginning in 2005, the TYC *Annual Report* is disseminated through a continuously updated web page that provides links to other sections of the agency's website. It includes commitment profiles for new commitments; reasons for commitment to TYC as a percentage of total new commitments by gender; commitments by county; average length of stay, residential end of year population, and bed capacity; reviews of agency treatment effectiveness; average cost per day per youth; agency funding; expenditures by county for TYC; and contracts greater than $100,000.

Research Note: The agency was previously called the Texas State Youth Development Council (1949–1957) and the Texas Youth Council (1957–1983).

397 *Commitment Profile for New Commitments.* Austin: Texas Youth Commission [annual, online only].

<http://www.tyc.state.tx.us/research/profile.html> [current edition]

<http://www.tyc.state.tx.us/archive/> [archived editions]

Provides a demographic profile of new commitments for the past five fiscal years as follows: TYC classification; felony vs. misdemeanor commitments; prior felony adjudications/referrals; TYC classifying offense; prior placement outside home; ethnicity, gender, and citizenship; age at commitment; committing state region; committing county (top fifteen with remainder grouped together as "other"); gang membership; parent marital status; prior runaway status; IQ and education; and median (50th percentile) IQ, age, last grade completed, and reading and math grade level at time of commitment.

398 *Coordinated Strategic Plan: Fiscal Years [year–year].* Austin: Texas Juvenile Probation Commission; Texas Youth Commission [biennial, 1995–date].

<http://www.tjpc.state.tx.us/publications/default.htm> [current edition]

<http://www.tyc.state.tx.us/archive/> [archived editions]

This plan for juvenile justice in Texas is developed jointly by TYC and the Texas Juvenile Probation Commission (see entry 383).

•399 *Criminal Justice Uniform Cost Report, Fiscal Years [year–year].* Austin: Legislative Budget Board, [online only, 2003–date].

<http://www.lbb.state.tx.us/PubSafety_CrimJustice/PubSafety_CrimJustice.htm>

This report utilizes agency budgets and reported expenditures to calculate uniform costs per day (with certain specified exclusions) for the Texas Youth Commission.

Research Note: Earlier data can be found in reports published by the Criminal Justice Policy Council (under varying titles).

•400 *Current Correctional Population Indicators: Adult and Juvenile Correctional Populations Monthly Report.* Austin: Legislative Budget Board [monthly, online only, 2004–date].

<http://www.lbb.state.tx.us/PubSafety_CrimJustice/PubSafety_CrimJustice.htm>

This continuously updated monthly report presents data on the TYC as follows: residential populations (institutions, halfway houses, contract care, and total residential); parole supervision populations (TYC, interstate compact (transfer-ins), and total parole); and monthly commitment activity (sentenced offenders, type A violent offenders, type B violent offenders, chronic serious offenders, controlled substances dealers, firearms offenders, general offenders, and total new monthly commitments).

401 *Directory: Adult and Juvenile Correctional Departments, Institutions, Agencies, and Probation and Parole Authorities* [cover title]. Alexandria, Va.: American Correctional Association [annual, 2001–date].

Provides profiles of juvenile institutions, juvenile community corrections, and juvenile contract facilities in Texas including the year opened, security level, capacity, average daily population, inmate gender, age limit, cost of care per day, and total staff.

Research Note: Published under slightly varying titles prior to 2001.

402 *Historical Criminal Justice Statistics: Juvenile Offender Characteristics.* Austin: Legislative Budget Board [online only, 2004–date].

<http://www.lbb.state.tx.us/PubSafety_CrimJustice/PubSafety_CrimJustice.htm>

Provides historical fiscal year statistics on TYC juvenile offender characteristics (on-hand population, admissions, and releases) by age, gender, race, citizenship, offense type, and commitment type.

403 *An Investigative Report on the Texas Youth Commission* [SAO Report]. Austin: State Auditor's Office, 2007. 07-022

<http://www.sao.state.tx.us/reports/main/07-022.html>

Reports the results of an investigation of physical security and the grievance process at youth facilities, the TYC organizational structure, the allocation of TYC resources, and the workloads, qualifications, and training of TYC facility staff. The report utilized survey responses from 3,279 youths in TYC and contract facilities and 1,672 TYC employees.

Research Note: An evaluation by the SAO of the TYC's compliance with the recommendations of this report can be found in *A Follow-up Audit Report on the Texas Youth Commission* (2009).

404 Kelly, William R. *Process Evaluation of the Texas Youth Commission's Chemical Dependency Treatment Program—Final Report*. Washington, D.C.: National Institute of Justice, Office of Justice Programs, U.S. Department of Justice, 2000. NCJ 182367

<http://www.ncjrs.gov/pdffiles1/nij/grants/182367.pdf>

Presents data from a process evaluation of the TYC's Chemical Dependency Treatment Program (CDTP), which was based on an analysis of 406 juveniles who entered the CDTP at five sites (Giddings State School, Evins Juvenile Facility, Jefferson County, Gainesville, and McFadden Ranch) from January through October 1998, and who were discharged by April 1, 1999.

Research Note: See also William R. Kelly, *Outcome Evaluation of the Texas Youth Commission's Chemical Dependency Treatment Program—Final Report* (NCJ 189032), which presents data from a follow-up outcome evaluation of the CDTP. <http://www.ncjrs.gov/pdffiles1/nij/grants/189032.pdf> Datasets are available through the National Archive of Criminal Justice Data, Inter-university Consortium for Political and Social Research (ICPSR), Institute for Social Research, University of Michigan.

<http://dx.doi.org/10.3886/ICPSR03141>

405 *Report on Customer Service*. Austin: Texas Youth Commission [biennial, 2004–date].

<http://austin.tyc.state.tx.us/cfinternet/customer_service/index.html>

Reports the results of customer service assessments regarding general measures, facilities, staff, communications, complaint-handling process, internet site, service timeliness, and printed information. The mail surveys are sent to Juvenile Court Judges and Chief Juvenile Probation Officers (the JPO Survey), TYC volunteers (the Volunteer Survey), and parents/guardians of youth in TYC custody (the Family Survey). Results are compared with previous surveys with percent changes noted. Statistics are also provided for allegations of abuse, neglect, and exploitation per 1,000 ADP (allegations confirmed, dismissed, and pending).

406 *Review of Agency Treatment Effectiveness*. Austin: Research and Planning Department, Texas Youth Commission [annual, 1999–date].

<http://www.tyc.state.tx.us/research/> [current edition]

<http://www.tyc.state.tx.us/archive/> [archived editions]

Provides fiscal year data on recidivism rates (rearrest and reincarceration) for offenders (capital and serious violent offenders, sex offenders, chemically dependent offenders, and mental health impaired offenders) who were amenable/not amenable to treatment in TYC programs.

407 *Self-Evaluation Report Provided to Sunset Advisory Commission.* Austin: Texas Youth Commission, 2007.

<http://www.state.tx.us/81streports/tyc/ser.pdf>

The Texas Sunset Act requires the automatic termination of designated State agencies twelve years after review unless the legislature extends the life of the agency by statute (Tex. Gov't Code Ann. §§ 325.001–.024 (Vernon 2005)). The Sunset Advisory Commission assists the legislature in making these determinations by evaluating the operations of agencies scheduled for termination. As a part of the review process, each agency submits a Self-Evaluation Report (SER) to the commission. This report provides statistics on fiscal matters (appropriations, revenues, expenditures, and federal aid); personnel; key performance measures; TYC programs and services (educational, mental health, aggression management, sex offender, and substance abuse treatment); and parole supervision.

Research Note: Earlier editions are available. See also the report of the commission's decisions regarding this review and their review of the TYC Office of Independent Ombudsman. <http://www.sunset.state.tx.us/81streports/tyc/tyc_dec.pdf>

408 Wallisch, Lynn S., and Lisa Kerber. *Substance Use and Delinquency Among Youths Entering Texas Youth Commission Facilities: 2000–2001.* Austin: Texas Commission on Alcohol and Drug Abuse, 2001.

<http://www.dshs.state.tx.us/sa/research/criminaljustice/youth_delinquency00-01.pdf

Reports random sample data collected between February 2000 and February 2001 on 1,026 youths entering the TYC intake facility at Marlin, Texas. Statistics are presented on the prevalence of substance use (alcohol, tobacco, marijuana, inhalants, powder cocaine, crack cocaine, heroin and other opiates, uppers, downers, and psychedelics), and criminal behavior (violent crimes and property crimes). The appendixes contain statistics on the prevalence and recency of substance use and crime among TYC youths by age in the following categories: total, male, female, Anglo, African American, Hispanic.

Research Note: Earlier editions are available.

Chapter 7

Capital Punishment and Death Row

Appellate Courts

•409 *Annual Statistical Report for the Texas Judiciary.* Austin: Office of Court Administration [2005–date].

<http://www.courts.state.tx.us/pubs/annual-reports.asp>

Presents data for the Texas Court of Criminal Appeals on direct appeals (death penalty and DNA appeals–death sentence); applications for writ of habeas corpus (death penalty); and motions for stay of execution. Also includes a county-level summary of death sentences and life sentences imposed in criminal cases in state district courts.

Research Note: Data is reported by fiscal year. Reports are available online back to 1996. Previously published under the titles *Texas Judicial Council Annual Report* (1974–1978), *Texas Judicial System Annual Report of Statistical and Other Data for Calendar Year [year]* (1979–1983), and *Texas Judicial System Annual Report Fiscal Year [year]* (1984–2004).

410 Fagan, Jeffrey, and James Liebman. *Processing and Outcome of Death Penalty Appeals after* Furman v. Georgia, *1973–1995: [United States].* Ann Arbor: National Archive of Criminal Justice Data, Inter-university Consortium for Political and Social Research, Institute for Social Research, University of Michigan, 2002.

<http://dx.doi.org/10.3886/ICPSR03468>

This data collection effort was undertaken to analyze the outcomes of capital appeals in the United States between 1973 and 1995. Datasets are provided as follows: state characteristics and death verdict reversals by state and year (DS1); state and county characteristics and death verdict reversals by county, state, and year (DS2); direct appeal data (DS3); state post-conviction data (DS4); and habeas corpus data (DS5).

411 Latzer, Barry, and James N.G. Cauthen. *Justice Delayed? Time Consumption in Capital Appeals: A Multistate Study.* New York: John Jay College of Criminal Justice, 2007. NCJ 217555

<http://www.ncjrs.gov/pdffiles1/nij/grants/217555.pdf>

Presents the results of a study that focused on the time consumed by capital appeals in fourteen representative states (including Texas) with enforceable death penalty laws. For each state, every capital case resolved on direct appeal by the court of last resort (COLR) between January 1, 1992, and December 31, 2002, was examined. Among the state-level data reported are frequency of decisions in direct appeals of capital cases (Fig. 5); median time (in days) from sentence to state supreme court decision (Fig. 9); median time (in days) from notice of appeal to state supreme court decision (Fig. 10); median time (in days) from sentence to notice of appeal (Fig. 13); median time (in days) from notice of appeal to last brief filed (Fig. 14); median time (in days) from last brief to oral argument (Fig. 15); and median time (in days) from oral argument to state supreme court decision (Fig. 16).

Research Note: Datasets are available through the National Archive of Criminal Justice Data, Inter-university Consortium for Political and Social Research (ICPSR), Institute for Social Research, University of Michigan.

<http://dx.doi.org/10.3886/ICPSR21680>

412 *Texas Court of Criminal Appeals: An Inventory of Court of Criminal Appeals Execution Case Files at the Texas State Archives, 1974–2008.* Austin: Texas State Library and Archives Commission.

<http://www.lib.utexas.edu/taro/tslac/30112/tsl-30112.html>

Contains individual files for executed inmates with records that include grand jury, hearing, trial, and *voir dire* examination transcripts; briefs; copies of exhibits; statements; correspondence, memoranda opinions; motions; death warrants; indexes; juror questionnaires; post-conviction writs of habeas corpus; and audio-visual materials.

Capital Punishment

•**413** *Capital Punishment—Statistical Tables* [National Prisoner Statistics NP-8]. Washington, D.C.: Bureau of Justice Statistics, Office of Justice Programs, U.S. Department of Justice [annual, 1980–date].

<http://purl.access.gpo.gov/GPO/LPS23986>

Reports the following state-level data: capital offenses; method of execution; prisoners under sentence of death, by region, jurisdiction, and race; Hispanics and women under sentence of death; number of persons executed, 1930–date; women under sentence of death, by race; and advance count of executions.

Research Note: Editions are available online back to 1993. Beginning with the 2006 edition, this report is available online only in the form of data tables on the BJS website ("Statistical Tables" was added to the title beginning with that edition). Statistics for 1971 through 1984 can be found in a separate overlapping publication in the National Prisoner Statistics series, which was also issued under the title *Capital Punishment*. This annual report was initially published by the National Criminal Justice Information and Statistics Service (1971–1979), and later by the Bureau of Justice Statistics (1980–1984). It subsequently merged with *Prisoners in State and Federal Institutions on . . .* to form *Correctional Populations in the United States* (see entry 414). Statistics prior to 1971 were reported by the Federal Bureau of Prisons in various publication series. Datasets are available (1973–date) through the National Archive of Criminal Justice Data, Inter-university Consortium for Political and Social Research (ICPSR), Institute for Social Research, University of Michigan.

<http://www.icpsr.umich.edu/icpsrweb/ICPSR/series/00010>

•414 *Correctional Populations in the United States.* Washington, D.C.: Bureau of Justice Statistics, Office of Justice Programs, U.S. Department of Justice [annual, 1985–1998, 2009–date].

<http://bjs.ojp.usdoj.gov/index.cfm?ty=pbse&sid=5>

Provides state-level data on movement of all prisoners under sentence of death, by race; movement of female prisoners under sentence of death, by race; movement of Hispanic prisoners under sentence of death; time between sentencing and the year-end for prisoners under sentence of death; age of prisoners under sentence of death; legal status at time of capital offense for prisoners under sentence of death; felony history of prisoners under sentence of death; age of prisoners received from court under sentence of death, by race; level of education completed by prisoners received from court under sentence of death; legal status at time of capital offense for prisoners received from court under sentence of death, by race; felony history of prisoners received from court under sentence of death, by race; means of removal for all prisoners who left death row, by race; status of prisoners removed from death row, by race; time between sentencing and removal for prisoners removed from death row; age of prisoners removed from death row; legal status at time of capital offense for prisoners removed from death row; felony history of prisoners removed from death row; prisoners executed under civil authority in the United States, by year, region, and jurisdiction; and prisoners executed under civil authority in the United States, by race and offense.

Research Note: See entry 229 for background on this publication series.

•415 *Death Row Information.* Huntsville: Texas Department of Criminal Justice [online only, 1982–date].

<http://www.tdcj.state.tx.us/stat/deathrow.htm>

Provides the following data on executed Texas inmates: roster of executed inmates (with links to profiles containing summaries of the crimes that sent them to death row and their last statements); county of conviction; number of executions by year; media witness list; and electrocutions (1923–1973).

Research Note: See also entry 419.

416 *Death Row U.S.A.: A Quarterly Report by the Criminal Justice Project of the NAACP Legal Defense and Educational Fund, Inc.* [online only, Summer 2000–date].

<http://naacpldf.org/death-row-usa>

The "Roster of the Executed" is a chronological list of executions since the 1976 reinstatement of capital punishment (date of execution, name of defendant, number if multiple victims, state, defendant/victim race, and victim gender). Each issue also provides an execution breakdown by state, including the race of the defendant and victim.

Research Note: See also entry 420.

417 Espy, M. Watt, and John Ortiz Smykla. *Executions in the United States, 1608–2002: The Espy File* [4th ICPSR ed.]. Ann Arbor: National Archive of Criminal Justice Data, Inter-university Consortium for Political and Social Research, Institute for Social Research, University of Michigan, 2004.

<http://dx.doi.org/10.3886/ICPSR08451>

Provides data on executions performed under civil authority in the United States between 1608 and 2002, including the age, race, name, sex, and occupation of the offender; place, jurisdiction, date, and method of execution; and the crime for which the offender was executed.

418 Perry, Steven W. *American Indians and Crime: A BJS Statistical Profile, 1992–2002.* Washington, D.C.: Bureau of Justice Statistics, Office of Justice Programs, U.S. Department of Justice, 2004. NCJ 203097

<http://purl.access.gpo.gov/GPO/LPS75639>

Provides statistics on capital punishment among American Indians, by state and status, 1973–2002 (Table 31).

Research Note: Earlier editions are available.

Death Row

•**419** *Death Row Information.* Huntsville: Texas Department of Criminal Justice [online only].

<http://www.tdcj.state.tx.us/stat/deathrow.htm>

Provides the following data on Texas death row inmates: roster of offenders on death row (with links to profiles containing summaries of the crimes that sent them to death row); gender and racial statistics of death row offenders; scheduled executions; county information for death row offenders; roster of women on death row; offenders no longer on death row; citizenship of death row offenders; death row facts; and historical death row data (1923–1973).

Research Note: See also entry 415.

420 *Death Row U.S.A.: A Quarterly Report by the Criminal Justice Project of the NAACP Legal Defense and Educational Fund, Inc.* [online only, 2000–date].

<http://naacpldf.org/death-row-usa>

Provides a state-level summary of prisoners currently on death row (total, by race, and percentage of total), along with a roster of federal and state death row prisoners (name, race, and if female or juvenile).

Research Note: See also entry 416.

Federal Criminal Justice System

421 *The Federal Death Penalty System: A Statistical Survey (1988–2000).* Washington, D.C.: U.S. Department of Justice, 2000.

<http://purl.access.gpo.gov/GPO/LPS6116>

The U.S. Department of Justice instituted a policy in 1988 that required United States Attorneys to submit to the United States Attorney General for review and approval any case in which they wanted to seek the death penalty (the decision not to seek the death penalty was left to their discretion). A revised protocol was instituted in 1995 that requires United States Attorneys to submit for review all cases in which a defendant is charged with a capital-eligible offense, regardless whether they actually favor seeking the death penalty in that case. These submissions are initially reviewed by a committee of senior U.S. Justice Department attorneys, known as the Attorney General's Review Committee on Capital Cases, which makes independent recommendations to the Attorney General. This report provides detailed statistics by federal judicial district, both before and after the revised Death Penalty Protocol of 1995, on recommendations to seek the death penalty by United States attorneys, the review committee, and the Attorney General, based on the race/ethnicity of the defendant and the victim(s), as well as the prevalence of agreement and disagreement among these three parties on recommendations to seek the death penalty based on the race/ethnicity of the defendant.

422 Klein, Stephen P., Richard A. Berk, and Laura J. Hickman. *Race and the Decision to Seek the Death Penalty in Federal Cases.* Santa Monica, Calif.: RAND Corporation, 2006. NCJ 214730

<http://www.ncjrs.gov/pdffiles1/nij/grants/214730.pdf>

This report examines possible defendant and victim race effects in capital decisions in the federal system. It presents an analysis of 312 cases, involving 657 defendants, received by the U.S. Department of Justice's Capital Case Unit (CCU) between January 1, 1995, and July 31, 2000, for which defendant- and victim-race data were available in the ninety-four federal judicial districts. The database was structured to allow the researchers to examine two stages in the federal prosecution process, i.e., the United States Attorney Office's recommendation to seek or not to seek the death penalty, and the final Attorney General charging decision.

Research Note: Readers are advised to review the critique of the report's methodology and conclusions authored by David C. Baldus, and the letter written by Baldus and other "expert consultants" recruited to work with RAND on the report. These are included in *Oversight of the Federal Death Penalty: Hearing before the Subcommittee on the Constitution of the Committee on the Judiciary, United States Senate, One Hundred Tenth Congress, First Session, June 27, 2007*, pp. 176–192, 326–329 (Washington, D.C.: G.P.O., 2009). <http://purl.access.gpo.gov/GPO/LPS112781>. Datasets are available through the National Archive of Criminal Justice Data, Inter-university Consortium for Political and Social Research (ICPSR), Institute for Social Research, University of Michigan. <http://dx.doi.org/10.3886/ICPSR04533>

Females

423 Streib, Victor L. *Death Penalty for Female Offenders, January 1, 1973, through June 30, 2009*. Ada, Ohio: College of Law, Ohio Northern University, 2009.

<http://www.law.onu.edu/faculty_staff/faculty_profiles/victorstreib.html>

Provides a state-by-state breakdown of death sentences for female offenders (Table 2); a list of executions of female offenders (January 1, 1900, through June 30, 2009), by state (Tables 3, 4); and a chronological roster of death sentences imposed on females (Appendix A). Case summaries are provided for female offenders under death sentences, by state (Appendix B).

Research Note: The report is periodically updated.

Habeas Corpus

424 King, Nancy J., Fred L. Cheesman II, and Brian J. Ostrom. *Final Technical Report: Habeas Litigation in U.S. District Courts: An Empirical Study of Habeas Corpus Cases Filed by State Prisoners Under the Antiterrorism and Effective Death Penalty Act of 1996* [Nashville, Tenn.]: Vanderbilt University Law School; [Williamsburg, Va.]: National Association for State Courts, 2007. NCJ 219559

<http://www.ncjrs.gov/pdffiles1/nij/grants/219559.pdf>

This report provides empirical information about the processing of state prisoner petitions seeking habeas corpus relief in U.S. District Courts under the Antiterrorism and Effective Death Penalty Act of 1996, also known as AEDPA (P.L. 104-132, 110 Stat. 1214). The study collected analyzed data from documents in a sample of habeas cases filed in U.S. District Courts. The non-capital case sample consisted of 2,384 cases randomly selected from nearly 37,000 non-capital habeas cases filed by state prisoners in federal district court during 2003 and 2004. The capital case sample consisted of cases begun in 2000, 2001, and 2002 in the thirteen federal districts with the highest volume of capital habeas filings, including the four Texas districts. This sample of

368 cases includes more than half of the capital habeas cases filed nationally during the period. District-level descriptive data is reported concerning the time elapsing from state conviction to federal filing; claims raised in habeas petitions; the application of defenses and limitations; case processing time; and merits review and outcome. Comparisons of post-AEDPA to pre-AEDPA case processing, and capital-case processing to non-capital-case processing, are provided. The report also provides results of regression analyses that examined which features are associated with variations in processing time for both capital and non-capital cases, variation in the time before capital cases are filed, and variation in the likelihood of relief in capital cases.

425 Liebman, James S., Jeffrey Fagan, and Valarie West. *A Broken System: Error Rates in Capital Cases, 1973–1995.* New York: Columbia Law School, Columbia University, 2000.

<http://www2.law.columbia.edu/instructionalservices/liebman/>

Presents the results of an analysis of all published state and federal judicial opinions in the United States between 1973 and 1995 that conducted direct and habeas review of state capital judgments, as well as many of the available opinions that conducted state post-conviction review of those judgments. The authors checked and catalogued every case revealed by these opinions, and hundreds of items of information about each case from the published decisions and the NAACP Legal Defense Fund's quarterly death row census were also collected. Section VIII presents state comparisons on rates of serious error found on state direct appeal; rates of serious error found on state post-conviction; rates of serious error found on state direct appeal and state post-conviction; rates of serious error found on federal habeas corpus; rates of serious error found by state versus federal courts; overall rates of error found on state direct appeal, state post-conviction, and federal habeas corpus; length of time of review; capital sentencing and execution rates and the two compared; demographic factors; and court factors. Section IX presents federal circuit court and regional comparisons. The appendixes contain state capital punishment report cards (Appendix A); federal circuit court and regional capital punishment report cards (Appendix B); incomplete list of capital judgments reversed on state post-conviction and related types of review, by state (Appendix C).

Research Note: Texas is in the U.S. Court of Appeals Fifth Circuit and has four districts: Eastern, Northern, Southern, and Western. Datasets are available through the Inter-university Consortium for Political and Social Research (ICPSR), Institute for Social Research, University of Michigan.

<http://dx.doi.org/10.3886/ICPSR03468>

Inmate Attitudes

426 Hilla, Derek Ian. "Capital Punishment: What Our Readers Say." *The Echo* 80, no. 9 (November 2007): 1, 7–9.

Reports the result of a poll of readers of *The Echo* (the newspaper published by and for inmates incarcerated in the Texas Department of Criminal Justice) on their opinions about capital punishment, including whether the death penalty should be a sentencing option, whether life without parole should be utilized in place of the death penalty, and whether the death penalty acts as a deterrent. Responses are categorized by age, gender, race, and conviction.

Juvenile Capital Punishment

427 Streib, Victor L. The *Juvenile Death Penalty Today: Death Sentences and Executions for Juvenile Crimes, January 1, 1973–February 28, 2005*. Ada, Ohio: College of Law, Ohio Northern University, 2005.

<http://www.law.onu.edu/faculty_staff/faculty_profiles/victorstreib.html>

Provides a roster of executions of juvenile offenders (Table 1); the minimum death penalty age by jurisdiction (Table 2); a state-by-state breakdown of juvenile death sentences (Table 4); and a chronological roster of juvenile death sentences imposed (Appendix A). Case summaries are provided for juvenile offenders under death sentences, by state (Appendix B).

Research Note: The report is periodically updated.

Wrongful Conviction

428 *The Innocence List*. Washington, D.C.: Death Penalty Information Center [online only, 1973–date].

<http://deathpenaltyinfo.org/innocence-list-those-freed-death-row>

A continuously updated list of defendants who (a) have been acquitted of all charges related to the crime that placed them on death row, or (b) had all charges related to the crime that placed them on death row dismissed by the prosecution, or (c) been granted a complete pardon based on evidence of innocence. The defendants are listed chronologically by the year of their exoneration along with the following information: state, race, year of conviction, number of years between conviction and exoneration, reason for exoneration, and if DNA testing was involved. The defendants' names are linked to brief summaries of their cases. The DPIC website also provides a state-by-state death penalty information database.

Research Note: Other lists of wrongful convictions, based on slightly different criteria, are maintained by the Center on Wrongful Convictions (Northwestern University School of Law) and the Innocence Project (Benjamin N. Cardozo School of Law at Yeshiva University).

Chapter 8

Victims of Crime

Child Victims

•**429** *Annual Report*. Austin: Texas Child Fatality Review Team [2006–date]. <http://www.dshs.state.tx.us/mch/Child_Fatality_Review.shtm>

Child fatality review teams are multidisciplinary, multi-agency working groups that review child deaths on a local level from a public health perspective with the goal of decreasing the incidence of preventable child deaths (Texas Fam. Code Ann. §§ 264.501–.515 (Vernon 2008 & Supp. 2010)). Their work is supported and coordinated by the Texas Department of State Health Services. This report contains data on child fatality victims as follows: race/ethnicity, age group, and gender of children who died from homicides (Table 5); place of homicide (Chart 4); perpetrator in homicide deaths (Chart 5); race/ethnicity, age group, and gender of children who died from firearms (Table 10); manner of death for firearm deaths (Chart 15); and owner of firearm in firearm deaths (Chart 16).

Research Note: Reports are available online back to 2000. Reports were biennial prior to 2006.

•**430** *Annual Report and Data Book.* Austin: Texas Department of Family and Protective Services [annual, 2009–date]. <http://www.dfps.state.tx.us/About/Data_Books_and_Annual_Reports/default.asp>

Child Protective Services (CPS), an agency within the Texas Department of Family and Protective Services, conducts civil investigations of reports of child abuse and neglect; protects children from child abuse and neglect; promotes the safety, integrity, and stability of families; and provides permanent placements for children who cannot safely remain with their own families. The *Data Book* provides statistics by fiscal year for the eleven DFPS regions as follows: daily caseload; Texas child population birth through seventeen years; completed investigations; total initial intakes and screened out cases; risk assessment findings of completed child abuse/neglect investigations; case action for risk indicated completed investigations; investigations of child abuse/neglect by source of report for completed investigations; number of child abuse/neglect completed investigations; family cases opened for services as a result of a completed investigation; confirmed allegations of child abuse/neglect by type of abuse; children in cases opened for services as a result of a completed investigation; point prevalence rate of child abuse/neglect per 1,000 children in Texas population per region; race/ethnicity of selected CPS statistics compared to Texas child population; confirmed victims of child abuse/neglect;

profile of confirmed child abuse/neglect victims; alleged and confirmed victims of child abuse/neglect; confirmed victims where the confirmed perpetrator was a parent; characteristics of perpetrators in confirmed investigations of child abuse/neglect; average number of families receiving preservation/reunification services per month; and family reunification services. The report also provides statistics on the living arrangements of children in DFPS substitute care. The County Charts section reports data at the county level.

Research Note: Editions of the *Data Book* are available online back to 1992 (it merged with the DFPS *Annual Report* to form a single publication beginning with the 2009 edition). Previously published under the title *Legislative Data Book* (1992–1999). The agency was called the Texas Department of Protective and Regulatory Services prior to 2004.

•431 *Child Maltreatment.* Washington, D.C: Children's Bureau, Administration on Children, Youth and Families, Administration for Children and Families, U.S. Department of Health and Human Services [1990–date].
<http://purl.access.gpo.gov/GPO/LPS3224>

The National Data Archive on Child Abuse and Neglect (NDACAN) is maintained at Cornell University by the Family Life Development Center in the College of Human Ecology. It was established as a voluntary national reporting clearinghouse by the Child Abuse Prevention, Adoption, and Family Services Act of 1988 (P.L. 100-294, 102 Stat. 102). *Child Maltreatment* reports the following state-level NDACAN data: screened-in and screened-out referrals (Table 2-1), report sources (Table 2-2); investigation dispositions (Table 2-3); report investigation trends (Table 2-4); PART (Program Assessment Rating Tool) measure: response time in hours (Table 2-6); child protective services workforce (Table 2-7); dispositions of children who received a CPS investigation (Table 3-1); victimization rates (Table 3-4); unique victims (Table 3-5); PART measure: first-time victims (Table 3-7); race and ethnicity of victims (Table 3-9); maltreatment types of victims (Table 3-10); race and maltreatment types of victims (Table 3-11); victims with a reported disability (Table 3-13); children with caregiver risk factor of domestic violence (Table 3-14); absence of maltreatment recurrence (Table 3-16); absence of maltreatment in foster care (Table 3-17); child fatalities (Table 4-1); prior CPS contact of child fatalities (Table 4-8); perpetrators by relationship to victims (Table 5-3); type of parental perpetrators (Table 5-4); children who received preventive services (Table 6-1); funding sources (Table 6-2); children who received post-investigation services (Table 6-3); average number of days to services (Table 6-4); children who received in-home services (Table 6-5); children who were removed from home (Table 6-6); maltreatment types of victims who were removed from home (Table 6-7); victims with court action and court-appointed representatives (Table 6-8); and victims who received family preservation or family reunification services within previous five years (Table 6-9).

Research Note: Editions are available online back to 1995. NDACAN requires preregistration in order to access restricted usage files of state case-level data on their website (2000–date). Unrestricted access to state-level aggregated counts of key indicators is also available (1990–date).

<http://www.ndacan.cornell.edu/>

432 *Child Welfare Outcomes . . . Report to Congress.* Washington, D.C.: Children's Bureau, Administration on Children, Youth and Families, Administration for Children and Families, U.S. Department of Health and Human Services [1998–date].

<http://purl.access.gpo.gov/GPO/LPS44444>

This report, which is developed in accordance with provisions of the Adoption and Safe Families Act of 1997 (P.L. 105-89, 111 Stat. 2115), contains chapters assessing each state's performance with regard to seven national child welfare outcomes. These outcomes were established by the U.S. Department of Health and Human Services in consultation with state and local child welfare agency administrators, child advocacy organizations, child welfare researchers, state legislators, and other experts in the child welfare field. The first two outcomes focus on reducing recurrence of child abuse and/or neglect, and reducing the incidence of child abuse and/or neglect in foster care. Statistics for each state are presented in four subsections (context data, outcomes data, state comment, and federal comment).

Research Note: Published under the title *Child Welfare Outcomes . . . Annual Report.* prior to the 2002–2005 edition. Reports of the Child and Family Service Reviews (CFSRs) are available for every state, including the Annual Progress and Services Report (APSR), Statewide Assessments, Final Reports (CFSR), Program Improvement Plans, and Individual Key Findings Reports. <http://basis.caliber.com/cwig/ws/cwmd/docs/cb_web/SearchForm>

433 *Kids Count Data Center.* Baltimore, Md.: Annie E. Casey Foundation [online only].

<http://datacenter.kidscount.org>

The Annie E. Casey Foundation, founded in 1948, is a private charitable organization dedicated to serving the needs of disadvantaged children, youth, and their families. Their data center provides statistics on over 100 indicators of child welfare at the national, state, and local levels. The Safety and Risky Behaviors subsection provides state profiles with county-level data (number and rates) for confirmed victims of child abuse (1990–date), and children in family violence shelters (2000–date).

Research Note: This information is not included in the foundation's annual print publication, *Kids Count Data Book.*

434 *National Data Analysis System (NDAS).* Arlington, Va.: National Center for Research, Data, and Technology, Child Welfare League of America [online only, 1990–date].

<http://ndas.cwla.org/>

The Child Welfare League of America, founded in 1920, is a coalition of more than 700 public and private child welfare agencies nationwide. The NDAS serves a clearinghouse for a wide range of statistics collected from federal and state sources. In addition, it provides proprietary data from the biennial CWLA State Child Welfare Agency Survey , which augments NDAS with data that is not available from other sources. The Child Abuse and Neglect subsection provide state-level data on preventative services; reports alleging maltreatment; investigations and dispositions; victims of maltreatment; perpetrators; and archived data. The Child Abuse and Neglect Fatalities subsection provides state-level data on reports of child abuse and neglect fatalities, child fatality review teams, perpetrators, and archived data.

Research Note: Data for all categories does not extend back to 1990.

College Students

435 Johnson, Matthew, and Glen Kercher. *Personal Victimization of College Students.* Huntsville: Crime Victims' Institute, Criminal Justice Center, Sam Houston State University, 2009.

<http://www.crimevictimsinstitute.org/pubs.html>

Reports the results of a survey of 3,894 undergraduate college students who were age eighteen or older, were currently enrolled at a Texas university, and had not taken the survey previously. The survey contains the following data: distribution, gender, race/ethnicity, employment status, and academic standing of respondents; living arrangements while at school; respondents living in a co-ed dorm; respondents who are a member of a fraternity or sorority; respondents living with roommates; primary caregiver of respondents; respondents witnessed physical violence between parents; type of personal victimization over lifetime; type of personal victimization over past two years; victim/offender relationship by victimization type; victims under the influence of alcohol and/or drugs for each type of victimization; victimization by gender, relationship status, ethnicity, employment status, academic standing, and living arrangements; victimization while living with or without a roommate; victimization and primary caregiver growing up; victimization and having witnessed physical violence between parents while growing up; involvement in personal criminal behavior in the past two years; and victimization and having been involved in personal criminal behavior in the past two years.

436 Johnson, Matthew, and Glen Kercher. *Property Victimization of College Students.* Huntsville: Crime Victims' Institute, Criminal Justice Center, Sam Houston State University, 2009.

<http://www.crimevictimsinstitute.org/pubs.html>

Reports the results of a survey of 3,894 undergraduate college students who were age eighteen or older, were currently enrolled at a Texas university, and had not taken the survey previously. The survey contains the following data: distribution, gender, race/ethnicity, employment status, and academic standing of respondents; living arrangements while at school; respondents living in a co-ed dorm; respondents a member of a fraternity or sorority; respondents living with roommates; weekly shopping habits of respondents; primary caregiver of respondents; respondents witnessed physical violence between parents; comparison of victimization by gender, relationship status, ethnicity, employment status, academic standing, living arrangements, membership in a fraternity or sorority, primary caregiver of respondents, and respondents having witnessed physical violence between parents; lifetime prevalence of property victimization; prevalence of property victimization over the past two years; prevalence of committing a property crime in the past two years; and victim/offender relationship by type of victimization.

Domestic Assault

•**437** *Easy Access to NIBRS: Victims of Domestic Violence*. Washington, D.C.: Office of Juvenile Justice and Delinquency Prevention, Office of Justice Programs, U.S. Department of Justice [online only].

<http://www.ojjdp.gov/ojstatbb/ezanibrsdv/>

Provides state-level data on victims of domestic violence based on information collected by the FBI's National Incident-Based Reporting System (NIBRS). The Inter-University Consortium of Political and Social Research (ICPSR), University of Michigan, prepared the data underlying this application by restructuring the original NIBRS data files into a series of "extracts" intended to facilitate access. Selection criteria include characteristics of the victim (most serious offense against the victim, victim-offender relationship, age of victim; sex of victim; race of victim; and most serious injury to victim); characteristics of first offender with a domestic relationship (age of offender, sex of offender, and race of offender); and characteristics of the incident (number of victims; victim(s) type; total number of offenders; type of weapon; location, day of week; and type of clearance).

Research Note: This website is maintained by the National Center for Juvenile Justice, which is the research division of the National Council of Juvenile and Family Court Judges, and sponsored by the Office of Juvenile Justice and Delinquency Prevention, Office of Justice Programs, U.S. Department of Justice.

438 Franklin, Courtney A. *The Intergenerational Transmission of Intimate Partner Violence.* Huntsville: Crime Victims' Institute, Criminal Justice Center, Sam Houston State University, 2010.

<http://www.crimevictimsinstitute.org/pubs.html>

This report is based on survey data gathered through the institute's 2007 *Criminal Victimization of Texas Residents* (see entry 463). It explores intergenerational transmission of adult intimate partner violence (IPV) and presents significant correlates of IPV perpetration and victimization.

439 Kercher, Glen A., Matthew C. Johnson, and Ilhong Yun. *Intimate Partner Violence.* Huntsville: Crime Victims' Institute, Criminal Justice Center, Sam Houston State University, 2008.

<http://www.crimevictimsinstitute.org/pubs.html>

Reports the results of a 2007 telephone survey of 700 randomly selected Texas residents on their experience with intimate partner violence, including distribution of survey respondents victims in each gender group; victims in each age group; victims in each ethnic group; victims in each education group; victims in each employment group; victims in each income group; victims in each relationship group; victims and alcohol use; victims and drug use; victims and psychological aggression; victims who witnessed intimate partner violence as a child; victims' spouses who witnessed intimate partner violence as a child; perpetrators in each gender group; perpetrators in each age group perpetrators in each ethnic group; perpetrators in each employment group; perpetrators in each income group; and perpetrators in each relationship group.

440 *Lesbian, Gay, Bisexual, Transgender and Queer Domestic Violence in the United States in [year].* New York: National Coalition of Anti-Violence Programs [annual, 1999–date].

<http://www.ncavp.org/publications/NationalPubs.aspx>

Contains data provided by the Montrose Counseling Center on domestic violence among lesbian, gay, bisexual, and transgender (LGBT) partners in Houston, including the gender and age of the victims, and the total calls per month requesting assistance.

Elderly and Physically Handicapped Victims

441 *The 2004 Survey of State Adult Protective Services: Abuse of Adults 60 Years of Age and Older.* Washington, D.C.: National Center on Elder Abuse, Administration on Aging, U.S. Department of Health and Human Services, 2006.

<http://www.ncea.aoa.gov/NCEAroot/Main_Site/pdf/2-14-06%20
FINAL%2060+REPORT.pdf>

442 *The 2004 Survey of State Adult Protective Services: Abuse of Vulnerable Adults 18 Years of Age and Older: A Report of the National Center on Elder Abuse.* Washington, D.C.: National Center on Elder Abuse, Administration on Aging, U.S. Department of Health and Human Services, 2007.
<http://www.ncea.aoa.gov/ncearoot/main_site/pdf/APS_2004NCEASurvey.pdf>

The National Center on Elder Abuse was established in 1988 as a national resource center for elder rights advocates, adult protective services agencies, law enforcement and legal professionals, medical and mental health providers, public policy leaders, educators, researchers, and concerned citizens. Two surveys of state adult protective service agencies were conducted for the center during FY2003 by the National Committee for the Prevention of Elder Abuse and the National Adult Protective Services Association. The first publication focuses on reports of abuse of individuals age sixty years and older and provides state-level abuse reporting rates (Table 3). The second focuses on reports of abuse of vulnerable adults age eighteen and older and provides state-level abuse reporting rates (Table 2) and adult protective services budgets (Table 3). A vulnerable adult was defined as a person who is either being mistreated or in danger of mistreatment and who, due to age and/or disability, is unable to protect themselves.

•443 *Annual Report and Data Book.* Austin: Texas Department of Family and Protective Services [annual, 2009–date].
<http://www.dfps.state.tx.us/About/Data_Books_and_Annual_Reports/default.asp>

Adult Protective Services (APS), an agency within the Texas Department of Family and Protective Services, investigates reports of abuse, neglect, and exploitation of adults in the community who are elderly or have disabilities; provides or arranges protective services as needed; and investigate reports of abuse, neglect, and exploitation of persons receiving services in state-operated and/or certain contracted settings that serve adults and children with mental illness or mental retardation. The *Data Book* provides statistics by fiscal year for the eleven DFPS regions as follows: Texas adult population ages sixty-five and over; Texas disabled adult population ages eighteen to sixty-four years; incidence of maltreatment per 1,000 adults in Texas adult population; in-home intake reports; intake reports by priority; in-home intake reports by source; in-home intakes, completed investigations, and confirmed cases; confirmed in-home investigations; completed in-home investigations; daily caseload;

completed in-home investigations by region and disposition; recidivism of in-home cases; characteristics of confirmed victims in completed in-home investigations; in-home confirmed victims in completed investigations; perpetrator characteristics in confirmed in-home investigations (characteristic as a percentage of total confirmed perpetrators); perpetrators in confirmed in-home investigations; number of referrals made to law enforcement in completed in-home cases; victims of family violence in confirmed investigations; confirmed allegations in in-home investigations by type of abuse/neglect; duration of in-home investigation and service delivery cases closed; purchased/non-purchased client services delivered for in-home cases; completed mental health (MH) and mental retardation (MR) settings by source of report; average length of completed MH/MR investigations; number of MH/MR investigations referred to law enforcement by setting; characteristics of victims in confirmed investigations in MHMR facilities; perpetrator characteristics in confirmed investigations in MHMR facilities; completed investigations in MH/MR settings; and dispositions of completed MH/MR investigations. The County Charts section reports data at the county level.

Research Note: Editions of the *Data Book* are available online back to 1992 (it merged with the DFPS *Annual Report* to form a single publication beginning with the 2009 edition). Previously published under the title *Legislative Data Book* (1992–1999). The agency was called the Texas Department of Protective and Regulatory Services prior to 2004.

444 Titterington, Victoria B. *Elder Abuse.* Huntsville: Crime Victims' Institute, Criminal Justice Center, Sam Houston State University, 2010.

<http://www.crimevictimsinstitute.org/pubs.html>

Presents data on personal and property victimization of Texas residents age sixty and over, based on the results of the 2005 and 2006 Texas Crime Victimization Surveys (see entry 463). Data is also reported on the survey respondents' firearms ownership, fear of crime, and experiences with identity theft.

Female Victims

445 *Texas Women Killed by their Intimate Partner in [year].* Austin: Texas Council on Family Violence [annual, 1998–date].

<http://www.tcfv.org/resources/abuse-in-texas/>

Provides an annual list of Texas women killed by their intimate partner along with brief accounts of the circumstances surrounding their deaths. The list is arranged by county and compiled using information gathered from the Texas Department of Public Safety, other Texas law enforcement agencies, and media reports.

446 *Violence Against Women Resource Guide.* Ann Arbor: National Archive of Criminal Justice Data, Inter-university Consortium for Political and Social Research Institute for Social Research, University of Michigan [online only]. <http://www.icpsr.umich.edu/NACJD/vaw/>

This website contains an interactive United States map (under "View VAW studies by state"), which provides access to state-level NACJD data collections on the topic of violence against women.

Human Trafficking

447 *The Texas Response to Human Trafficking: Report to the 81st Legislature.* Austin: Texas Health and Human Services Commission, 2008. <http://www.hhsc.state.tx.us/reports/TexasResponseHumanTrafficking.pdf>

The Victims of Trafficking and Violence Protection Act of 2000 (P.L. 106-386,114 Stat. 1464) established human trafficking as a federal crime and made trafficking victims eligible for federally funded or administered health and social services. This report was prepared under legislative mandate and addresses issues surrounding how existing social services address or fail to address the needs of human trafficking victims. It contains the results of a internet-based survey of fifty-nine direct service providers in the five geographical areas of the state that receive federal funding to combat human trafficking (Austin, Dallas/Fort Worth, El Paso, Houston, and San Antonio). In addition, thirty state agency personnel participated in the survey. Among the survey data reported include the number and type of human trafficking victims served, age and national origin of victims, agency interaction with victims, barriers to providing services, efforts to track the success of programs and client services, collaboration with federal agencies that fund services for victims, sources of referral, policies on protection of victims, and training needs.

Research Note: The complete survey, *Human Trafficking in Texas: Statewide Evaluation of Existing Laws and Social Services,* was conducted for the HHSC by the Institute on Domestic Violence and Sexual Assault, Center for Social Work Research, School of Social Work, University of Texas at Austin. It is reprinted in its entirety in this report. See also the Texas Attorney General's report to the 81st Texas Legislature on human trafficking.

<http://www.oag.state.tx.us/AG_Publications/pdfs/human_trafficking.pdf>

Immigrants

448 Kercher, Glen, and Connie Kuo. *Victimization of Immigrants.* Huntsville: Crime Victims' Institute, Criminal Justice Center, Sam Houston State University, 2008. <http://www.crimevictimsinstitute.org/pubs.html>

Reports the results of a 2007 survey of 907 Chinese, Korean, Vietnamese, and Hispanic immigrants in Houston, Texas, regarding the types of criminal victimization they experienced, the contexts in which this victimization occurred, and their reporting behavior.

Institutional Elder Abuse

•**449** *Nursing Home Compare.* Baltimore, Md.: Centers for Medicare and Medicaid Services, U.S. Dept. of Health and Human Services [online only].

<http://www.medicare.gov/nhcompare/home.asp>

Provides continuously updated data for Medicare- or Medicaid-certified nursing homes complied from two sources. The first is the Centers for Medicare and Medicaid Services' Online Survey, Certification, and Reporting (OSCAR) database. This includes nursing home characteristics and health deficiencies issued during the three most recent state inspections and recent complaint investigations. State survey agencies inspect the homes utilizing Centers for Medicare and Medicaid Services' regulations, enter the data into OSCAR, and update it as necessary. The second is data for quality measures extracted from the Minimum Data Set (MDS) repository. Regulations require that a MDS assessment be performed by the nursing home itself at admission, quarterly, annually, and whenever the resident experiences a significant change in status. Inspection data for the current and previous two inspections is available for download. The health deficiencies category includes mistreatment deficiencies along with an indication of their scope and level of harm. Nursing homes are searchable by name, city, county, state, or ZIP code.

Juvenile Victims

•**450** Snyder, Howard N., and Melissa Sickmund. *Juvenile Offenders and Victims: 2006 National Report.* Washington, D.C.: Office of Juvenile Justice and Delinquency Prevention, Office of Justice Programs, U.S. Department of Justice, 2006. NCJ 212906

<http://www.ojjdp.ncjrs.gov/ojstatbb/nr2006/index.html>

Chapter 2 provides data on juvenile victims as follows: juvenile homicide victims, firearm-related homicides of juveniles, juvenile suicide, victimization survey of juveniles, victims of school crime, victimization risk factors, juvenile victims of reported violent crimes, offenders who victimize juveniles, time-of-day analysis of juvenile victimization, location of juvenile victimization, juvenile victims of statutory rape, juvenile victimization on the Internet, juvenile kidnap victims, missing children, runaway and thrownaway children, missing children trends, child maltreatment (case processing and trends, demographics, and perpetrators), child maltreatment fatalities, foster care, and adoption.

Research Note: Earlier editions are available. Not all subsections contain state-level data. This report incorporates data from some earlier specialized OJJDP reports individually authored by Sickmund and Snyder that are not otherwise included in this book.

•451 "Youth Risk Behavior Surveillance—United States." [Surveillance Summaries]. *Morbidity and Mortality Weekly Report* (*MMWR*) [biennial, 1993–date].

<http://www.cdc.gov/mmwr/mmwr_ss/ss_cvol.html>

One report is published biennially under this title (authors and cover dates vary). It provides survey results (total, male, and female), for the following categories: percentage of high school students who were in a physical fight or who were injured in a physical fight; percentage of high school students who experienced dating violence or who were ever physically forced to have sexual intercourse; percentage of high school students who carried a weapon on school property or were threatened or injured with a weapon on school property; and percentage of high school students who were in a physical fight on school property or who were bullied on school property; percentage of high school students who did not go to school because they felt unsafe at school or on their way to or from school.

Research Note: The survey is conducted in odd-numbered years and the report is published the following year. Online access to current and past editions is also available on the website of the Division of Adolescent and School Health, National Center for Chronic Disease Prevention and Health Promotion, Centers for Disease Control and Prevention, U.S. Department of Health and Human Services. <http://www.cdc.gov/healthyyouth/yrbs/index.htm>

Missing Person Investigation

452 Hughes, Kristen. *Unidentified Human Remains in the United States, 1980–2004* [Fact Sheet]. Washington, D.C.: Bureau of Justice Statistics, Office of Justice Programs, U.S. Department of Justice, 2007. NCJ 219533

<http://www.ojp.usdoj.gov/bjs/pub/pdf/uhrus04.pdf>

Provides the number of unidentified human remains in five-year periods from 1980 to 2004, by state, as reported to the National Death Index. This database is maintained by the Division of Vital Statistics, National Center for Health Statistics, Centers for Disease Control and Prevention, U.S. Department of Health and Human Services. It includes homicides, accidental deaths, deaths from natural causes, and suicides.

Research Note: The database is available to investigators solely for statistical purposes in medical and health research. It is not accessible to organizations or the general public for legal, administrative, or genealogical purposes. Preregistration is required. <http://www.cdc.gov/nchs/ndi.htm>

•**453** *Missing and Unidentified Persons Online Bulletin*. Austin: Missing Persons Clearinghouse, Bureau of Information Analysis, Texas Department of Public Safety [online only, 1986–date].
<http://www.txdps.state.tx.us/mpch/>

This website provides three searchable repositories: Missing Persons Bulletin, Abductors/Companions Bulletin, and Unidentified Persons Bulletin. These bulletins provide information on missing persons (photograph, name, date of birth, race, case number, case type, location last seen, and date last seen); abductors/companions (photograph, date of birth, race, case number, case type, location last seen, and date last seen); and unidentified persons (forensic drawing/photograph, case number, agency, date found, gender, race, hair, and estimated date of death).

Sexual Assault Victims

454 Busch, Noël B., Holly Bell, Diana M. DiNitto, and James A. Neff. *A Health Survey of Texans: A Focus on Sexual Assault* [Final Report]. Austin: Institute on Domestic Violence and Sexual Assault, University of Texas at Austin, 2003.
<http://www.taasa.org/publications/Prevalence_Final.pdf>

Reports the results of a telephone survey of 1,200 adult Texans conducted by the School of Social Work at the University of Texas at Austin in collaboration with the Public Policy Research institute (PPRI) at Texas A&M University. The following estimates for Texas were calculated based on the number of participants in the survey and Census 2000 population data: estimated percentage who experienced sexual assault by gender, by gender and age at time of assault, and by gender, race/ethnicity, income, and education (Tables 1–3); estimated percentage of females who experienced sexual assault (before age fourteen, between ages fourteen and seventeen, and since age eighteen) by race/ethnicity, income, and education (Tables 4–6); relationship of females who experienced sexual assault to perpetrator (Table 7); estimated percentage reporting that a family member experienced sexual assault (Table 8); estimated percentage who experienced sexual assault whose most recent assault was reported to police (Table 9); estimated percentage of adults who experienced sexual assault and who experienced other violence during most recent assault (Table 10); location of most recent sexual assault by gender (Table 11); location of most recent sexual assault by age group and race/ethnicity, females (Table 12); estimated percentage of females who experienced sexual assault by mental/physical disability, by age group and mental/physical disability, and by mental/physical disability and race/ethnicity (Tables 13–15); estimated percentage of females who experienced sexual assault who received medical care for most recent assault by gender, by race/ethnicity, and by age at time of assault (Tables 16–18); estimated percentage of sexual assaults of females resulting in pregnancy (Table 19); estimated percentage who experienced sexual assault and reported most recent assault involved a weapon or threat by gender and by race/ethnicity (Tables 20–21); estimated percentage of females who experienced sexual assault and most recent assault involved a weapon by weapon type (Table 22); estimated percentage of females who experienced sexual assault (victims), and those who have not (non-victims), by drug and alcohol use (Table 23); estimated percentage who experienced sexual assault by whether they were incapacitated and unable to give consent (Table 24); estimated percentage of females who experienced sexual assault and screened positive for drug/alcohol problems (Table 25); estimated percentage of perpetrators who used drugs and/or alcohol at time of assault (Table 26); and estimated percentage of females who experienced sexual assault and were influenced by drugs and/or alcohol (Table 27).

Research Note: The survey was jointly funded by the Office of the Texas Attorney General, Sexual Assault Prevention and Crisis Services, and the Texas Association Against Sexual Assault.

455 Garcia, Mimi, and Torie Hilton. *A Report on the Level of Care of Sexual Assault Survivors in Texas Hospital Emergency Rooms.* Austin: Texas Association Against Sexual Assault, 2003.

<http://www.taasa.org/publications/sa_treatment.pdf>

Reports the results of a mail survey of 107 Texas hospital emergency rooms on their policies, protocols, procedures, and staffing relating to the treatment of sexual assault victims.

456 Kilpatrick, Dean G., and Kenneth J. Ruggiero. *One in Eight: Rape in Texas: A Report to the State.* Charleston: National Violence Against Women Prevention Research Center, Medical University of South Carolina, 2003.

<http://academicdepartments.musc.edu/ncvc/grants/50_states_reports/texas.pdf>

Presents estimates of the prevalence of rape victimization in Texas based on data extracted from National Women's Study (NWS) and the National Violence Against Women Survey (NVAWS).

Stalking

457 Kercher, Glen, and Matthew Johnson. *Stalking in Texas.* Huntsville: Crime Victims' Institute, Criminal Justice Center, Sam Houston State University, 2008.

<http://www.crimevictimsinstitute.org/pubs.html>

Reports the results of a 2006 telephone survey of 701 Texas residents on the frequency and types of individual stalking experiences, their emotional reactions to these experiences, their relationship to the stalker, violent actions by the stalker toward the victim before the stalking began, reasons for stalking behavior from the victims' perspective, and reporting behavior.

Victim Compensation

•**458** *Annual Report.* Austin: Crime Victim Services Division, Office of the Attorney General [1991–date].

<http://www.oag.state.tx.us/victims/publications_cv.shtml>

The Texas Crime Victims' Compensation Act (Tex. Code Crim. Proc. Ann. arts. 56.31–.64 (Vernon 2006 & Supp. 2010)) stipulates that an individual who suffers personal injury or death as a result of criminally injurious conduct or as a result of actions taken by the individual as an interventor, is entitled to file (or have a claimant file on their behalf) an application for compensation not later than three years after the criminally injurious conduct. A victim or claimant may not file such an application unless they report the criminally injurious conduct to the appropriate state or local law enforcement agency within a reasonable period of time, but not so late as to interfere with or hamper the investigation and prosecution of the crime after the criminally injurious conduct is committed (this requirement is waived if the victim is a child). The program is funded by legislative appropriations and administered by the Texas Attorney General, who is required to annually file a report with the governor and the legislature that includes a statistical summary of claims and awards made and denied. The fund also supports grants and contracts that focus on victim-related services or assistance. This report provides a financial summary, activity summary, applications received (total, by type of crime, by age, and by gender); payments (by benefit, type of crime, age, and gender); annual payout summary; activity summary by county; and victim assistance program funding by county.

Research Note: Data is reported by fiscal year. Reports are available online back to 2003. Each edition also has an individual title. The Grants and Contracts annual report merged with the Crime Victims Services annual report in 2005. Earlier data was reported by the Texas Workers' Compensation Commission.

459 *OVC Links to Victim Assistance & Compensation Programs.* Washington. D.C.: Office for Victims of Crime, Office of Justice Programs, U.S. Department of Justice [online only].

<http://www.ojp.usdoj.gov/ovc/help/links.htm>

The Crime Victims Fund was established by the Victims of Crime Act of 1984 (P.L 98-473, Title II, Ch. XIV, 98 Stat. 2170). The Office of Victims of Crime, Office of Justice Programs, U.S. Department of Justice, provides state-level funding through formula and discretionary grants to victim assistance and victim compensation programs. In Texas the former is administered by the Criminal Justice Division, Office of the Governor, and the latter by the Crime Victims Services Division, Office of the Attorney General. An interactive United States map provides links to the websites of these two agencies. VOCA Funded State Wide Analysis is also provided, which is a continuously updated list of VOCA Victim Assistance grants/programs funded for the State of Texas listed by city (the date of the latest update is posted at the bottom of the list).

460 *Report to the Nation.* Washington, D.C.: Office for Victims of Crime, Office of Justice Programs, U.S. Department of Justice [biennial, 2003–date].

<http://www.ojp.usdoj.gov/ovc/welcovc/repcong.htm>

Reports state victim assistance distributions (Appendix A); state victim compensation distributions (Appendix B); and Trafficking Victims Discretionary Grant Program allocations (Appendix F).

Research Note: Data is reported by fiscal year. Reports are available online back to 1996. Previously published under the title *Victims of Crime Act of 1984, as Amended: A Report . . .* (subtitle varies).

Victim Services

461 *Report on States Adult Protective Services Training Programs.* [Boulder, Colo.]: National Association of Adult Protective Services Administrators, 2002.

<http://www.ncea.aoa.gov/ncearoot/main_site/pdf/publication/
TrainingLibraryforAPS040603.pdf>

The National Association of Adult Protective Services Administrators conducted a baseline study of state adult protective services (APS) programs in 2001 for the National Center on Elder Abuse, Administration on Aging, U.S. Department of Health and Human Services. This publication reports results from that study on APS staff and supervisory training budgets, requirements, and competencies; educational requirements; and professional certification requirements.

Research Note: The National Association of Adult Protective Services Administrators (NAAPSA) merged with the National Adult Protective Services Association (NAPSA) during FY2009.

462 Yun, Ilhong, and Glen Kercher. *Victim Services in Texas: Where We Are and Where We Need to Be.* Huntsville: Crime Victims' Institute, Criminal Justice Center, Sam Houston State University [2007].

<http://www.crimevictimsinstitute.org/pubs.html>

Reports the results of a 2006 survey of 407 Texas victim service providers, including victim assistance coordinators, victim liaison offers, and community victim advocates. Topics covered include funding sources, personnel, demographic characteristics of providers, staffing increase versus victim increase (over past three years), agency mission statements that specifically address victim services, method of victim contact, services provided, services requested across all providers but not available, reasons some victims do not use services, degree of inter-agency communication and cooperation as perceived by victim assistance coordinators/victim liaison officers/community victim advocates, providers reporting a community committee or task force, and rural versus urban service providers.

Victimization Surveys

•463 *Criminal Victimization of Texas Residents.* Huntsville: Crime Victims' Institute, Criminal Justice Center, Sam Houston State University [annual, 2006–date].

<http://www.crimevictimsinstitute.org/pubs.html>

Presents the results of annual telephone surveys of approximately 700 randomly selected Texas residents on their experiences with violent victimization and property victimization. Demographic characteristics of the respondents are provided (including firearm ownership).

Research Note: Previously published under the title, *Texas Crime Victimization Report* (2004–2005).

•464 *National Crime Victimization Survey: MSA Data, 1979–2004.* Ann Arbor: National Archive of Criminal Justice Data, Inter-university Consortium for Political and Social Research, Institute for Social Research, University of Michigan, 2007.

<http://dx.doi.org/10.3886/ICPSR04576>

The National Crime Victimization Survey (NCVS) has been the nation's primary source of information on the frequency, characteristics, and consequences of criminal victimization since its inception in 1973. It comprises an annual data collection conducted by the Census Bureau for the Bureau of Justice Statistics, Office of Justice Programs, U.S. Department of Justice. The NCVS collects information on personal and property crimes, reported and not reported to the police, from a nationally representative stratified multistage cluster sample of U.S. households. Beginning in 1992, the NCVS categorizes crimes as "personal" or "property," which covers the personal crimes of rape and sexual attack, robbery, aggravated and simple assault and purse-snatching/pocket-picking; and the property crimes of burglary, theft, and motor vehicle theft. A rotating panel design is utilized in which households remain in the sample for three years. All residents age twelve or older are interviewed at six-month intervals for a total of seven interviews. The survey data include type of crime; month, time, and location of the crime; relationship between victim and offender; characteristics of the offender; self-protective actions taken by the victim during the incident and results of those actions; consequences of the victimization; type of injuries suffered; type of property lost; whether the crime was reported to police and reasons for reporting/not reporting; and offender use of weapons, drugs, and alcohol. Basic demographic information such as age, race, gender, marital status, and household income of the victim is also collected. This sampling strategy was developed explicitly to yield national estimates of criminal victimization. Therefore, given the sample design, the smallest geographic areas at which data is generally available to make estimates are Census Bureau regions (i.e., Northeast, Midwest, South, and West). However, the Census Bureau and the BJS have developed special subsets of NCVS data that are capable of providing reliable survey-based estimates of crime and victimization for the core counties within the nation's largest Metropolitan Statistical Areas (MSAs), given that heavily populated metropolitan areas constitute unique self-representing portions of the NCVS sample. This study contains two such data files, a weighted person-based file, and a weighted incident-based file, which contain the core counties within the top forty NCVS MSAs (which includes Dallas, Fort Worth–Arlington, Houston, and San Antonio). The person-based file contains select household and person variables for all people in NCVS-interviewed households in the core counties of these MSAs from January 1979 through December 2004. The incident-based file contains select household, person, and incident variables for persons who reported a violent crime within any of the core counties of these MSAs from January 1979 through December 2004. Household, person, and incident information for persons reporting non-violent crime are excluded from this file.

Chapter 9

Driving/Boating Under the Influence and Traffic Fatalities

Driving Under the Influence

465 *Alcohol-Impaired Drivers Involved in Fatal Crashes, by Gender and State, 2007–2008* [Traffic Safety Facts/Research Note]. Washington, D.C.: National Center for Statistics and Analysis, National Highway Traffic Safety Administration, U.S. Department of Transportation, 2009. DOT HS 811 195

<http://www-nrd.nhtsa.dot.gov/Pubs/811195.pdf>

Provides data on alcohol-impaired drivers involved in fatal crashes by gender and state, 2007–2008 (Table 6).

•466 *Alcohol-Impaired Driving* [Traffic Safety Facts]. Washington, D.C.: National Center for Statistics and Analysis, National Highway Traffic Safety Administration, U.S. Department of Transportation [annual, online only, 2006–date].

<http://purl.access.gpo.gov/GPO/LPS11019>

Provides data on traffic fatalities by state and the highest driver or motorcycle rider BAC (blood alcohol concentration) in the crash.

Research Note: Previously published under the title *Alcohol* (1994–2005).

467 *Alcohol-Related Fatalities and Alcohol Involvement Among Drivers and Motorcycle Operators in 2005.* [Traffic Safety Facts/Crash•Stats]. Washington, D.C.: National Center for Statistics and Analysis, National Highway Traffic Safety Administration, U.S. Department of Transportation, 2006. DOT HS 810 644

<http://purl.access.gpo.gov/GPO/LPS96237>

Provides state-level 2005 data on drivers and motorcycle operators with a BAC (blood alcohol concentration) $\geq$ 0.08 grams per deciliter involved in fatal crashes by age (Table 4), and alcohol-related fatalities, fatalities in crashes involving a BAC $\geq$ 0.08 grams per deciliter, and percent change, 2004–2005 (Table 5).

Research Note: Earlier editions are available (published under slightly varying titles).

468 *Drug Involvement of Fatally Injured Drivers: A Brief Statistical Summary.* [Traffic Safety Facts/Crash•Stats]. Washington, D.C.: National Center for Statistics and Analysis, National Highway Traffic Safety Administration, U.S. Department of Transportation, 2010. DOT HS 811 415

<http://www-nrd.nhtsa.dot.gov/Pubs/811415.pdf>

Reports the following state-level data (number and percentage) for fatally injured drivers: not tested for drugs; tested, no drugs reported; tested, drugs found; tested, results unknown; unknown if tested; and total.

469 *Fatalities and Fatality Rates in Alcohol-Impaired Driving Crashes by State* [Traffic Safety Facts/Research Note]. Washington, D.C.: National Center for Statistics and Analysis, National Highway Traffic Safety Administration, U.S. Department of Transportation [annual, 2001–date].

<http://www-nrd.nhtsa.dot.gov/Cats/listpublications.aspx?Id=B&ShowBy=DocType>

Provides state-level data on total alcohol-impaired fatalities and the corresponding fatality rates per 100 million VMT (vehicle miles travelled).

Research Note: Published under slightly varying titles.

470 *Fatalities in Crashes Involving Alcohol-Impaired 21- to 24-Year-Old Drivers During the December Holidays: A Brief Statistical Summary* [Traffic Safety Facts/Crash•Stats]. Washington, D.C.: National Center for Statistics and Analysis, National Highway Traffic Safety Administration, U.S. Department of Transportation, 2008. DOT HS 811 063

<http://www-nrd.nhtsa.dot.gov/Pubs/811063.pdf>

Reports fatalities in crashes involving an alcohol-impaired twenty-one- to twenty-four-year-old driver, by state, 2007 (Table 4).

•471 *Fatality Analysis Reporting System (FARS) Encyclopedia.* Washington, D.C.: National Center for Statistics and Analysis, National Highway Traffic Safety Administration, U.S. Department of Transportation [online only, 1994–date].

<http://purl.access.gpo.gov/GPO/LPS38001>

The Fatality Analysis Reporting System (FARS) is a census of all crashes involving motor vehicles traveling on public roadways in which a person (either a vehicle occupant or pedestrian) died within thirty days of the crash. It provides state-and county-level reports covering alcohol (number and percentage) for the following categories: highest blood alcohol concentration in crash, total killed in alcohol-related crashes, and total killed; blood alcohol concentration of the driver and total drivers involved in fatal crashes; blood alcohol concentration of the driver and total drivers killed in fatal crashes; and blood alcohol concentration of the driver and total surviving drivers involved in fatal crashes.

Research Note: See also entry 502. County-level data can be accessed in the States subsection. For background on FARS, see *Fatality Analysis Reporting System: Fatal Crash Data Overview.*

<http://www-nrd.nhtsa.dot.gov/pubs/farsbrochure.pdf>

472 Fell, James C., Elizabeth A. Langston, John H. Lacey, A. Scott Tippetts, and Ray Cotton. *Evaluation of Seven Publicized Enforcement Demonstration Programs to Reduce Impaired Driving: Georgia, Louisiana, Pennsylvania, Tennessee, Texas, Indiana, and Michigan* [Draft Report]. Washington, D.C.: National Highway Traffic Safety Administration, U.S. Department of Transportation, 2008.

<http://ntlsearch.bts.gov/tris/ntlc/nhtsa/record30205.shtm>

This report summarizes the evaluations of NHTSA-sponsored demonstration projects in seven states (including Texas), which emphasized highly visible law enforcement coupled with intensive publicity to reduce impaired driving. The Texas project targeted fourteen highly populated counties. In addition to a summary table showing the overall results of the study (p. 13), data is provided as follows: summary of state enforcement efforts (Table 1); summary of state public information, education, and media efforts (Table 2); Texas average monthly rates of fatalities and DWI arrests by year in the fourteen intervention counties (Table 8); annual DWI arrests for selected communities participating in the project in Texas (Table 9); summary of the equipment purchases in the Texas project (Table 10); observed and fitted bimonthly ratios of drinking drivers to non-drinking drivers in fatal crashes in Texas intervention counties (Fig. 17); FARS (Fatality Analysis Reporting System) analysis of seven states' alcohol demonstration program results (Table 19); and results of the impact of seven-state publicized enforcement programs on drinking drivers in fatal crashes in relation to comparison states (Fig. 20).

473 McKnight, A. Scott, Derrik E. Watson, Robert B. Voas, and James C. Fell. *Update of Vehicle Sanction Laws and Their Application.* Volume 2, *Vehicle Sanctions Status by State* [Final Report]. Washington, D.C.: National Highway Traffic Safety Administration, U.S. Department of Transportation, 2008. DOT HR 811 028B

<http://ntlsearch.bts.gov/tris/ntlc/nhtsa/record32848.shtm>

Provides a summary of legal sanctions directed at the vehicles owned by convicted DWI offenders to limit their illicit driving. These sanctions fall into three broad categories: (1) programs that require special license plates on the vehicles of DWI offenders and/or confiscating the vehicle plates and vehicle registration; (2) devices installed in the vehicle that prevent its operation if the driver has been drinking (alcohol ignition interlock); and (3) programs that impound, immobilize, confiscate, or forfeit the offender's vehicle. Appendix A, "Presence and Status of Vehicle Sanction Laws in the States," presents 2004 data on six sanctions (alcohol ignition interlock, vehicle impoundment, vehicle immobilization, vehicle forfeiture, license plate and vehicle registration suspension, and special license plates) as follows: presence of vehicle sanction laws in the states and their usage (Table A-2); presence of vehicle sanction laws in the states and type of offender application (Table A-3); presence of vehicle sanction laws in the states and mandatory or discretionary application (Table A-4); and presence of vehicle sanction laws in the states and their system application (Table A-5).

•**474** *Motorcycles* [Traffic Safety Facts]. Washington, D.C.: National Center for Statistics and Analysis, National Highway Traffic Safety Administration, U.S. Department of Transportation [annual, online only, 1993–date].
<http://purl.access.gpo.gov/GPO/LPS11107>

Provides data on motorcycle rider fatalities by state, helmet use, and BAC (blood alchohol concentration).

475 *Percentage of Adults Who Reported Drinking and Driving by State and Gender, BRFSS, 1984–2008.* Bethesda, Md.: Alcohol Epidemiologic Data System, Division of Epidemiology and Prevention Research, National Institute on Alcohol Abuse and Alcoholism, U.S. Department of Health and Human Services (updated, 2009).
<http://www.niaaa.nih.gov/Resources/DatabaseResources/QuickFacts/Adults/brfss04.htm>

The Behavioral Risk Factor Surveillance System (BRFSS), established in 1984, is a state-based system of ongoing health surveys that collects information on health risk behaviors, preventive health practices, and health care access through random-digit-dialed household telephone surveys of noninstitutionalized adults aged eighteen years and over residing in the United States. This report presents state-level statistics on self-reported adult drinking and driving.

•**476** *State Alcohol-Impaired Driving Estimates* [Traffic Safety Facts]. Washington, D.C.: National Center for Statistics and Analysis, National Highway Traffic Safety Administration, U.S. Department of Transportation [annual, online only, 2007–date].
<http://purl.access.gpo.gov/GPO/LPS11122>

Provides state-level data (for 1982 and the reporting year) on fatalities by highest driver or motorcycle rider BAC (blood alcohol concentration) in the crash; drivers involved in fatal crashes by BAC of the driver; driver fatalities by state and BAC test status; surviving drivers by state and BAC test status; BAC test status for drivers involved in fatal traffic crashes; and estimated percentage of fatalities in alcohol-impaired-driving crashes and estimated percentage of drivers involved in fatal crashes with a BAC ≥ 0.08.

Research Note: Previously published under the title *State Alcohol Estimates* (1994–2006).

477 *State Data System Crash Data Report: 1990–1999.* Washington, D.C.: National Center for Statistics and Analysis, National Highway Traffic Safety Administration, U.S. Department of Transportation, 2002. DOT 809 301
<http://purl.access.gpo.gov/GPO/LPS22532>

Contains nine tables of descriptive statistics summarizing alcohol-related motor vehicle crashes that occurred from 1990–1999 in each of the seventeen states (including Texas) that participate in the State Data System.

Research Note: See also entry 521.

478 "State Estimates of Persons Aged 18 or Older Driving Under the Influence of Alcohol or Illicit Drugs." *The NSDUH Report* (April 17, 2008), pp. 1–4.
<http://www.oas.samhsa.gov/2k8/stateDUI/stateDUI.cfm>

Presents state-level estimates of past year driving under the influence of alcohol and illicit drugs among current drivers aged eighteen or older utilizing annual averages based on combined data from the 2004, 2005, and 2006 National Surveys on Drug Use and Health (NSDUH). State estimates are rank ordered from highest to lowest and divided into quintiles.

Research Note: The annual NSDUH is conducted by the Office of Applied Studies, Substance Abuse and Mental Health Services Administration, U.S. Department of Health and Human Services. The survey defines "illicit drugs" to include marijuana/hashish, cocaine (including crack), inhalants, hallucinogens, heroin, or prescription-type drugs used non-medically. The HTML version also contains the data table that was used to construct each map, which is not found in the print or PDF versions.

479 *State Traffic Data* [Traffic Safety Facts]. Washington, D.C.: National Center for Statistics and Analysis, National Highway Traffic Safety Administration, U.S. Department of Transportation [annual, online only, 1993–date].
<http://purl.access.gpo.gov/GPO/LPS16516>

Provides data on alcohol involvement in fatal traffic crashes for the reporting year and the year one decade previous (with percentage change); and states with 0.08 BAC illegal per se laws.

Research Note: See also entry 522.

•480 *State Traffic Safety Information for Year [year].* Washington, D.C.: National Center for Statistics and Analysis, National Highway Traffic Safety Administration, U.S. Department of Transportation [annual, online only, 2001–date].
<http://purl.access.gpo.gov/GPO/LPS43372>

Provides detailed county-level statistics on alcohol-related motor vehicle crash fatalities and alcohol-related fatalities as a percentage of all motor vehicle crash fatalities; and a ranking of the top ten counties for both.

Research Note: See also entry 523.

•481 *State Transportation Statistics.* Washington, D.C. Bureau of Transportation Statistics, Research and Innovative Technology Administration, U.S. Department of Transportation [annual, 2004–date].

<http://purl.access.gpo.gov/GPO/LPS74934>

Contains statistics on fatalities in motor vehicle crashes involving high blood alcohol concentration (Section B).

Research Note: See also entry 524.

482 *State Trends in Drinking Behaviors, 1984–2001* [U.S. Alcohol Epidemiologic Data Reference Manual, Vol. 7]. Bethesda, Md.: National Institute on Alcohol Abuse and Alcoholism, National Institutes of Health, Public Health Service, U.S. Department of Health and Human Services, 2003. NIH 02-5213

Presents state-level survey results on percentage distribution of driving after having too much to drink one or more times in the past month for selected demographic characteristics, 1984–2000 (Table 3).

483 Subramanian, Rajesh. *State Alcohol Related Fatality Rates 2002* [Technical Report]. Washington, D.C.: National Center for Statistics and Analysis, National Highway Traffic Safety Administration, U.S. Department of Transportation, 2003. DOT HS 809 673

<http://purl.access.gpo.gov/GPO/LPS85958>

Provides individual state profiles showing estimated rates of alcohol involvement in traffic fatalities from 1982, the first data year for which NHTSA began reporting alcohol data, to 2002. Reports fatalities and fatality rates (total and alcohol-related) per 100 million vehicle miles traveled (VMT), and the change in alcohol-related fatality rates over time for Texas versus the United States. Color maps show alcohol-related fatalities by county and alcohol-related fatalities as a percentage of total fatalities by county.

•484 *Texas Motor Vehicle Crash Statistics.* Austin: Traffic Operations Division, Texas Department of Transportation [annual, online only, 2003–date].

<http://www.dot.state.tx.us/txdot_library/drivers_vehicles/publications/crash_statistics/default.htm>

Provides data on Texas motor vehicle crashes under the following categories: DUI drivers in fatal crashes by driver age; alcohol testing in fatal crashes; BAC test results on fatally injured drivers; BAC tests on fatally injured drivers; DUI fatalities by age; total and DUI fatal and injury crashes comparison; DUI crashes and injuries in cities and towns; DUI crashes and injuries by county—Texas map; DUI crashes and injuries by county; DUI driver fatalities by county and age; DUI related fatalities by county and age; DUI drivers involved in crashes by age; DUI related crashes by hour and day of the week; DUI crashes by hour of the day; DUI related fatal crashes by hour; DUI related total crashes by hour of the day; DUI fatal crashes and fatalities by month and day; fatalities in crashes involving DUI; and alcohol testing in fatal crashes with DUI drivers.

Research Note: See also entry 528. Information contained in these reports represents reportable data collected from Texas Peace Officer's Crash Reports received and processed by TXDOT. Earlier data can be found in various report series published by the Texas Department of Public Safety.

485 *Traffic Safety Annual Assessment—Highlights: A Brief Statistical Summary* [Traffic Safety Facts/Crash•Stats]. Washington, D.C.: National Center for Statistics and Analysis, National Highway Traffic Safety Administration, U.S. Department of Transportation [annual, online only, 2007–date].
<http://www-nrd.nhtsa.dot.gov/cats/index.aspx>

Reports state-level driving fatalities (total and alcohol-impaired) for the most recent two reporting years.

Research Note: Publications in the Traffic Safety Annual Assessment report major findings from the Annual Assessment of Motor Vehicle Traffic Crash Fatalities and Injuries, which is based on the Fatality Analysis Reporting System (FARS) and the National Automotive Sampling System General Estimates System (NASS GES).

•486 *Traffic Safety Facts: A Compilation of Motor Vehicle Crash Data from the Fatality Analysis Reporting System and the General Estimates System.* Washington, D.C.: National Center for Statistics and Analysis, National Highway Traffic Safety Administration, U.S. Department of Transportation [annual].
<http://purl.access.gpo.gov/GPO/LPS16514>

Provides the following state-level data in Chapter 5: persons killed by highest blood alcohol concentration (BAC) in the crash; drivers involved in fatal crashes, by BAC of the driver; drivers killed in fatal crashes, by BAC of the driver; and surviving drivers involved in fatal crashes by BAC of the driver.

Research Note: See also entry 529.

487 Yi, Hsiao-ye, Chiung M. Chen, and Gerald D. Williams. *Trends in Alcohol-Related Fatal Traffic Crashes, United States, 1982–2004* [Surveillance Report]. Bethesda, Md.: Alcohol Epidemiologic Data System, Division of Epidemiology and Prevention Research, National Institute on Alcohol Abuse and Alcoholism, U.S. Department of Health and Human Services, 2006.

<http://purl.fdlp.gov/GPO/gpo703>

Provides state-level data for 1998 and 2004 on total and alcohol-related traffic fatalities (Table 6), and drivers involved in fatal traffic crashes and given blood alcohol concentration (BAC) tests, according to injury severity (Table 9).

Research Note: Earlier editions are available.

488 "Youth Risk Behavior Surveillance Survey—United States." [Surveillance Summaries]. *Morbidity and Mortality Weekly Report* (*MMWR*) [biennial, 1993–date].

<http://www.cdc.gov/mmwr/mmwr_ss/ss_cvol.html>

One report is published biennially under this title (authors and cover dates vary). It provides survey results on the percentage of high school students who rode in a car or other vehicle driven by someone who had been drinking alcohol, or who drove a car or other vehicle when they had been drinking alcohol (total, male, and female), by state and selected local areas.

Research Note: The survey is conducted in odd-numbered years and the report is published the following year. Online access to current and past editions is also available on the website of the Division of Adolescent and School Health, National Center for Chronic Disease Prevention and Health Promotion, Centers for Disease Control and Prevention, U.S. Department of Health and Human Services. <http://www.cdc.gov/healthyyouth/yrbs/index.htm>

Boating Under the Influence

•489 *Boating Statistics*. Washington, D.C.: U.S. Coast Guard, U.S. Department of Homeland Security [annual].

<http://purl.access.gpo.gov/GPO/LPS27443>

Provides state-level accident data (total, fatal, non-fatal injury, number killed, number injured, and property damage); and five-year state-level summaries of boating accidents (total, fatal, and number killed); alcohol involvement in boating accidents (total, number killed, and number injured); and alcohol use as a contributing factor in boating accidents (total accidents and fatalities).

490 *State Transportation Statistics*. Washington, D.C.: Bureau of Transportation Statistics, Research and Innovative Technology Administration, U.S. Department of Transportation [annual].

<http://purl.access.gpo.gov/GPO/LPS74934>

Section B ("Safety") contains statistics from the U.S. Coast Guard on alcohol involvement in recreational boating accidents.

Traffic Fatalities

•491 *Annual Report*. Austin: Texas Child Fatality Review Team [2006–date].
<http://www.dshs.state.tx.us/mch/Child_Fatality_Review.shtm>

Child fatality review teams are multidisciplinary, multi-agency working groups that review child deaths on a local level from a public health perspective with the goal of decreasing the incidence of preventable child deaths (Tex. Fam. Code Ann. §§ 264.501–.515 (Vernon 2008 & Supp. 2010)). Their work is supported and coordinated by the Texas Department of State Health Services. This report contains data on child fatalities in motor vehicle crashes as follows: race/ethnicity, age, and sex of child who died of motor vehicle crashes (Table 9); position of child in motor vehicle crash (Chart 12); causes listed for motor vehicle crash (Chart 13); and car or booster seat usage for children less than nine years old (Chart 14).

Research Note: Reports are available online back to 2000–2001. Reports were biennial prior to 2006.

492 *Bicyclists and Other Cyclists* [Traffic Safety Facts]. Washington, D.C.: National Center for Statistics and Analysis, National Highway Traffic Safety Administration, U.S. Department of Transportation [annual, online only, 2005–date].
<http://purl.access.gpo.gov/GPO/LPS111171>

Provides state-level data on traffic fatalities and fatality rates of bicyclists and other cyclists.

Research Note: Previously published under the title *Pedalcyclists* (1993–2004).

493 Burgess, Marilouise. *Contrasting Rural and Urban Fatal Crashes 1994–2003* [Technical Report]. Washington, D.C.: National Center for Statistics and Analysis, National Highway Traffic Safety Administration, U.S. Department of Transportation, 2005. DOT HS 809 896
<http://purl.access.gpo.gov/GPO/LPS97980>

Reports the percentage of rural fatal crashes from 1994 to 2003, by state (Table 1).

494 *Buses Involved in Fatal Accidents Factbook.* Ann Arbor: Center for Truck and Bus Statistics, Transportation Research Institute, University of Michigan [annual].
<http://www.umtri.umich.edu/divisionPage.php?pageID=4>

Provides state-level statistics for bus involvement in fatal traffic accidents by year and bus type.

Research Note: Factbooks are located in the Publications subsection.

495 Cejun Liu, Chou-Lin Chen, Rajesh Subramanian, and Dennis Utter. *Analysis of Speeding-Related Fatal Motor Vehicle Traffic Crashes* [Technical Report]. Washington, D.C.: National Center for Statistics and Analysis, National Highway Traffic Safety Administration, U.S. Department of Transportation, 2005. DOT HS 809 839

<http://purl.access.gpo.gov/GPO/LPS98245>

Reports speeding-related fatalities as a percentage of total fatalities, and total fatalities, speeding-related fatalities, and their percentage of the total, by state, 1983–2002 (Appendix 6.17a–b).

496 Chang, Dow. *National Pedestrian Crash Report.* Washington, D.C.: National Center for Statistics and Analysis, National Highway Traffic Safety Administration, U.S. Department of Transportation, 2008. DOT HS 810 968

<http://purl.access.gpo.gov/GPO/LPS98115>

Provides statistics on pedestrian crash deaths (1997–2006), by state (Table A-6) and city (Table A-7).

497 *Children* [Traffic Safety Facts]. Washington, D.C.: National Center for Statistics and Analysis, National Highway Traffic Safety Administration, U.S. Department of Transportation [annual, online only, 1994–date].

<http://purl.access.gpo.gov/GPO/LPS11150>

Provides data on total traffic fatalities among children age fourteen and under by state and age group.

498 *Comparison of Motorcycle Rider Fatalities in Traffic Crashes, 2005–2006: A Brief Statistical Summary* [Traffic Safety Facts/Crash•Stats]. Washington, D.C.: National Center for Statistics and Analysis, National Highway Traffic Safety Administration, U.S. Department of Transportation, 2007. DOT HS 810 820

<http://purl.access.gpo.gov/GPO/LPS96241>

Presents data on motorcycle rider fatalities in traffic crashes by state, year, change, percentage change, and motorcycle rider fatalities as percentage of total fatalities (Table 2).

499 *Crash Statistics—State Profiles.* Washington, D.C.: Federal Motor Carrier Safety Administration, U.S. Department of Transportation [annual, online only, 2001–date].

<http://ai.volpe.dot.gov/CrashProfile/StateCrashProfileMain.asp>

This website provides statistics on fatal and non-fatal large truck crashes organized into seven focus areas: summary, vehicle, driver, environment, crash, carrier, and maps.

•**500** "Deaths: Final Data for [year]." *National Vital Statistics Reports.* Hyattsville, Md.: National Center for Health Statistics, Centers for Disease Control and Prevention, U.S. Department of Health and Human Services [annual, 1997–date].

<http://purl.access.gpo.gov/GPO/LPS2365>

One report is published annually under this title (authors and cover dates vary). It presents state-level data for number of deaths, death rates, and age-adjusted death rates for major causes of death utilizing the *International Classification of Diseases—Tenth Revision (ICD-10)*. Major causes of death listed include motor vehicle accidents.

Research Note: This series supersedes *Monthly Vital Statistics Reports (MVSR)*.

501 *Drivers 65 and Older Have Lower Involvement Rates in Fatal Crashes: A Brief Statistical Summary* [Traffic Safety Facts/Crash•Stats]. Washington, D.C.: National Center for Statistics and Analysis, National Highway Traffic Safety Administration, U.S. Department of Transportation, 2007. DOT HS 810 779

<http://purl.access.gpo.gov/GPO/LPS96240>

Provides data on drivers sixty five and older involved in fatal crashes by state, year, and involvement rate, 2001–2005 (Table 2).

•**502** *Fatality Analysis Reporting System (FARS) Encyclopedia.* Washington, D.C.: National Center for Statistics and Analysis, National Highway Traffic Safety Administration, U.S. Department of Transportation [online only, 1994–date].

<http://purl.access.gpo.gov/GPO/LPS38001>

The Fatality Analysis Reporting System (FARS) is a census of all crashes involving motor vehicles traveling on public roadways in which a person (either a vehicle occupant or pedestrian) died within thirty days of the crash. It provides the following state- and county-level reports: crashes and all victims (traffic fatalities and percentage change from previous year; and fatal crashes by first harmful event, roadway function class, person type, and age group); occupants (occupants killed by vehicle type and passenger vehicle restraint use); pedestrians (fatality rates); and fatalities and fatality rates.

Research Note: See also entry 471. County-level data can be accessed in the States subsection. For background on FARS, see *Fatality Analysis Reporting System: Fatal Crash Data Overview.*

<http://www-nrd.nhtsa.dot.gov/pubs/farsbrochure.pdf>

503 *Fatally Injured Motorcycle Operators by License Status*: *A Brief Statistical Summary* [Traffic Safety Facts/Crash•Stats]. Washington, D.C.: National Center for Statistics and Analysis, National Highway Traffic Safety Administration, U.S. Department of Transportation, 2008. DOT HS 810 892

<http://purl.access.gpo.gov/GPO/LPS96247>

Provides state-level data on fatally injured motorcycle operators by license status, 2002–2006 (Table 2).

504 *Federal Railroad Administration Office of Safety Analysis*. Washington, D.C.: Office of Safety Analysis, Federal Railroad Administration, U.S. Department of Transportation [annual, online only, 1975–date].

<http://safetydata.fra.dot.gov/officeofsafety/>

Provides detailed county-level statistics on fatal and nonfatal highway–rail incidents and trespassing incidents (not at crossings). The data is searchable by railroad.

Research Note: A highway-rail incident is any impact between a rail and a highway user at a crossing site, regardless of severity. Includes motor vehicles and other highway/roadway/sidewalk users at both public and private crossings.

•505 *Highway Statistics*. Washington, D.C.: Federal Highway Administration, U.S. Department of Transportation [annual, 1945–date].

<http://purl.access.gpo.gov/GPO/LPS4717>

Contains state-level statistics for persons fatally injured in motor vehicle crashes by federal-aid highways and by function system (Section V).

Research Note: Editions are available online back to 1945.

506 *Large Truck Crash Facts.* Washington, D.C.: Analysis Division, Federal Motor Carrier Safety Administration, U.S. Department of Transportation [annual, 1999–date].

<http://purl.access.gpo.gov/GPO/LPS11206>

Provides state-level data—for the reporting year and the previous decade—on fatalities in crashes involving large trucks (Table 30); fatal crashes involving large trucks (Table 31); large trucks involved in fatal crashes (Table 32); single-vehicle fatal crashes involving large trucks (Table 33); and multiple-vehicle fatal crashes involving large trucks (Table 34).

507 *Large Trucks* [Traffic Safety Facts]. Washington, D.C.: National Center for Statistics and Analysis, National Highway Traffic Safety Administration, U.S. Department of Transportation [annual, online only, 1993–date].

<http://purl.access.gpo.gov/GPO/LPS11109>

Provides data on large truck involvement in fatal crashes by state.

508 *Most Fatalities in Young (15- to 20-Year-Old) Driver Crashes Are Young Drivers and Their Young Passengers: A Brief Statistical Summary* [Traffic Safety Facts/Crash•Stats]. Washington, D.C.: National Center for Statistics and Analysis, National Highway Traffic Safety Administration, U.S. Department of Transportation, 2006. DOT HS 810 597

<http://purl.access.gpo.gov/GPO/LPS96236>

Provides state-level 2004 data on fatalities in crashes involving a fifteen- to twenty-year-old driver by person type (Table 2).

509 "Motor Vehicle-Related Death Rates—United States, 1999–2005." *Morbidity and Mortality Weekly Report (MMWR)* 58, no. 7 (February 27, 2009): 161–165.

<http://www.cdc.gov/mmwr/preview/mmwrhtml/mm5807a1.htm>

Reports the number of motor-vehicle deaths and death rates, by state and U.S. Census region, 1999–2005 (Table 1).

510 *Motorcycles* [Traffic Safety Facts]. Washington, D.C.: National Center for Statistics and Analysis, National Highway Traffic Safety Administration, U.S. Department of Transportation [annual, online only, 1993–date].

<http://purl.access.gpo.gov/GPO/LPS11107>

Provides data on motorcycle rider fatalities by state, helmet use, and operator alcohol use.

511 Nguyen, Nhatthien Q. "Traffic Crash Investigation Units." *TELEMASP Bulletin* [Texas Law Enforcement Management and Administrative Statistics Program] 16, no. 3 (May/June 2009): 1–8.

<http://www.lemitonline.org/telemasp/>

Presents data from a survey of sixty-three Texas law enforcement agencies on their traffic crash investigation units as follows: criteria used for selection of crash investigators (Fig. 1); initial training required for crash investigators (Fig. 2); sources of funding for equipment (Fig. 3); permanently assigned equipment to crash investigators (Fig. 4); type of crashes handled (Fig. 5); type of crash engendering downloading the Event Data Recorder (Fig. 6); and comparison of review processes (Fig. 7). Nguyen notes that "Despite the enormous impact of traffic accidents, especially fatalities, they are often overlooked in the criminal justice system."

512 *Occupant Protection* [Traffic Safety Facts]. Washington, D.C.: National Center for Statistics and Analysis, National Highway Traffic Safety Administration, U.S. Department of Transportation [annual, online only, 1993–date].

<http://purl.access.gpo.gov/GPO/LPS11092>

Provides data on passenger vehicle occupants killed by state and restraint use.

513 *Older Population* [Traffic Safety Facts]. Washington, D.C.: National Center for Statistics and Analysis, National Highway Traffic Safety Administration, U.S. Department of Transportation [annual, online only, 1993–date].
<http://purl.access.gpo.gov/GPO/LPS16515>

Provides data on driver involvement in fatal traffic crashes and fatalities in traffic crashes, by state and age group.

514 *Passenger Vehicles* [Traffic Safety Facts]. Washington, D.C.: National Center for Statistics and Analysis, National Highway Traffic Safety Administration, U.S. Department of Transportation [annual, online only, 2008–date].
<http://purl.access.gpo.gov/GPO/LPS11066>

Provides data on passenger vehicle occupant fatalities, number and percentage, by state and vehicle type.

515 *Pedestrians* [Traffic Safety Facts]. Washington, D.C.: National Center for Statistics and Analysis, National Highway Traffic Safety Administration, U.S. Department of Transportation [annual, online only, 1993–date].
<http://purl.access.gpo.gov/GPO/LPS11066>

Provides state-level data on pedestrian traffic fatalities and fatality rates.

516 *Race and Ethnicity* [Traffic Safety Facts]. Washington, D.C.: National Center for Statistics and Analysis, National Highway Traffic Safety Administration, U.S. Department of Transportation [annual, online only, 2006–date].
<http://www-nrd.nhtsa.dot.gov/Pubs/810995.pdf>

Reports motor vehicle traffic fatalities by region, state, and race/ethnicity (Table 7).

517 *Rural/Urban Comparison* [Traffic Safety Facts]. Washington, D.C.: National Center for Statistics and Analysis, National Highway Traffic Safety Administration, U.S. Department of Transportation [annual, online only, 2001–date].
<http://purl.access.gpo.gov/GPO/LPS65248>

Provides data on total fatalities (number and percentage) by state and location (urban, rural, and unknown).

Research Note: The 2006 edition was the first to report state-level data.

518 Shankar, Umesh. *Pedestrian Roadway Fatalities* [Technical Report]. Washington, D.C.: National Center for Statistics and Analysis, National Highway Traffic Safety Administration, U.S. Department of Transportation, 2003. DOT HS 809 456

<http://purl.access.gpo.gov/GPO/LPS49031>

Ranks pedestrian fatality rates from all crashes by U.S. cities with populations of 100,000 or more (Table B-25).

519 Schrock, Steven D., et al. *An Analysis of Fatal Work Zone Crashes in Texas*. College Station, Tex: Texas Transportation Institute, Texas A&M University System, 2004. FHWA/TX-05/0-4028-1

<http://tti.tamu.edu/documents/0-4028-1.pdf>

Presents data collected by a Texas Transportation Institute research team between February 1, 2003, and April 30, 2004, who received notification and responded to seventy-seven fatal work zone crash locations in twenty-one of the twenty-five Texas Department of Transportation (TxDOT) districts. These incidents resulted in the deaths of eighty-eight persons, including seventy-seven motorists or passengers, one bicyclist, two pedestrians, six contractor workers, one police officer, and one TxDOT employee. Factors investigated included roadway type, crash location within the work zone, work zone activity type, weather conditions, lighting conditions, alcohol involvement, large truck involvement, and level of work zone influence.

520 *Speeding* [Traffic Safety Facts]. Washington, D.C.: National Center for Statistics and Analysis, National Highway Traffic Safety Administration, U.S. Department of Transportation [annual, online only, 1994–date].

<http://purl.access.gpo.gov/GPO/LPS11144>

Provides data on speeding-related traffic fatalities by state, road type, and speed limit.

521 *State Data System Crash Data Report: 1990–1999.* Washington, D.C.: National Center for Statistics and Analysis, National Highway Traffic Safety Administration, U.S. Department of Transportation, 2002. DOT 809 301

<http://purl.access.gpo.gov/GPO/LPS22532>

Contains forty-two tables of descriptive statistics summarizing motor vehicle traffic crashes that occurred from 1990–1999 in each of the seventeen states (including Texas) that participate in the State Data System, in the following categories: crashes, vehicles, people, speeding, rollovers, motorcycles, large trucks, fatalities and injuries by age, and safety equipment.

Research Note: See also entry 477.

522 *State Traffic Data* [Traffic Safety Facts]. Washington, D.C.: National Center for Statistics and Analysis, National Highway Traffic Safety Administration, U.S. Department of Transportation [annual, online only, 1993–date]. <http://purl.access.gpo.gov/GPO/LPS16516>

Provides data on traffic fatalities and fatality rates; traffic fatalities and percentage change, 1975–date; speeding-related traffic fatalities by road type and speed limit; passenger vehicle occupants and motorcyclists killed; traffic fatalities and vehicles involved in fatal crashes by type; fatalities in the beds of pickup trucks by age; key provisions of occupant restraint laws and seat belt use rates; and a history of state motorcycle helmet laws.

Research Note: See also entry 479.

•523 *State Traffic Safety Information for Year [year].* Washington, D.C.: National Center for Statistics and Analysis, National Highway Traffic Safety Administration, U.S. Department of Transportation [online only, 2001–date]. <http://purl.access.gpo.gov/GPO/LPS43372>

Provides detailed county-level statistics on motor vehicle crash fatalities and fatality rank (rate per 100,000 population as compared to rates for all U.S. counties) for the following categories: total, single vehicle, non-junction, intersection, intersection-related, speeding involved, pedestrians, bicyclists and other cyclists, large truck involved, roadway departure, passenger car occupants, light truck/van occupants, other/unknown occupants (not including motorcycles), total occupants (not including motorcyclists), and motorcycle riders. Also included are top ten county rankings for total fatalities/rates and motorcyclists fatality/rates, general statewide data on the use of occupant restraints and motorcycle helmets, and state GIS location-based fatal traffic crash maps.

Research Note: See also entry 480.

•524 *State Transportation Statistics.* Washington, D.C.: Bureau of Transportation Statistics, Research and Innovative Technology Administration, U.S. Department of Transportation [annual, 2004–date]. <http://purl.access.gpo.gov/GPO/LPS74934>

Section B contains statistics on highway traffic fatalities and fatality rates; passenger car and light truck occupants killed and restraint use; large truck involvement in fatal crashes; safety belt laws and use; pedestrian fatalities involving motor vehicles; rail incidents and fatalities (including freight railroad, Amtrak, and commuter rail operations); highway-rail grade crossing incidents and fatalities (including freight railroad, Amtrak, and commuter rail operations); train accident/incident fatalities, including at highway-rail crossings, by category of person killed; and transit incidents/fatalities (all transit modes).

Research Note: See also entry 481.

525 *States with Primary Enforcement Laws Have Lower Fatality Rates (Updated)* [Traffic Safety Facts/Research Note]. Washington, D.C.: National Center for Statistics and Analysis, National Highway Traffic Safety Administration, U.S. Department of Transportation, 2008. DOT HS 810 921

<http://purl.access.gpo.gov/GPO/LPS99445>

Reports state-level 2006 data on passenger vehicle occupant fatality rates per 100,000 population by age (Table 4). States with primary safety belt use laws at the end of 2006 are highlighted in the table.

Research Note: This is an update of *States with Primary Enforcement Laws Have Lower Fatality Rates* (DOT HS 810 557). <http://purl.access.gpo.gov/GPO/LPS99450>

526 Subramanian, Rajesh, and Louis Lombardo. *Analysis of Fatal Motor Vehicle Traffic Crashes and Fatalities at Intersections, 1997 to 2004.* Washington, D.C.: National Center for Statistics and Analysis, National Highway Traffic Safety Administration, U.S. Department of Transportation, 2007. DOT HS 810 682

<http://purl.access.gpo.gov/GPO/LPS98035>

Provides state-level statistics for 1997–2004 on fatal crashes and fatalities at intersections by type of traffic control device (Table 5), and fatal two-vehicle crashes and fatalities at intersections that were not part of the National Highway System (NHS) by type of traffic control device (Table 35).

527 *Texas Selected Health Facts.* Austin: Center for Health Statistics, Texas Department of State Health Services [annual, online only, 2000–date].

<http://www.dshs.state.tx.us/chs/cfs/>

Provides statistics on traffic fatalities at the state, public health region, and county levels. Beginning with 2006 data, searches can be conducted utilizing an array of other geographical limiters, including Metropolitan Statistical Areas (MSAs).

•528 *Texas Motor Vehicle Crash Statistics.* Austin: Traffic Operations Division, Texas Department of Transportation [annual, online only, 2003–date].

<http://www.dot.state.tx.us/txdot_library/drivers_vehicles/publications/crash_statistics/default.htm>

Provides data on Texas motor vehicle crashes under the following categories: motor vehicle traffic crash highlights; statewide traffic crash rates; fatal crashes and fatalities by month and road type; fatalities by age, person type (driver, passenger, pedestrian, pedalcyclist), and gender; restraint use by injury severity and seat position; motorcyclist fatalities and serious injuries by age group with seat position and helmet use; rural and urban crashes and injuries by severity; crashes and injuries in cities and towns; fatal crashes and fatalities by county and road type; crashes and injuries by county; crashes and injuries by date; fatal and non-fatal crashes by month and day of the week; fatal and non-fatal crashes by hour and day of the week; fatal motor vehicle traffic crashes and fatalities during holiday periods; first harmful event of crashes and injuries by severity; fatalities in crashes involving speed—over limit; crash contributing factors light conditions for crashes; weather conditions for crashes; road surface condition for crashes; ages of drivers in crashes; count of units in crashes by unit type; and crashes by vehicle contributing factor.

Research Note: See also entry 484. Information contained in these reports represents reportable data collected from Texas Peace Officer's Crash Reports received and processed by TX-DOT. Earlier data can be found in various report series published by the Texas Department of Public Safety.

•529 *Traffic Safety Facts: A Compilation of Motor Vehicle Crash Data from the Fatality Analysis Reporting System and the General Estimates System.* Washington, D.C.: National Center for Statistics and Analysis, National Highway Traffic Safety Administration, U.S. Department of Transportation [annual].
<http://purl.access.gpo.gov/GPO/LPS16514>

Provides the following state-level data: traffic fatalities and percentage change from the previous year; fatal crashes by first harmful event; fatal crashes by roadway function class; fatalities by roadway function class; persons killed, licensed drivers, registered vehicles, population, and fatality rates; persons killed by person type (driver, passenger, motorcyclist, pedestrian, pedalcyclist, and other/unknown); persons killed by age group; occupants killed by vehicle type; passenger car and light truck occupants killed by restraint use; ranking of pedestrian fatality rates; speeding-related traffic fatalities, by road type and speed limit; rural/urban fatal crashes and average emergency medical services (EMS) response times; persons killed, population, and fatality rates by city; and fatalities and fatality rates, 1975–date (Chapter 5).

Research Note: See also entry 486.

530 *Trends in Fatal Crashes Among Drivers With Invalid Licenses* [Research Note]. Washington, D.C.: National Center for Statistics and Analysis, National Highway Traffic Safety Administration, U.S. Department of Transportation, 2009. DOT HS 811 229
<http://www-nrd.nhtsa.dot.gov/Pubs/811229.pdf>

Reports state-level data on the number of drivers sixteen and older in fatal crashes with invalid licenses by year, 1998–2007 (Table 2), and by selected statistics (Table 3).

531 *Trucks Involved in Fatal Accidents Factbook.* Ann Arbor: Center for Truck and Bus Statistics, Transportation Research Institute, University of Michigan [annual].

<http://www.umtri.umich.edu/divisionPage.php?pageID=4>

Provides state-level statistics for medium and heavy truck involvement in fatal traffic accidents by year and truck configuration.

Research Note: Factbooks are located in the Publications subsection.

532 Varghese, Cherian, and Umesh Shankar. *Passenger Vehicle Occupant Fatalities by Day and Night —A Contrast* [Traffic Safety Facts/Crash•Stats]. Washington, D.C.: National Center for Statistics and Analysis, National Highway Traffic Safety Administration, U.S. Department of Transportation, 2007. DOT HS 810 637

<http://purl.access.gpo.gov/GPO/LPS99420>

Presents passenger vehicle occupant fatalities in 2005 by state, time of day, and restraint use (Table 1).

•533 *WISQARS*™ [Web-based Injury Statistics Query and Reporting System]. Atlanta, Ga.: National Center for Injury Prevention and Control, Centers for Disease Control and Prevention, U.S. Department of Health and Human Services [online only, 1981–date].

<http://www.cdc.gov/injury/wisqars/index.html>

This database allows users to generate reports on injury mortality utilizing the *International Classification of Diseases—Tenth Revision (ICD-10)*. Output can be customized using the following variables: intent or manner of the injury; cause or mechanism of the injury (e.g., motor vehicle—traffic); census region or state; race; Hispanic origin; sex and age group; and year(s). Injury rates can be compared using the age adjusting option. Reports can also be generated utilizing the same variables for the leading cause of death for all causes with drill down to ICD codes (1994–date).

Research Note: Data prior to 1999 is presented in tables utilizing the *International Classification of Diseases—Ninth Revision (ICD-9)*.

534 *Young Drivers* [Traffic Safety Facts]. Washington, D.C.: National Center for Statistics and Analysis, National Highway Traffic Safety Administration, U.S. Department of Transportation [annual, online only, 1994–date].

<http://purl.access.gpo.gov/GPO/LPS11020>

Provides data on fatalities in crashes involving young drivers (ages fifteen to twenty) by state and fatality type.

Chapter 10

Substance Abuse and Treatment

Drug-related Fatalities

•535 "Deaths: Final Data for [year]." *National Vital Statistics Reports.* Hyattsville, Md.: National Center for Health Statistics, Centers for Disease Control and Prevention, U.S. Department of Health and Human Services [annual, 1997–date].

<http://purl.access.gpo.gov/GPO/LPS2365>

One report is published annually under this title (authors and cover dates vary). It presents state-level data for number of deaths, death rates, and age-adjusted death rates for major causes of death utilizing the International Classification of Diseases—Tenth Revision (ICD-10). Major causes of death listed include alcohol-induced causes and drug-induced causes.

Research Note: This series supersedes *Monthly Vital Statistics Reports (MVSR).*

•536 *Drug Abuse Warning Network, [year]: Area Profiles of Drug-Related Mortality* [DAWN Series]. Rockville, Md.: Office of Applied Studies, Substance Abuse and Mental Health Services Administration, U.S. Department of Health and Human Services [2003–date].

<http://purl.access.gpo.gov/GPO/LPS79143>

Provides data on drug-related deaths as reported to the Drug Abuse Warning Network (DAWN) by medical examiners and coroners (ME/Cs). In 2004 the network received reports from 150 jurisdictions in forty-six metropolitan areas; six states report data from statewide ME/C networks (Texas is not included in this group). Data is reported for deaths associated with substance abuse and drug misuse (intentional and accidental); homicide by drug (i.e., malicious poisonings); deaths related to the use of drugs for legitimate therapeutic purposes; and deaths with drug involvement when the manner of death could not be determined by the ME/Cs. The Metropolitan Area Profiles include a profile of Houston–Sugar Land–Baytown, with tabular and graphical statistics on drug-related deaths by drug category; deaths by case type; cause and place of death; and drug-related deaths involving drug misuse and suicide (rates by gender and age, and top five drugs involved for each category). The Abbreviated Profiles for Areas with Less than 50% Population Coverage include a profile of Dallas–Fort Worth–Arlington.

Research Note: Following a major redesign of its reporting criteria and quality controls initiated in January 2003, the network is now referred to as "New DAWN" in order to clearly demarcate the mortality data it reports, which is not comparable to data from any previous years. For a compilation of statistics gathered under the previous criteria, see *Emergency Department Trends from the Drug Abuse Warning Network, Final Estimates 1995–2002,* which provides tables for "ED drug mentions: estimated rates per 100,000 population by metropolitan area by half year." <http://dawninfo.samhsa.gov/old_dawn/pubs_94_02/edpubs/2002final/>

537 Fingerhut, Lois A. *Increases in Poisoning and Methadone-Related Deaths: United States, 1999–2005* [Health E-Stats]. Atlanta, Ga.: National Center for Health Statistics, Centers for Disease Control and Prevention, U.S. Department of Health and Human Service, 2008.

<http://www.cdc.gov/nchs/data/hestat/poisoning/poisoning.htm>

Presents statistics on methadone-related poisoning deaths in 1999–2005, ratio of deaths in 2005 to deaths in 1999, and crude death rates for 2005, by state (Table 3a), and methadone-related poisoning deaths in 1999–2005, by state for states with fewer than twenty deaths in any of the years 2003–2005 (Table 3b).

538 *National Drug Control Strategy: Data Supplement.* Washington, D.C.: Office of National Drug Control Policy, Executive Office of the President [annual, 2004–date].

<http://purl.access.gpo.gov/GPO/LPS6500> [current edition]

<http://purl.access.gpo.gov/GPO/LPS94333> [archived editions]

The State Data section provides the number of deaths from drug-induced causes and age-adjusted death rates from drug-induced causes (deaths per 100,000 population).

539 "Unintentional Poisoning Deaths—United States, 1999–2004." *Morbidity and Mortality Weekly Report* (*MMWR*) 56, no. 5 (February 9, 2007): 93–96.

<http://www.cdc.gov/mmwr/PDF/wk/mm5605.pdf>

Provides a map showing the percentage change in unintentional poisoning mortality rates, by rural status of state, United States, 1999–2004. The report notes that "Nearly all poisoning deaths in the United States are attributed to drugs, and most drug poisonings result from the abuse of prescription and illegal drugs."

540 Warner, Margaret, Li Hui Chen, and Diane M. Makuc. "Increase in Fatal Poisonings Involving Opioid Analgesics in the United States, 1999–2006." *NCHS Data Brief,* no. 22 (September 2009), pp. 1–8.

<http://www.cdc.gov/nchs/data/databriefs/db22.htm>

Provides a United States map, along with an accompanying state-level data table, showing age-adjusted death rates for poisoning deaths involving opioid analgesics in terms of a comparison of state and U.S. rates for 2006 (Fig. 5). Opioid analgesics are drugs that are usually prescribed to relieve pain and include: methadone, which is used to treat opioid dependency as well as pain;

other opioids, such as oxycodone and hydrocodone; and synthetic narcotics such as fentanyl and propoxyphene. Opium, heroin, and cocaine are not included in this class. Estimates are based on the National Vital Statistics System multiple cause of death mortality files and are for poisoning deaths of any intent (unintentional, suicide, homicide or legal intervention, or undetermined).

Employee Drug Testing

541 *Drug Testing Index®*. Madison, N.J.: Quest Diagnostics [online only, 2001–date].

<http://www.questdiagnostics.com/employersolutions/
drug_testing_index_es.html>

Quest Diagnostics performs more than 8.5 million drug tests annually utilizing six SAMHSA-certified laboratories. The Quest Diagnostics Drug Testing Index® contains data on positivity rates to yield a comprehensive analysis of workplace drug-use trends among three major testing populations: federally mandated, safety-sensitive workers; general workforce; and combined U.S. workforce. This website provides United States maps that depict annual drug test rates for three-digit zip code areas in the following categories: overall positivity, amphetamines positivity, cocaine positivity, marijuana positivity, opiate positivity, phencyclidine positivity.

Research Note: This data is referenced in reports of the National Drug Intelligence Center, U.S. Department of Justice, and the Office of National Drug Control Policy, Executive Office of the President.

Substance Abuse

542 *Apparent Per Capita Alcohol Consumption: National, State, and Regional Trends* [Surveillance Report]. Bethesda, Md.: Alcohol Epidemiologic Data System, Division of Epidemiology and Prevention Research, National Institute on Alcohol Abuse and Alcoholism, U.S. Department of Health and Human Services [annual, 1977–date].

<http://pubs.niaaa.nih.gov/publications/surveillance.htm>

Provides data for the most recent reporting year on apparent alcohol consumption for states, census regions, and the United States (volume and ethanol in thousands of gallons, per capita consumption in gallons, based on population age fourteen and older) (Table 2). Also, per capita ethanol consumption is reported for states, census regions, and the United States (gallons of ethanol, based on population age fourteen and older), 1977–date (Table 3).

543 *Changes in Prevalence Rates of Drug Use between 2002–2003 and 2004–2005 among States.* Rockville, Md.: Office of Applied Studies, Substance Abuse and Mental Health Services Administration, U.S. Department of Health and Human Services, 2007.

<http://oas.samhsa.gov/stateTrends.htm>

Presents state-level average percentages, by age group, based on the annual National Surveys on Drug Use and Health (2002–2005), for the following: illicit drug use in past month (Table D.1); marijuana use in past year (Table D.2); marijuana use in past month (Table D.3); perceptions of great risk of smoking marijuana once a month (Table D.4); first use of marijuana (Table D.5); illicit drug use other than marijuana in past month (Table D.6); cocaine use in past year (Table D.7); nonmedical use of pain relievers in past year (Table D.8); alcohol use in past month (Table D.9); binge alcohol use in past month (Table D.10); perceptions of great risk of having five or more drinks of an alcoholic beverage once or twice a week (Table D.11); alcohol use and binge alcohol use in past month among persons aged twelve to twenty (Table D.12); tobacco product use in past month (Table D.13); cigarette use in past month (Table D.14); perceptions of great risk of smoking one or more packs of cigarettes per day (Table D.15); alcohol dependence or abuse in past year (Table D.16); alcohol dependence in past year (Table D.17); illicit drug dependence or abuse in past year (Table D.18); illicit drug dependence in past year (Table D.19); dependence on or abuse of illicit drugs or alcohol in past year (Table D.20); needing but not receiving treatment for illicit drug use in past year (Table D.21); needing but not receiving treatment for alcohol use in past year (Table D.22). These tables are followed by a second series that present P values of no change between combined year prevalence rates (2002–2003, 2003–2004, and 2004–2005) for the same set of categories.

544 *Epidemiologic Trends in Drug Abuse.* Vol. 1, *Proceedings of the Community Epidemiology Work Group: Highlights and Executive Summary.* Bethesda, Md.: National Institute on Drug Abuse, National Institutes of Health, U.S. Department of Health and Human Services [annual, 1988–date].

545 *Epidemiologic Trends in Drug Abuse.* Vol. 2, *Proceedings of the Community Epidemiology Work Group.* Bethesda, Md.: National Institute on Drug Abuse, National Institutes of Health, U.S. Department of Health and Human Services [annual, 1988–date].

<http://www.drugabuse.gov/about/organization/cewg/Reports.html>

These proceedings contain Texas reports prepared by Jane C. Maxwell, which are based on data compiled for the publication *Substance Abuse Trends in Texas* (see entry 549).

Research Note: Reports are available online back to June 1999. Published biannually prior to 2007.

546 Hourani, Laurel L., Carol L. Council, and Weihua Shi. *Substance Abuse and Mental Health in Texas, 2001.* Rockville, Md: Office of Applied Studies, Substance Abuse and Mental Health Services Administration, U.S. Department of Health and Human Services, 2005.

<http://oas.samhsa.gov/8states/texas2k1.doc>

Presents the following finding (including standard errors) from 2001 National Household Survey on Drug Abuse (NHSDA) for adult Texans aged eighteen and older by socio-demographic characteristics: estimated numbers of past month tobacco use (Table 1); percentages of past month tobacco use (Table 2); estimated numbers of alcohol use and dependence or abuse (Table 3); percentages of alcohol use and dependence or abuse (Table 4); estimated number of past year illicit drug use and dependence or abuse (Table 5); percentages of past year illicit drug use and dependence or abuse (Table 6); estimated numbers of alcohol or illicit drug dependence or abuse and treatment need and receipt for alcohol or illicit drugs in the past year (Table 7); percentages of alcohol or illicit drug dependence or abuse and treatment need and receipt for alcohol or illicit drugs in the past year (Table 8); estimated numbers of co-occurring disorders (substance abuse and serious mental illness) and treatment in the past year (Table 11); percentages co-occurring disorders (substance abuse and serious mental illness) and treatment in the past year (Table 12); estimated numbers of alcohol or illicit drug dependence/abuse or serious mental illness and treatment receipt in the past year (Table 13); percentages of alcohol or illicit drug dependence/abuse or serious mental illness and treatment receipt in the past year (Table 14); and percentage distributions of selected characteristics of people who had serious mental illness or alcohol/ illicit drug dependence/abuse and received treatment and had unmet need for treatment in the past year (Table 15).

547 *Impact of Hurricanes Katrina and Rita on Substance Use and Mental Health: Detailed Tables.* Rockville, Md.: Office of Applied Studies, Substance Abuse and Mental Health Services Administration, U.S. Department of Health and Human Services, 2008.

<http://oas.samhsa.gov/2k8/katrina/katrina.cfm>

Presents the following state-level data, for the periods June 2004–July 2005 and January–December 2006, on Gulf States disaster area residents, age eighteen and over, who were affected by hurricanes Katrina and Rita: substance use disorder in the past year—numbers and percentages (Tables 24A–B); past month illicit drug use—numbers and percentages (Tables 25A–B); past month marijuana use—numbers and percentages (Tables 26A–B); past month cigarette use—numbers and percentages (Tables 27A–B); past month binge alcohol use—numbers and percentages (Tables 28A–B); nonmedical use of prescription type drugs—numbers and percentages (Tables 29A–B); and past month nonmedical use of pain relievers—numbers and percentages (Tables 30A–B).

Research Note: These tables serve as a supplement to "Impact of Hurricanes Katrina and Rita on Substance Use and Mental Health," *The NSDUH Report* (January 31, 2008).

548 Liu, Liang Y. *2005 Texas Survey of Substance Use Among College Students: Main Findings Report.* Austin: Texas Department of State Health Services, 2007.

<http://www.dshs.state.tx.us/sa/Research/college/2005/2005_
CollegeSurvey_lliu043007.pdf>

Reports the results of a spring 2005 survey of 4,634 undergraduate students aged eighteen to twenty-six from forty randomly selected Texas public and private universities, colleges, and community colleges. The survey covered alcohol, tobacco, and illicit drugs. Appendix A contains tables showing prevalence and recency of substance use among college students by gender (A1), race/ethnicity (A2), age (A3), membership in a fraternity/sorority (A4), class standing (A5), parental annual household income (A6), and type of institution (A7).

•**549** Maxwell, Jane C. *Substance Abuse Trends in Texas.* Austin: Gulf Coast Addiction Technology Transfer Center, Addiction Research Institute of the Center for Social Work Research, School of Social Work, University of Texas at Austin [annual, 1995–date].

<http://www.utexas.edu/research/cswr/gcattc/drugtrends.html>

A compilation of statistics from federal and state sources prepared as a report for the Community Epidemiology Work Group (CEWG) meetings sponsored by the National Institute on Drug Abuse (NIDA). Data is presented on the availability, street price, purity, trafficking, distribution, and prevalence of use of illegal substances; alcohol abuse and treatment; items analyzed by the Texas Department of Public Safety (DPS) laboratories; poison control center calls for assistance or to report misuse; admission to the Texas Department of State Health Service (DSHS) treatment programs; hospital emergency room visits and deaths related to substance use; substance abuse in schools and colleges; drug- and alcohol-related arrests; and prevalence of infectious diseases relating to drug abuse, including AIDS, HIV, and syphilis.

Research Note: Published biannually prior to 2007.

550 *National Drug Control Strategy: Data Supplement.* Washington, D.C.: Office of National Drug Control Policy, Executive Office of the President [annual, 2004–date].

<http://purl.access.gpo.gov/GPO/LPS6500> [current edition]

<http://purl.access.gpo.gov/GPO/LPS94333> [archived editions]

The State Data section provides the estimated number and percentages of users, age twelve or older, of the following: any illicit drugs, marijuana, cocaine, or nonmedical use of pain relievers. It also provides data on the percentage of high school students who used the following: marijuana or cocaine, inhalants or illegal steroids, or cigarettes or alcohol; and for selected cities, the percentage of high school students who used selected drugs, cigarettes, or alcohol. For selected metropolitan areas, data is provided for the estimated number of emergency department drug episodes, cocaine mentions, heroin/morphine mentions, marijuana/hashish mentions, and methamphetamine/speed mentions. The economic costs of drug abuse for selected Metropolitan Statistical Areas (MSAs) is also reported.

551 Pemberton, Michael R., James D. Colliver, Tania M. Robbins, and Joseph C. Gfroerer. *Underage Alcohol Use: Findings from the 2002–2006 National Surveys on Drug Use and Health* [Analytic Series]. Rockville, Md.: Office of Applied Studies, Substance Abuse and Mental Health Services Administration, U.S. Department of Health and Human Services, 2008. <http://oas.samhsa.gov/underage2k8/underage.pdf>

Reports state-level annual averages for persons aged twelve to twenty, based on combined data from the 2002–2006 National Surveys on Drug Use and Health (NSDUH), on the following: alcohol use in the lifetime, past year, and past month; binge and heavy alcohol use in the past month; and alcohol dependence or abuse in the past year—numbers (Table 3.10A); and alcohol use in the lifetime, past year, and past month; binge and heavy alcohol use in the past month; and alcohol dependence or abuse in the past year—percentages (Table 3.10B).

552 *Percentage of Adults Who Reported Binge Drinking by State and Gender, BRFSS, 1984–2008.* Bethesda, Md.: Alcohol Epidemiologic Data System, Division of Epidemiology and Prevention Research, National Institute on Alcohol Abuse and Alcoholism, U.S. Department of Health and Human Services (updated, 2009).

<http://www.niaaa.nih.gov/Resources/DatabaseResources/QuickFacts/Adults/brfss03.htm>

553 *Percentage of Adults Who Reported Heavy Drinking by State and Gender, BRFSS, 1984–2008.* Bethesda, Md.: Alcohol Epidemiologic Data System, Division of Epidemiology and Prevention Research, National Institute on Alcohol Abuse and Alcoholism, U.S. Department of Health and Human Services, 2009.
<http://www.niaaa.nih.gov/Resources/DatabaseResources/QuickFacts/Adults/brfss02.htm>

Presents state-level statistics on self-reported adult heavy drinking and adult binge drinking, based on the Behavioral Risk Factors Surveillance System (BRFSS) (see entry 556).

Research Note: The report defines heavy drinking as on average having greater than two drinks per day for men, and one drink per day for women during the past month. Binge drinking is defined as the reported consumption of five or more drinks of alcoholic beverages on at least one occasion during the past month.

554 *Pulse Check: Trends in Drug Abuse* [Cover title: *Pulse Check: Drug Markets and Chronic Users in 25 of America's Largest Cities; Special Topic: Local Drug Markets—A Decade of Change.*] Washington, D.C.; Office of National Drug Control Policy, Executive Office of the President, 2004. NCJ 201398
<http://purl.access.gpo.gov/GPO/LPS1762>

Presents data on drug abuse patterns and drug illicit drug markets in twenty-five metropolitan areas (including Dallas and Houston) as reported by ethnographers, epidemiologists, treatment providers, and law enforcement officials.

Research Note: Last report in this series (earlier editions focus on other special topics).

555 *Shoveling Up II: The Impact of Substance Abuse on Federal, State, and Local Budgets.* New York: National Center on Addiction and Substance Abuse at Columbia University, 2009.
<http://www.casacolumbia.org/templates/publications_reports.aspx>

Provides individual state summaries along with data for spending by category, and spending related to substance abuse and addiction (amount, percentage, as percentage of state budget, and per capita), as follows: burden spending (justice, elementary/secondary education, health, child/family assistance, mental health/developmental disabilities, public safety, and state workforce); regulation/compliance (licensing and control, collection of taxes, and liquor store expenses); prevention, treatment, and research; and total (Appendix D).

Research Note: Earlier editions are available. The State and Local Survey Instruments are available in a separate file (Appendix A).

556 *SMART: BRFSS City and County Data—Local Health Risk Prevalence Data.* Atlanta, Ga.: Division of Adult and Community Health, National Center for Chronic Disease Prevention and Health Promotion, Centers for Disease Control and Prevention, U.S. Department of Health and Human Services [online only, 2002–date].

<http://apps.nccd.cdc.gov/BRFSS-SMART/SelMMSAPrevData.asp>

The Behavioral Risk Factor Surveillance System (BRFSS), established in 1984, is a state-based system of ongoing health surveys that collects information on health risk behaviors, preventive health practices, and health care access through random-digit-dialed household telephone surveys of noninstitutionalized adults aged eighteen years and over residing in the United States. The Selected Metropolitan/Micropolitan Area Risk Trends (SMART) is a documented and verified subset of the BRFSS. It reports estimates of adults who reported having consumed at least one drink of alcohol within the past thirty days; heavy drinkers (adult men having consumed more than two drinks per day and adult women having consumed more than one drink per day); and binge drinkers (males having consumed five or more drinks on one occasion, females having consumed four or more drinks on one occasion).

Research Note: Datasets are available for download. This data is also reported in *MMWR [Morbidity and Mortality Weekly Report] Surveillance Summaries* under the title "Surveillance of Certain Health Behaviors Among States and Selected Local Areas—Behavioral Risk Factor Surveillance System (BRFSS), United States, [year]." <http://purl.access.gpo.gov/GPO/LPS57591>

•557 *State Level Data on Alcohol, Tobacco, and Illegal Drug Use.* Rockville, Md.: Office of Applied Studies, Substance Abuse and Mental Health Services Administration, U.S. Department of Health and Human Services [online only, 1999–date].

<http://www.oas.samhsa.gov/states.cfm>

This website provides access to extensive statistical data and trends based on state estimates of licit and illicit substance use, treatment needs, and mental health factors (serious psychological distress and major depressive episodes) from the annual National Survey on Drug Use and Health (NSDUH), which has been conducted since 1971 and is the leading source of data on illicit substance use by the U.S. civilian population aged twelve and older. The website also contains links to the current and previous editions of the annual *State Estimates of Substance Use from the National Surveys on Drug Use and Health* (the HTML format contains additional tables not found in the print or PDF versions).

Research Note: The survey was called the National Household Survey on Drug Abuse (NHSDA) prior to 2002. Datasets are available through the Inter-university Consortium for Political and Social Research (ICPSR), Institute for Social Research, University of Michigan.

<http://www.icpsr.umich.edu/icpsrweb/ICPSR/series/00064>

558 *State Trends in Drinking Behaviors, 1984–2001* [U.S. Alcohol Epidemiologic Data Reference Manual, Vol. 7]. Bethesda, Md.: National Institute on Alcohol Abuse and Alcoholism, National Institutes of Health, Public Health Service, U.S. Department of Health and Human Services, 2003. NIH 02-5213

Presents state-level survey results on percentage distribution of drinking status and drinking level in the past month for selected demographic characteristics (Table 1), and percentage distribution of drinking five or more drinks on a single occasion one or more times in the past month for selected demographic characteristics (Table 2).

559 *Substate Estimates from the National Surveys on Drug Use and Health.* Rockville, Md.: Office of Applied Studies, Substance Abuse and Mental Health Services Administration, U.S. Department of Health and Human Services [1999–date].

<http://www.oas.samhsa.gov/substate.cfm>

Reports the following statistics for states and substate regions from the annual National Survey on Drug Use and Health (NSDUH) for persons aged twelve or older (unless otherwise specified): illicit drug use in past month and illicit drug use other than marijuana in past month; marijuana use in past month, average annual rate of first use of marijuana, and perceptions of great risk of smoking marijuana once a month; marijuana use in past year, cocaine use in past year, and nonmedical use of pain relievers in past year; alcohol use in past month, binge alcohol use in past month, and perceptions of great risk of having five or more drinks of an alcoholic beverage once or twice a week; alcohol use in past month and binge alcohol use in last month among persons aged twelve to twenty; cigarette use in past month, tobacco product use in past month, and perceptions of great risk of smoking one or more packs of cigarettes per day; alcohol dependence in past year and illicit drug dependence in past year; alcohol dependence or abuse in past year, illicit drug dependence or abuse in past year, and dependence on or abuse of illicit drugs or alcohol in past year; needing but not receiving treatment for alcohol use in past year and needing but not receiving treatment for illicit drug use in past year; and serious psychological distress in past year and having at least one major depressive episode in past year among persons aged eighteen or older.

Research Note: The survey was called the National Household Survey on Drug Abuse (NHSDA) prior to 2002. Substate region definitions for Texas were obtained from the Texas Department of State Health Services and are defined in terms of the state's 254 counties. Datasets are available through the Inter-university Consortium for Political and Social Research (ICPSR), Institute for Social Research, University of Michigan.

<http://www.icpsr.umich.edu/icpsrweb/ICPSR/series/00064>

•560 *Texas School Survey of Substance Use Among Students: Grades 4–6.* Austin: Mental Health and Substance Abuse Program Services, Texas Department of State Health Services [biennial, 1990–date].
<http://www.dshs.state.tx.us/sa/Research/SchoolSurveys.shtm>

Reports the results of the Texas School Survey of Substance Use, which is conducted by the Texas Department of State Health Services, in conjunction with the Public Policy Research Institute at Texas A&M University. It contains data derived from a sample of approximately seventy school districts statewide on patterns of substance use (alcohol, tobacco, inhalants, and marijuana), demographic correlates of substance use, and protective and risk factors related to substance use. The appendixes provide data on the prevalence and recency of substance use by grade—for border and non-border counties—in the following categories: total, male, female, Anglo, African American (non-border counties), and Hispanic.

Research Note: Beginning in 2006, data is also available for each Health and Human Services Commission (HHSC) state planning region. Prior to 2004, the survey was conducted jointly with the legacy agency Texas Commission on Alcohol and Drug Abuse. School-district level data (1996–date) is available through the Public Policy Research Institute at Texas A&M University (on-site access only).

•561 *Texas School Survey of Substance Use Among Students: Grades 7–12.* Austin: Mental Health and Substance Abuse Program Services, Texas Department of State Health Services [biennial, 1988–date].
<http://www.dshs.state.tx.us/sa/Research/SchoolSurveys.shtm>

Reports the results of the Texas School Survey of Substance Use, which is conducted by the Texas Department of State Health Services, in conjunction with the Public Policy Research Institute at Texas A&M University. It contains data derived from a sample of approximately seventy school districts statewide on patterns of substance use, demographic correlates of substance use, protective and risk factor related to substance use, alcohol- and drug-related problems, and sources of information and assistance for substance problems. One set of appendices provide data on the prevalence and recency of substance use by grade—for students in border and non-border counties combined—in the following categories: total, male, female, Anglo, African American, Hispanic, students who reported earning A's/B's, students who reported earning C's, D's, or F's, students who were living/not living with both parents, students who would/would not seek help from adults for substance abuse problems, students living in school district three years or less/more than three years, and type of extracurricular activity. Responses are also provided by grade to specific questions on alcohol, inhalants, and other illegal drugs (use, availability, perceived dangers, seeking help, etc.). Other appendices provide data on the prevalence and recency of substance use by grade for students in border counties and in non-border counties, and prescription-type drug use prevalence.

Research Note: Beginning in 2006, data is also available for each Health and Human Services Commission (HHSC) state planning region. Prior to 2004, the survey was conducted jointly with the legacy agency Texas Commission on Alcohol and Drug Abuse. School-district level data (1996–date) is available through the Public Policy Research Institute at Texas A&M University (on-site access only). Summary survey results are reported under the title "Adolescent Substance Use in Texas" in *The EpiLink*, the public health news bulletin of the Texas Department of State Health Services Infectious Disease Control Unit. <http://www.dshs.state.tx.us/idcu/epilink/>

562 Wallisch, Lynn S. *2000 Texas Survey of Substance Use Among Adults.* Austin: Texas Commission on Alcohol and Drug Abuse, 2001.

<http://www.dshs.state.tx.us/sa/research/adult/AdultHousehold.pdf>

Presents the results of a statewide telephone survey of 10,227 Texas adults conducted between July 2000 to March 2001. Data is reported by gender, age, race/ethnicity, region, and major metropolitan area on the prevalence and recency of substance use (including illicit drugs, alcohol, and tobacco); and alcohol- and drug-related problems; treatment experience and current needs; and related problems (e.g., mental health problems among adults with substance problems and co-occurrence of gambling and substance problems).

Research Note: Earlier editions are available.

563 "Youth Risk Behavior Surveillance—United States." [Surveillance Summaries]. *Morbidity and Mortality Weekly Report* (*MMWR*), [biennial, 1993–date].

<http://www.cdc.gov/mmwr/mmwr_ss/ss_cvol.html>

One report is published biennially under this title (authors and cover dates vary). It provides survey results (total, male, and female) by state and selected local areas, for the following categories: percentage of high school students who ever smoked cigarettes; percentage of high school students who currently smoked cigarettes; percentage of high school students who currently smoked more than ten cigarettes/day and who tried to quit smoking cigarettes; percentage of high school students who usually obtained their own cigarettes by buying them in a store or gas station or who currently used smokeless tobacco; percentage of high school students who currently smoked cigars or who currently used tobacco; percentage of high school students who drank alcohol; percentage of high school students who had five or more drinks of alcohol in a row or who usually obtained the alcohol they drank by someone giving it to them; percentage of high school students who used marijuana; percentage of high school students who used cocaine; percentage of high school students who used inhalants or ecstasy; percentage of high school students who used heroin or methamphetamines; percentage of high school students who took steroids without a doctor's prescription or who injected any illegal drug; percentage of high school students who used hallucinogenic drugs or who took prescription drugs without a doctor's prescription; percentage of high school students who smoked a whole cigarette before age thirteen years or who drank alcohol for the first time before age thirteen years; percentage of high school students who tried marijuana for the first time before age thirteen years; percentage of high school students who used tobacco on school property; percentage of high school students who drank alcohol on school property or who used marijuana on school property; and percentage of high school students who were offered, sold, or given an illegal drug by someone on school property.

Research Note: The survey is conducted in odd-numbered years and the report is published the following year. Online access to current and past editions is also available on the website of the Division of Adolescent and School Health, National Center for Chronic Disease Prevention and Health Promotion, Centers for Disease Control and Prevention, U.S. Department of Health and Human Services. <http://www.cdc.gov/healthyyouth/yrbs/index.htm>

Substance Abuse Treatment

564 *Inventory of State Substance Abuse Prevention and Treatment Activities and Expenditures.* Washington, D.C.: Office of National Drug Control Policy, Executive Office of the President, 2006. NCJ 216918

<http://purl.access.gpo.gov/GPO/LPS93674>

Provides state-level statistics on expenditures of funds allocated by the Substance Abuse and Mental Health Services Administration's Block Grant Program for substance abuse prevention and treatment services and how states allocate their own funding for these services. The data includes the following Texas State agency expenditures: from all funding sources (total and by activity); block grant funds by activity, core strategy, and resource development activity; state funds by activity; and prevention services and treatment services from all funding sources. Also includes data (number and total dollar amounts) for discretionary prevention grants awarded by the Center for Substance Abuse Prevention and discretionary treatment grants awarded by the Center for Substance Abuse Treatment.

565 *National Drug Control Strategy: Data Supplement.* Washington, D.C.: Office of National Drug Control Policy, Executive Office of the President [annual, 2005–date].

<http://purl.access.gpo.gov/GPO/LPS6500> [current edition]

<http://purl.access.gpo.gov/GPO/LPS94333> [archived editions]

The State data section provides the estimated number of persons, age twelve or older, needing but not receiving treatment for an illicit drug problem in the past year, number of clients in any substance abuse treatment, and number of clients in drug abuse treatment.

•566 *National Survey of Substance Abuse Treatment Services (N-SSATS): Data on Substance Abuse Treatment Facilities.* Rockville, Md.: Office of Applied Studies, Substance Abuse and Mental Health Services Administration, U.S. Department of Health and Human Services [annual, 2000–date]. <http://purl.access.gpo.gov/GPO/LPS32188>

The State Data chapter provides statistics on N-SSATS forms accounting, response rate, and mode of response (Table 6.1). It also includes data on the number and percentage distribution of all the following categories: facilities and clients in treatment (Tables 6.2a–b); clients under age eighteen in treatment, and clients under age eighteen in facilities offering special programs or groups for adolescents (Tables 6.3a–b); facilities with managed care agreements or contracts, and clients in facilities with managed care agreements or contracts (Tables 6.4a–b); facility operation (Tables 6.5a–b); primary focus of facility (Table 6.6); type of care offered (Table 6.7a–b); client substance abuse problem treated (Table 6.8); facility size (Table 6.10); type of counseling used (Table 6.12); clinical/therapeutic approaches used often or sometimes (Tables 6.13a–b); facilities offering special programs or groups for specific client types (Tables 6.14a–b); facilities offering services in sign language for the hearing impaired and in languages other than English (Tables 6.15a–b); facilities detoxifying clients from various substances (opiates, alcohol, and cocaine) (Table 6.16); facilities with client outreach (Table 6.17); facility licensing, certification, or accreditation (Tables 6.18a–b); facilities employing specific practices as part of their standard operating procedures (Tables 6.19a–b); facility payment options (Tables 6.20a–b); facility funding (Table 6.21); facilities with Opioid Treatment Programs (OTPs) and clients receiving medication-assisted opioid therapy (Table 6.22); type of care offered in facilities with Opioid Treatment Programs (OTPs) (Tables 6.23a–b); facility licensing, certification, or accreditation of facilities with Opioid Treatment Programs (OTPs) (Tables 6.24a–b); clients in treatment, according to facility operation (Tables 6.25a–b); clients in treatment, according to primary focus of facility (Table 6.26); clients in treatment, according to type of care received (Tables 6.27a–b); clients in treatment, according to substance abuse problem and co-occurring mental heath disorders (Table 6.28); clients in treatment according to counseling type (Table 29); clients under age eighteen in treatment, according to facility operation (Tables 6.30a–b); clients under age eighteen in treatment, according to primary focus of facility (Table 6.31). Finally, it includes data on clients under age eighteen in treatment, according to type of care received (Table 6.32); clients in treatment aged eighteen and over, and clients per 100,000 population aged eighteen and over, according to substance abuse problem treated (Table 6.33); facility size, according to type of care offered: median number of clients (Table 6.9); and facility capacity and utilization of residential (non-hospital) and hospital inpatient care: number and utilization rate (Table 6.11). Types of facilities covered include private non-profit; private for-profit; local, county, or community government; state government; federal government (Department of Veterans Affairs, Department of Defense, Indian Health Service); and tribal government.

Research Note: Datasets are available through the Inter-university Consortium for Political and Social Research (ICPSR), Institute for Social Research, University of Michigan.

<http://www.icpsr.umich.edu/icpsrweb/ICPSR/series/00058>

567 *Quick Statistics from the Drug and Alcohol Services Information System.* Rockville, Md.: Office of Applied Studies, Substance Abuse and Mental Health Services Administration, U.S. Department of Health and Human Services [online only].

<http://wwwdasis.samhsa.gov/webt/NewMapv1.htm>

An interactive map allows users access to state-level data from two databases: the Treatment Episode Data Set (TEDS), which presents information on the demographic and substance abuse characteristics of annual admissions to treatment for abuse of alcohol and drugs in facilities that report to individual state administrative data systems (updated quarterly), and the National Survey of Substance Abuse Treatment Services (N-SSATS), an annual survey that collects information from all facilities in the United States, both public and private, that provide substance abuse treatment.

•568 *Substance Abuse Research: Statewide Data.* Austin: Mental Health and Substance Abuse Program Services, Texas Department of State Health Services [annual].

<http://www.dshs.state.tx.us/sa/default.shtm>

Provides the following spreadsheet data: statewide adult admissions, statewide youth admissions, admissions by county where client resides, admissions by primary substance by region, admissions by service type by region, assessments by region, BHIPS wait list entries by region, COPSD statistics (region and statewide), OSR assessments/referrals, priority population admissions by region, referrals entered in BHIPS by region, screening by region, and licensed outpatient slots and residential beds by region.

Research Note: Reports are located in the Research and Media subsection. Data for the first two categories is provided by calendar year, and the remaining categories by fiscal year. Regional data is based on the eleven DSHS Health Service Regions. <http://www.dshs.state.tx.us/regions/default.shtm>

•569 *Treatment Episode Data Set (TEDS): National Admissions to Substance Abuse Treatment Services* [DASIS Series]. Rockville, Md.: Office of Applied Studies, Substance Abuse and Mental Health Services Administration, U.S. Department of Health and Human Services [annual, 2003–date].

<http://purl.access.gpo.gov/GPO/LPS7070>

Reports state-level data from the Treatment Episode Data Set (TEDS) for admissions to substance abuse treatment, primarily at facilities that receive some public funding, in the following categories: primary alcohol admissions, number and admissions per 100,000 population (Tables 2.3a–b); primary heroin admissions, number and admissions per 100,000 population (Tables 2.4a–b); primary non-heroin opiates/synthetics admissions, number and admissions per 100,000 population (Tables 2.5a–b); primary cocaine admissions, number and admissions per 100,000 population (Tables 2.6a–b); primary marijuana admissions, number and admissions per 100,000 population (Table 2.7a–b); primary methamphetamine/amphetamine admissions, number and admissions per 100,000 population (Tables 2.8a–b); admissions, number (Table 4.2a); transfers, number (Table 4.2b) and codependents, number (Table 4.2c); item percentage response rate, TEDS Minimum Data Set (Table 4.3); item percentage response rate, TEDS Supplemental Data Set (Table 4.4); admissions, number (Table 4.5); admissions per 100,000 population (Table 4.6a); admissions per 100,000 population, adjusted for age, sex, and race/ethnicity (Table 4.6b); admissions according to primary substance of abuse, number (Table 4.7); admissions per 100,000 population, according to primary substance of abuse (Table 4.8a); and admissions per 100,000 population, adjusted for age, sex, and race/ethnicity, according to primary substance of abuse (Table 8.b). Substances covered include alcohol, opiates, heroin, cocaine, marijuana/hashish, methamphetamine/amphetamine, tranquilizers, sedatives, hallucinogens, PCP, and inhalants.

Research Note: Selected tables present annual data for the reporting year and the previous decade. Data is reported for clients age twelve years and over with the exception of Tables 4.2a–c, 4.3, and 4.4. Since a client can be admitted to substance abuse treatment more than once during a single year, TEDS records represent admissions rather than individuals. Datasets are available through the Inter-university Consortium for Political and Social Research (ICPSR), Institute for Social Research, University of Michigan.

<http://www.icpsr.umich.edu/icpsrweb/ICPSR/series/00056>

•570 *Treatment Episode Data Set (TEDS): Discharges from Substance Abuse Treatment Services* [DASIS Series]. Rockville, Md.: Office of Applied Studies, Substance Abuse and Mental Health Services Administration, U.S. Department of Health and Human Services [annual, 2002–date].

<http://purl.access.gpo.gov/GPO/LPS7070>

Reports annual state-level data from the Treatment Episode Data Set (TEDS) for discharges from substance abuse treatment, primarily at facilities that receive some public funding, in the following categories: discharges and year of admission, number and percentage distribution (Tables 2.2a–b); discharges and type of service, number and percentage distribution (Tables 2.3a–b); discharges and reason for discharge, number and percentage distribution (Table 2.4); discharges by type of service and reason for discharge—number, percentage distribution, and median and average length of stay (Table 2.5); discharges from opioid replacement therapy, by type of service, according to reason for discharge—number, percentage distribution, and median and average lengths of stay (Table 2.6); discharges from outpatient treatment according to reason for discharge, number and percentage distribution (Table 3.1); discharges from intensive outpatient treatment according to reason for discharge, number and percentage distribution (Table 4.1); discharges from short-term residential treatment according to reason for discharge, number and percentage distribution (Table 5.1); discharges from long-term residential treatment according to reason for discharge, number and percentage distribution (Table 6.1); discharges from hospital residential treatment according to reason for discharge, number and percentage distribution (Table 7.1); discharges from detoxification according to reason for discharge, number and percentage distribution (Table 8.1); discharges from outpatient opioid replacement therapy according to reason for discharge, number and percentage distribution (Table 9.1); and discharges from opioid replacement detoxification according to reason for discharge, number and percentage distribution (Table 10.1). Substances covered include alcohol, opiates, heroin, nonprescription methadone, cocaine, marijuana/hashish, methamphetamine/amphetamine, barbiturates, benzodiazepine, hallucinogens, PCP, and inhalants.

Research Note: Since a client can be discharged from substance abuse treatment more than once during a single year, TEDS records represent discharges rather than individuals. Data-sets are available through the Inter-university Consortium for Political and Social Research (ICPSR), Institute for Social Research, University of Michigan. <http://www.icpsr.umich.edu/icpsrweb/ICPSR/series/00056>

•571 *Treatment Episode Data Set (TEDS) Highlights: National Admissions to Substance Abuse Treatment Services* [DASIS Series]. Rockville, Md.: Office of Applied Studies, Substance Abuse and Mental Health Services Administration, U.S. Department of Health and Human Services [annual, 2002–date].

<http://purl.access.gpo.gov/GPO/LPS7070>

Reports annual state-level data from the Treatment Episode Data Set (TEDS) for admissions to substance abuse treatment, primarily at facilities that receive some public funding, according to primary substance of abuse: number and percentage distribution (Tables 6a-b). Substances covered include alcohol, opiates, heroin, nonprescription methadone, cocaine, marijuana/ hashish, methamphetamine/amphetamine, barbiturates, benzodiazepine, hallucinogens, PCP, and inhalants.

Research Note: This report is published annually in advance of the full TEDS report. Since a client can be admitted to substance abuse treatment more than once during a single year, TEDS records represent admissions rather than individuals. Datasets are available through the Interuniversity Consortium for Political and Social Research (ICPSR), Institute for Social Research, University of Michigan.

<http://www.icpsr.umich.edu/icpsrweb/ICPSR/series/00056>

572 *Undocumented Immigrants in Texas: A Financial Analysis of the Impact to the State Budget and Economy* [Special Report]. Austin: Texas Comptroller of Public Accounts, 2006.

<http://www.window.state.tx.us/specialrpt/undocumented/>

Provides the Comptroller's estimate of the State's cost for providing substance abuse services to undocumented immigrants (Section IV).

Chapter 11

Appropriations, Revenues, Expenditures, and Federal Aid

Appropriations and Revenues

573 *Agency Legislative Appropriations Requests.* Austin: Legislative Budget Board [biennial].

<http://www.lbb.state.tx.us/External_Links/LAR/Agency_LAR_ Listing_0808.htm>

Provides the legislative appropriations requests of all State agencies for the forthcoming biennium as submitted to the Governor's Office of Budget, Planning and Policy and the Legislative Budget Board. These contain data extracted from the Automated Budget and Evaluation System of Texas (ABEST) and include, depending on the individual agency, the following: summary of request, strategy request (by agency goal), rider revisions and additions request, rider appropriations and unexpended balances request, sub-strategy request, sub-strategy summary, exceptional item request schedule, exceptional item strategy allocation schedule, exceptional item strategy request, capital budget, supporting schedules, and administrative and support costs (direct and indirect).

574 *Biennial Revenue Estimate.* Austin: Texas Comptroller of Public Accounts [1969–date].

<http://www.window.state.tx.us/finances/>

The Texas Comptroller of Public Accounts is required to prepare and submit to the governor and the legislature, in advance of each regular legislative session, a biennial revenue estimate (Tex. Const. art. III, § 49a). Each report covers the remainder of the current fiscal year and the upcoming biennium. Schedule I provides Estimates of Revenue by Source, Fund, Account, and Object. The sources include General Revenue, General Revenue Dedicated, Federal Funds, Appropriated Receipts, and Other Funds. Schedule II provides estimated fund balances for the current fiscal year (beginning balance, estimated revenues, estimated transfers, estimated expenditures, and ending balance).

Research Note: Editions are available online back to FY2007.

<http://www.window.state.tx.us/publications/archive.html>

575 *Budget and Performance Assessments: State Agencies and Institutions, Fiscal Years [year] to [year].* Austin: Legislative Budget Board [biennial].

<http://www.lbb.state.tx.us/Performance%20Reporting/Other_Budget_Perf_ Assesments.htm>

This report, which is prepared for and submitted to the legislature in accordance with the provisions of Tex. Gov't Code Ann. § 322.011 (Vernon 2005), is organized by government function (e.g., Public Safety and Criminal Justice) and subdivided by agency. It contains overviews of each agency's fiscal year budget highlights and full-time equivalent positions. The Performance Highlights provide a summary of the percentage of each agency's fiscal year performance measures (i.e., outcome/results/impact, output/volume, and efficiency) in which 95 percent of the targeted level was attained or exceeded. The Measures Assessments contain audits of performance targets that the agency met, exceeded, or failed to meet.

Research Note: Reporting year ends August 31. Reports are available online back to FY1999. The date range designated for each edition covers both actual and targeted performance measures.

576 *CSHB 1: The House Appropriations Committee's Proposed Budget for Fiscal [year–year]* [State Finance Report]. Austin: House Research Organization, Texas House of Representatives [biennial].

<http://www.hro.house.state.tx.us/frame4.htm#budget>

Provides an analysis of the Texas House Appropriations Committee's version (i.e., committee substitute) of the proposed biennial General Appropriations Bill, and follows the arrangement of the bill's articles.

Research Note: The House and the Senate traditionally take turns originating the General Appropriations Bill. Therefore, alternate editions are published under the title *CSSB 1: The House Appropriations Committee's Proposed Budget for Fiscal [year–year]*. Published under varying titles prior to 2001.

•**577** *Fiscal Size-up.* Austin: Legislative Budget Board [biennial, 2004–date].

<http://www.lbb.state.tx.us/>

Provides a detailed analysis of the Texas State budget for each biennium, a description of the major state revenue sources and funds, appropriated federal funds, and the overall economic outlook for Texas. Each edition also contains in-depth narrative profiles of every state agency, board, bureau, council, commission, department, and institution of higher education that receives state funding. These profiles include their mission, goals, strategies for delivery of services, selected performance measures, significant recent legislation, and biennial appropriations. Chapter 4 covers General Government (including the Office of the Governor's Criminal Justice Division and the Office of the Attorney General); Chapter 5 covers Health and Human Services (including the Department of Regulatory and Protective Services, which oversees Child Protective Services and Adult Protective Services); Chapter 7 covers the Judiciary; and Chapter 8 covers Public Safety and Criminal Justice.

Research Note: Previously published under the title *Fiscal Size-up: Texas State Services* (1970–2002).

578 *Fiscal [year–year] State Budget: Background on the Issues* [State Finance Report]. Austin: House Research Organization, Texas House of Representatives [biennial, 2009–date].

<http://www.hro.house.state.tx.us/frame4.htm#budget>

Provides an overview of the budget drivers, revenue streams, and selected budget issues for each article in the biennial Texas State budget.

•**579** *General and Special Laws of the State of Texas.* [General Appropriations Act.] Austin: Secretary of State [biennial].

<http://www.lbb.state.tx.us>

The biennial General Appropriations Act appropriates funding to State agencies and sets forth provisions for spending authority. It takes effect on September 1 of each odd-numbered year following the regular session of the legislature and is implemented over the next two years. The Act is divided into administrative sections, known as "articles," under which State agencies are organized by similar type and purpose, e.g., the Judiciary (Article IV) and Public Safety and Criminal Justice (Article V). Other sections are devoted to General Government (Article I), General Provisions (Article IX), and the Legislature (Article X). The governor has statutory authority to initiate a process called "budget execution" by proposing, during times when the legislature is not in session, that certain transfers of appropriations be made from one agency to another; that certain appropriations be retained by an agency and available for expenditure for a different purpose; or that a certain appropriation distribution or utilization time frame be changed. The Legislative Budget Board, after holding a public hearing, may approve, modify, or reject the proposal (Tex. Gov't Code Ann. §§ 317.001–.053 (Vernon 2005)).

Research Note: For an overview of the biennial Texas budget cycle, see *Budget 101: A Guide to the Budget Process in Texas* (Senate Research Center). See also *Writing the State Budget*, which summarizes the steps in the budget process and reviews the filed version of the General Appropriations Bill for each legislative session (House Research Organization). A general summary is provided in the chapter "Public Safety and Criminal Justice Spending" in *Texas Budget Highlights—Fiscal [year–year]* (House Research Organization).

580 *Governor's Proposed State Budget for the . . . Biennium, Presented to the . . . Legislature.* Austin: Office of the Governor [biennial].

<http://www.governor.state.tx.us/bpp>

The governor's proposed biennial State budget, which is delivered to all legislators at the beginning of each regular legislative session in accordance with the provisions of Tex. Gov't Code Ann. § 401.046 (Vernon 2005). It is organized by the articles of the General Appropriations Bill.

Research Note: Some editions have subtitles. Previously published under the titles *Executive Budget, Texas Executive Budget* and *State of Texas Executive Budget.* A summary edition is also published.

581 *Legislative Budget Estimates for the . . . Biennium Submitted to the . . . Texas Legislature.* Austin: Legislative Budget Board [biennial].

<http://www.lbb.state.tx.us/>

The Legislative Budget Board is required to compile an overview of the biennial General Appropriations Bill draft (excluding riders) and submit it to the legislature not later than the fifth day after a regular legislative session convenes (Tex. Gov't Code Ann.§ 322.008 (Vernon 2005)). The report compares the budget requests of State agencies with the LBB's recommendations, and is accompanied by data on the estimated, expended, and budgeted allocations for each agency from previous years. The number of FTE positions for each agency is listed along with a schedule of salaries for exempt positions.

Research Note: Editions are available online back to FY1999. A summary edition is also published that contains narratives for each agency outlining significant budget issues and setting forth the rationale for the board's recommendations.

•582 *Open Data Center.* Austin: Texas Comptroller of Public Accounts [online only, 2008–date].

<http://www.texastransparency.org/opendata/catalog.php>

Provides direct access to machine-readable, platform-independent raw datasets, as well as other important data tools created by the Texas Comptroller of Public Accounts. State revenue collection information is reported by fiscal year, including comptroller revenue object, and the appropriated funds into which the revenues were deposited. Only deposits to the State Treasury are included.

583 *Sources of Revenue Growth: A History of State Taxes and Fees in Texas, 1972–2003,* rev. ed. Austin: Texas Comptroller of Public Accounts, 2004.

<http://www.window.state.tx.us/taxbud/sources/>

Provides historical statistics on sources of revenue growth in terms of net collections (base, legislation, total, and percentage change) for concealed handgun fees (p. 65), and misdemeanor and felony court case fees (p. 66).

584 *State of Texas Annual Cash Report: Revenue and Expenditures of State Funds for the Year Ending August 31, [year].* Austin: Texas Comptroller of Public Accounts [1989–date].

<http://www.window.state.tx.us/finances/pubs/cashrpt/>

The Texas Comptroller of Public Accounts is required annually (by the first Monday in November) to exhibit to the governor an exact and complete statement showing the funds and revenues of the state, and public expenditures during the preceding year or during another period required by the governor (Tex. Gov't Code Ann. § 403.013 (Vernon 2005)). Revenue is reported in the period when cash is collected, and expenditures are reported in the period when cash disbursements are made. Net revenue is reported for the prior and current fiscal year for these object codes relating to criminal justice, which are listed within receipt category and type: Concealed Handgun Fees (3126), Private Sector Prison Industries Oversight Receipts (3134), Sale of Confiscated Alcoholic Beverages (3269), Controlled Substances Act Forfeited Property Sales (3582), Arrest Fees (3706), Court Fines (3710), Fees from Criminal Offenses (3712), Fees from Misdemeanor or Felony Cases (3713), Recovery of Parole Costs (3735), Prison Industry Sales (3756), Fingerprint Record Fees (3776), and Bail Bond Surety Fees (3858). Beginning cash balances, total net revenues and expenditures, and ending cash balances, are reported for these General Revenue Accounts, Dedicated, within Group 01 (General State Operating and Disbursing Funds) that relate to criminal justice: Law Enforcement Officer Standards and Education (0116), Criminal Justice Planning (0421), Bill Blackwood Law Enforcement Management Institute (0581), Parolee Court Ordered Restitution Trust Fund (0984), Attorney General Law Enforcement (5006), Commission on State Emergency Communications (5007), Sexual Assault Program (5010), Crime Stoppers Assistance (5012), Breath Alcohol Testing (5013), Fugitive Apprehension (5028), Center for Study and Prevention of Juvenile Crime and Delinquency (5029), Sexual Assault Prevention and Crisis Services (5037), 9-1-1 Service Fees (5050), Private Sector Prison Industries Expansion (5060), Fair Defense (5073), Correctional Management Institute and Criminal Justice Center (5083), and Child Abuse and Neglect Prevention (5084/Trust Fund 5085). This data is also reported within Group 02 (Constitutional Funds Expendable for Specific Purposes) for Compensation to Victims of Crime (0469/Auxiliary Fund 0494).

Research Note: Reports are available online back to FY2001. The report is also cited as *Annual Cash Report* and *Texas Annual Cash Report*.

585 *The State of Texas Comprehensive Annual Financial Report: Fiscal Year Ending August 31, [year].* Austin: Texas Comptroller of Public Accounts [1991–date].

<http://www.window.state.tx.us/finances/pubs/cafr/>

The Texas Comptroller of Public Accounts is required annually (by the last day in February) to exhibit to the governor an audited comprehensive annual financial report that includes all State agencies determined to be part of the statewide accounting entity and that is prepared in accordance with generally accepted accounting principles (Tex. Gov't Code Ann. § 403.013 (Vernon 2005)). The Statistical Section (under Financial Trends—Changes in Net Assets) provides data for the government function Public Safety and Corrections as follows: governmental activities (expenses and program revenues charges for services), and business-type activities (expenses and program revenues charges for services).

Research Note: Reports are available online back to FY2000. Each report provides data for the most recent seven fiscal years. The report is also cited as *Comprehensive Annual Financial Report for the State of Texas for the Fiscal Year Ending August 31, [year]*. This is one of two annual financial reports issued by the Comptroller. The other is the *State of Annual Cash Report*, which contains a section devoted to outlining the differences between the two reports (see entry 584).

•586 *Texas Budget Source*. Austin: Legislative Budget Board [biennial, online only, 2002–date].

<http://tbs.lbb.state.tx.us/>

This website allows access to data in the Legislative Budget Board's Automated Budget and Evaluation System of Texas (ABEST). Users can generate agency-level reports or reports organized by the articles of the General Appropriations Bill.

Expenditures

•587 *Census of Governments: Government Finance Statistics*. Washington, D.C.: Governments Division, U.S. Census Bureau, U.S. Department of Commerce [quinquennial, 1957–date].

<http://purl.access.gpo.gov/GPO/LPS33151>

The Census of Governments is conducted in years ending in "2" and "7" as mandated by 13 U.S.C. § 161 (2009). The Annual Survey of Government Finances series is conducted in the intervening years under the provisions of 13 U.S.C. § 182 (2009). One component of this series is the Annual Survey of State and Local Government Finances, which comprises a sample of state and local governments, with a new sample being selected every five years (years ending in "4" and "9"). Another component, the Annual Survey of State Government Finances, serves as a supplement. Data is presented for expenditures at the levels of state government, local government (county, municipal, and township), and a combination of state and local government, for the government functions "public safety" (which includes the subcategories "police protection" and "corrections"), and "governmental administration" (which includes the subcategory "judicial and legal").

Research Note: Editions are available online back to 1992. Definitions are provided for the various government function categories covered in the report. Datasets are available through the

Inter-university Consortium for Political and Social Research (ICPSR), Institute for Social Research, University of Michigan. <http://www.icpsr.umich.edu/icpsrweb/ICPSR/series/00012>

•588 *Justice Expenditure and Employment.* Washington, D.C.: Bureau of Justice Statistics, Office of Justice Programs, U.S. Department of Justice [annual, 1982–date].

<http://bjs.ojp.usdoj.gov/index.cfm?ty=daa>

Presents data extracted from the Census Bureau's Annual Survey of Government Finances and Annual Survey of Government Employment, which provide state-level estimates of per capita total justice expenditures and per capita expenditures by government function (police protection, judicial/legal, and corrections). State-level spending estimates are reported for correctional institutions (including construction) and other correctional functions (including capital outlay).

Research Note: Definitions are provided for the various government function categories covered in the report. Prior data is reported in various publications series of the U.S. Department of Justice's Law Enforcement Assistance Administration and the Census Bureau's Governments Division. Datasets are available through the Inter-university Consortium for Political and Social Research (ICPSR), Institute for Social Research, University of Michigan. <http://www.icpsr.umich.edu/icpsrweb/ICPSR/series/00087>

•589 *Open Data Center.* Austin: Texas Comptroller of Public Accounts [online only, 2008–date].

<http://www.texastransparency.org/opendata/catalog.php>

Provides direct access to machine-readable, platform-independent raw datasets, as well as other important data tools created by the Texas Comptroller of Public Accounts. Detailed expenditure information is reported by fiscal year, including comptroller object, vendor name, payment date, appropriation number, appropriation year, and appropriated fund. In addition, detailed purchasing information is reported for NIGP (National Institute of Governmental Purchasers) class and item numbers by fiscal year, as reported to the Comptroller from the purchasing systems of the largest State agencies.

589A *State Contracts.* Austin: Legislative Budget Board [online only, 2007–date].

<http://www.lbb.state.tx.us/Contracts/Contracts.htm>

This website provides information on State contracts and bid solicitations (Tex. Gov't Code Ann. § 322.020 (Vernon Supp. 2010)). Searches can be conducted using a combination of document type, agency, fiscal year, vendor, and contract value.

Research Note: The LBB's related publication, *Contracts Reported by Texas State Agencies and Institutions of Higher Education: Construction, Consulting, Major Information Systems, Professional Services, and Other,* is available online back to FY2003.

590 *State of Texas Annual Cash Report: Revenue and Expenditures of State Funds for the Year Ending August 31, [year].* Austin: Texas Comptroller of Public Accounts [1989–date].

<http://www.window.state.tx.us/finances/pubs/cashrpt/>

Reports net fiscal year expenditures for all State funds by department within governmental functions, and by object code within expenditure categories (see entry 584).

591 *The State of Texas Comprehensive Annual Financial Report: Fiscal Year Ending August 31, [year].* Austin: Texas Comptroller of Public Accounts [1991–date].

<http://www.window.state.tx.us/finances/pubs/cafr/>

The Texas Comptroller of Public Accounts is required annually (by the last day in February) to exhibit to the governor an audited comprehensive annual financial report that includes all State agencies determined to be part of the statewide accounting entity and that is prepared in accordance with generally accepted accounting principles (Tex. Gov't Code Ann. § 403.013 (Vernon 2005)). The Statistical Section (under Financial Trends—Changes in Fund Balances: Government Funds) provides data on expenditures for the government function Public Safety and Corrections.

Research Note: Reports are available online back to FY2000. Each report provides data for the most recent ten fiscal years. This publication also reports statistics on full-time equivalent employees (last ten fiscal years); capital asset statistics (most recent three fiscal years); and operating indicators (most recent three fiscal years), for the government function Public Safety and Corrections. The report is also cited as *Comprehensive Annual Financial Report for the State of Texas for the Fiscal Year Ending August 31, [year].* This is one of two annual financial reports issued by the Comptroller. The other is the *State of Texas Annual Cash Report*, which contains a section devoted to outlining the differences between the two reports (see entry 584).

•592 *Texas State Expenditures by County.* Austin: Texas Comptroller of Public Accounts [annual, 1991–date].

<http://www.window.state.tx.us/taxbud/expbyco/>

Reports fiscal year State expenditures for all Texas counties. The tabular data is arranged by agency, with columns designated for totals as well as selected parameters such as intergovernmental payments, labor costs, public assistance, operating expenses, and capital outlays. The same data is also provided for each Texas Council of Governments region.

Research Note: Editions are available online back to 1998.

593 *Unit Costs and the "Price" of Government: A New Way to Examine State Spending* [Special Report]. Austin: Comptroller of Public Accounts, 2003.

<http://www.window.state.tx.us/specialrpt/unitcost03/>

The Texas Comptroller of Public Accounts formulated a special index of Texas State government spending (FY1990 through FY2002) based on the Uniform Statewide Accounting System (USAS), which provided statewide total expenditures, agency totals, and figures for a large number of expenditure codes. An analysis of expenditures based on this index for the Texas Department of Criminal Justice, Texas Youth Commission, Texas Juvenile Probation Commission, and Texas Department of Public Safety, is contained in the chapter "Article V Expenditures: Public Safety and Criminal Justice."

•**594** *Where the Money Goes.* Austin: Texas Comptroller of Public Accounts [online only, 2001–date].

<http://www.window.state.tx.us/comptrol/expendlist/cashdrill.php>

This website provides the following check register search tools to access fiscal year State expenditures: spending by agency, spending by category, spending by detailed purchase code, payments to vendors, and travel expenses by agency.

Research Note: Coverage for some categories does not extend back to 2001.

Federal Aid, Grants, Loans, and Contracts—General Sources

595 *Biennial Report to the . . . Texas Legislature.* Austin: Criminal Justice Division, Office of the Governor [2001–date].

<http://www.governor.state.tx.us/cjd>

Provides fiscal year data on federal and state funds administered by the Office of the Governor's Criminal Justice Division (Appendix A), and a comparative funding summary arranged by fund source (Appendix B).

•**596** *Consolidated Federal Funds Report.* Washington, D.C.: Governments Division, U.S. Census Bureau, U.S. Department of Commerce [annual, online only, 1993–date].

<http://www.census.gov/govs/cffr/>

The On-Line Query System provides access to state- and county-level data for annual federal government funding received through grants and loans to state and local governments, federal procurement awards and contracts, salaries and wages of federal employees, direct payments to individuals, and other selected major programs. The data is searchable by object area, agency, and program code.

Research Note: Earlier data is available on CD-ROMs issued by the U.S. Census Bureau (1983–1992). Datasets are available through the Inter-university Consortium for Political and Social Research (ICPSR), Institute for Social Research, University of Michigan.

<http://www.icpsr.umich.edu/icpsrweb/ICPSR/series/00019>

•597 *Consolidated Federal Funds Report for Fiscal Year . . . State and County Areas.* Washington, D.C.: Governments Division, U.S. Census Bureau, U.S. Department of Commerce [1998–date].
<http://purl.access.gpo.gov/GPO/LPS7000>

Provides state-level consolidated fiscal year data on federal government expenditures or obligations, by agency, for grants and loans to state and local governments, procurement contracts, salaries and wages, direct payments for individuals, and other selected major programs. In addition, county-level data is provided for federal government expenditures (total and for five major object categories).

Research Note: Reports are available online back to 1995. Previously published under the titles *Consolidated Federal Funds Report, Volume I: County Areas; Vol. 2: Subcounty Areas* (1983–1993*)* and *Consolidated Federal Funds Report: County Areas* (1994–1997). This report is one of two publications comprising the Consolidated Federal Funds Report (CFFR) series. The other is *Federal Aid to States* (see entry 599). Data for both publications has been consolidated and tabulated in a standard format by the Census Bureau under the auspices of the Office of Management and Budget (OMB). The statistics are based primarily on agency data submitted quarterly to the Federal Assistance Award Data System (see entry 600). Therefore, grant amounts listed represent the federal obligation incurred at the time the grant is awarded and do not represent actual expenditures. Furthermore, the grant data reported includes all grants, regardless of whether the recipient is a government entity. *Federal Aid to* States reports actual expenditures to governmental recipients only. Datasets are available through the Interuniversity Consortium for Political and Social Research (ICPSR), Institute for Social Research, University of Michigan. <http://www.icpsr.umich.edu/icpsrweb/ICPSR/series/00019>

598 *Excluded Parties List System (EPLS).* Washington,. D.C.: U.S. General Services Administration [online only, 1988–date].
<http://purl.access.gpo.gov/GPO/LPS49844>

The EPLS provides a single comprehensive list of individuals and firms excluded by federal government agencies from receiving federal contracts or federally approved subcontracts, and from certain types of federal financial and nonfinancial assistance and benefits. It was established "to ensure that agencies solicit offers from, award contracts, grants, or financial or non-financial assistance and benefits to, and consent to subcontracts with responsible contractors only and not allow a party to participate in any affected program if any Executive department or agency has debarred, suspended, or otherwise excluded (to the extent specified in the exclusion action) that party from participation in an affected program." The Bureau of Justice Assistance, U.S. Department of Justice, is one such agency that submits names of individuals to the EPLS under the authority of the Denial of Federal Benefits Program. This program was established by the Anti-Drug Abuse Act of 1988 (P.L. 100-690 § 5301, 102 Stat. 4181), and provides a sentencing option for federal and state courts to deny all or selected benefits available from the federal government to individuals convicted of drug trafficking or possession.

Research Note: Searches for current and past exclusions can be conducted by utilizing an array of advanced search criteria. The print edition, *Lists of Parties Excluded from Federal Procurement or Nonprocurement Programs as of . . .*, was discontinued effective July 11, 2003.

•599 *Federal Aid to States for Fiscal Year [year].* Washington, D.C.: Governments Division, U.S. Census Bureau, U.S. Department of Commerce [1998–date].

<http://purl.access.gpo.gov/GPO/LPS4561>

Provides state-level data on actual federal government expenditures through grants to state and local governments, by agency and for selected programs.

Research Note: Reports are available online back to 1998. This data was reported from 1981 through 1997 in Table 2 of *Federal Expenditures by State for Fiscal Year [year]: A Report Prepared Pursuant to the Consolidated Federal Funds Report Act of 1982 (Public Law 97-236).* <http://purl.access.gpo.gov/GPO/LPS2879> *Federal Aid to States* is one of two publications comprising the Consolidated Federal Funds Report (CFFR) series. The other is *Consolidated Federal Funds Report for Fiscal Year . . . State and County Areas* (see entry 597). Data for both publications has been consolidated and tabulated in a standard format by the Census Bureau under the auspices of the Office of Management and Budget (OMB). Datasets are available through the Inter-university Consortium for Political and Social Research (ICPSR), Institute for Social Research, University of Michigan. <http://www.icpsr.umich.edu/icpsrweb/ICPSR/series/00019>

•600 *Federal Assistance Award Data System.* Washington, D.C.: Governments Division, U.S. Census Bureau, U.S. Department of Commerce [quarterly, 1981–date].

<http://www.census.gov/govs/www/faads.html>

The Federal Assistance Award Data System (FAADS) is authorized under the provisions of 31 U.S.C. § 6102(a) (2003). It comprises a repository of federal financial assistance award transactions of approximately 600 federal programs that focus primarily on assistance to state and local governments. However, all major programs providing transfer payments to individuals, discretionary project grants, loans, or insurance are also covered. Data is currently received from thirty-three executive departments and agencies with grant making authority. Each transaction record identifies, by the *Catalog of Federal Domestic Assistance* (CFDA) program code number and name, the type and amount of financial assistance, the type and location of the recipient and the geographic place of performance. The recipient location and place of performance are identified by name and by the geographic code for the state/territory, county area and/or place. The federal agency that made each award is identified by code and by name. Reporting in FAADS is based on the geographic location of the initial recipient, which may be different from the location of the funded project and could also be different from the location of secondary recipients or the prime beneficiaries. Each quarterly report is a discrete entity and no summation, consolidation, or other linkage with previous or future quarterly data is provided to users.

Research Note: State-level reports, displayed as spreadsheets, are available through the Census Bureau website beginning with first quarter of FY2008. Earlier data files, beginning with the first quarter of FY1982 , are available through the National Archives and Records Administration website (Record Group 29). <http://aad.archives.gov/aad/>

600A *Federal Audit Clearinghouse.* Washington, D.C.: Governments Division, U.S. Census Bureau, U.S. Department of Commerce [online only, 1997–date].

<http://harvester.census.gov/sac/>

Non-federal entities (i.e., state and local governments, non-profit entities, and Indian tribes) that annually expend $300,000 or more in federal awards ($500,000 for fiscal periods ending after December 31, 2003) are required under provisions of 31 U.S.C. §§ 7501–7507 (2003) to undergo a single or program-specific audit in accordance with Office of Management and Budget (OMB) Circular A-133 (2003 revision). The OMB designated the Census Bureau to serve as the clearinghouse for these audits, which are searchable through the Internet Data Dissemination System (IDDS) by the auditee name, EIN (Employer Identification Number), or state.

•601 *Federal Procurement Data System—Next Generation (FPDS-NG).* Washington, D.C.: Office of Federal Procurement Policy, Office of Management and Budget, Executive Office of the President [online only, 1978–date].

<https://www.fpds.gov/>

The Office of Federal Procurement Policy Act (P.L. 93-400, 88 Stat. 796) established the Office of Federal Procurement Policy (OFPP) in the Office of Management and Budget (OMB). It was required, inter alia, to "establish a system for collecting, developing, and disseminating the procurement data which takes into account the needs of the Congress, the executive branch, and the public sector." Data collection was initiated at the beginning of FY1979. Researchers can use the "ezSearch" function to generate reports on unclassified federal executive branch procurement contracts estimated at $3,000 or more. Four optional filters are available (department, agency, vendor, and vendor state). Search results can be further refined by drilling down the links within individual documents and then displayed as graphs or exported to Acrobat, MS Excel, CSV, or HTML.

Research Note: Advanced search capabilities are also available. Users must register to access reports and retrieve data. The FAQ section enumerates the agencies and types of data that are excluded from the database. Published reports of the OFPP are available online beginning with *Federal Procurement Data System. Special Analysis 1, Federal Acquisition Awards Over $10,000 by Type of Contractor: Fourth Quarter Fiscal Year 1981.*

602 *State of Texas Annual Cash Report: Revenue and Expenditures of State Funds for the Year Ending August 31, [year].* Austin: Texas Comptroller of Public Accounts [1989–date].

<http://www.window.state.tx.us/finances/pubs/cashrpt/>

Reports federal revenue for all funds (excluding trust), by selected State agency and by government function and program, for the most recent five fiscal years (see entry 584).

•**603** *Top 100 Federal Funding Sources in the Texas State Budget.* Austin: Legislative Budget Board [biennial, 2004–date].

<http://www.lbb.state.tx.us/Federal_Funds/Federal_Funds.htm>

This report, prepared by the LBB's Federal Funds Analysis Team, ranks the top 100 sources for federal grant expenditures in Texas by federal agency source. More detailed information on these sources is provided in chapters organized by subject (e.g., Justice). Data reported includes the recipient agency and proportionate shares (if the grant is shared among multiple agencies); purpose of the grant; match or maintenance of effort provisions; allowable uses and restrictions; and eligibility criteria.

Research Note: The Introduction enumerates the types of federal funds received by the State that are not included in the report. A summary of the report is published as a special issue of *Federal Funds Watch.*

•**604** *USASpending.gov.* Washington, D.C.: Office and Management of Budget, Executive Office of the President [online only, 2000–date].

<http://purl.access.gpo.gov/GPO/LPS91044>

The provisions of the Federal Funding Accountability and Transparency Act of 2006 (P.L. 109-282, 120 Stat. 1186) mandated that the Office of Management and Budget (OMB) establish a free, searchable, publically accessible website, beginning with FY2007 and each fiscal year thereafter, detailing for each federal award of financial assistance and expenditures (with a few exceptions) the following information: (1) the amount; (2) the transaction type, funding agency, the North American Industry Classification System (NAICS) code or *Catalog of Federal Domestic Assistance* entry number, program source, and an award title that describes the purpose of each funding action; (3) the name and location of the recipient and the primary location of performance; and (4) a unique identifier of the recipient and any parent entity. The act further stipulates that the website must provide for separate searches that distinguish between awards that are grants, sub-grants, loans, cooperative agreements, and other forms of financial assistance and awards that are contracts, subcontracts, purchase orders, task orders, and delivery orders. The website contains all the information reported to the Federal Assistance Award

Data System (see entry 600) and the Federal Procurement Data System—Next Generation (see entry 601), as well as other agency specific data sources. Federal assistance is searchable by recipient; by place of performance (state, county, or city); by major agency; or by type of assistance (e.g., grants and cooperative agreements, direct payments, loans, and insurance). Federal contracts are searchable by contractor; by place of performance (state, county, congressional district, or zip code); by contracting agency; by competition type; or by product/service provided.

Research Note: This website incorporates data from and supersedes *FederalSpending.gov*.

Federal Aid, Grants, Loans, and Contracts—Individual Programs

605 *Bulletproof Vest Partnership Award Notifications: FY[year] Funds.* Washington, D.C.: Office of Justice Programs, Bureau of Justice Assistance, U.S. Department of Justice [online only, 1999–date].

<http://www.ojp.usdoj.gov/bvpbasi/bvpprogramresources.htm>

The Bulletproof Vest Partnership Grant Act of 1998 (P.L. 105-181, 112 Stat. 512) established a matching grant program to assist state and local jurisdictions to purchase armor vests for use by law enforcement departments. This report provides data on fiscal year funding decisions (grant amount and number of vests) by state and jurisdiction.

606 *COPS Quick Facts for the State of Texas.* Washington, D.C.: Office Community Oriented Policing Services, U.S. Department of Justice [annual, online only].

<http://www.cops.usdoj.gov/Default.asp?Item=1082>

The Community Oriented Policing Services (COPS) program was established by the Violent Crime Control and Law Enforcement Act of 1994 (P.L. 103-322, Title I, 108 Stat. 1796). It distributes funding to eligible state, local, and tribal law enforcement agencies—through program grants and cooperative agreements—to hire and train community policing professionals, acquire cutting-edge crime fighting technologies, and develop and implement innovative community policing strategies. This report provides data on accepted COPS grants by agency/program as follows: award date, type, number of officers, funding amount, and whether the grantee is located in more than one congressional district. Additional state-level data on COPS grants is provided under Grants Announcements (FY2001–date).

Research Note: The Audit Division, Office of the Inspector General, U.S. Department of Justice, reports on the expenditure of federal funds by selected recipients of COPS grants. Executive summaries of these audits are available on the OIG's website, arranged alphabetically by state. <http://www.usdoj.gov/oig/grants/_cops.htm>

607 *Correctional Facilities on Tribal Lands Program.* Washington, D.C.: Bureau of Justice Assistance, Office of Justice Programs, U.S. Department of Justice [online only, 2007–date].

<http://www.ojp.usdoj.gov/BJA/grant/tribal_correction.html>

The Correctional Facilities on Tribal Lands Discretionary Grant Program was established by the Violent Crime Control and Law Enforcement Act of 1994 (P.L. 103-322, Title II, 108 Stat. 1796). Funding may be used to help tribes construct or renovate correctional facilities on tribal lands used for the incarceration of offenders subject to tribal jurisdiction. Applicants are limited to federally recognized tribal governments. Data on annual funding for both planning and renovation (state, grantee, and amount) is provided in the Related Information and Resources section.

Research Note: Reports are available online back to 2007.

608 *DNA Initiative: Advancing Criminal Justice Through DNA Technology.* Washington, D.C.: National Institute of Justice, Office of Justice Programs, U.S. Department of Justice [online only, 2004–date].

<http://www.dna.gov/funding/>

The Department of Justice's DNA Initiative was established to provide funding, training and assistance to federal, state, and local forensic labs; police departments; medical professionals; victim service providers; and prosecutors, defense lawyers, and judges, with the goal of ensuring that forensic DNA reaches its full potential to solve crimes, protect the innocent, and identify missing persons. Data on grant awards and outsourcing contracts is provided for the following programs funded through the initiative: Forensic DNA Backlog Reduction Program; Offender/Arrestee DNA Backlog Reduction Program; Solving Cold Cases with DNA; Postconviction DNA Testing Assistance Program; Forensic Science Training Development and Delivery Program; Using DNA Technology to Identify the Missing; Forensic DNA Unit Efficiency Improvement Program; and Forensic DNA Research and Development.

Research Note: Depending on the program, data is provided at the state, jurisdictional, or agency level. Data for some programs does not extend back to 2004. In 2007 the NIJ merged the Forensic DNA Capacity Enhancement and Forensic Casework Backlog Reduction programs to form the Forensic DNA Backlog Reduction Program.

609 *Drug Court Discretionary Grant Program.* Washington, D.C.: Bureau of Justice Assistance, Office of Justice Programs, U.S. Department of Justice [annual, online only, 2002–date].

<http://www.ojp.usdoj.gov/BJA/grant/drugcourts.html>

The Drug Court Discretionary Grant Program was established by the Violent Crime Control and Law Enforcement Act of 1994 (P.L. 103-322, Title V, 108 Stat. 1796). It provides financial and technical assistance to states, state courts, local courts, units of local government, and Indian tribal governments to develop and implement treatment drug courts that effectively integrate substance abuse treatment, mandatory drug testing, sanctions and incentives, and transitional services in judicially supervised court settings with jurisdiction over nonviolent, substance-abusing offenders.

Research Note: Award data is presented by fiscal year.

610 *Drug-Free Communities Support Program.* Washington, D.C.: Office of National Drug Control Policy, Executive Office of the President [annual, on-line only].

<http://www.ondcp.gov/dfc/grantee_map.html>

The Drug-Free Communities Support Program was authorized by the Drug-Free Communities Act of 1997 (P.L. 105-20, 111 Stat. 224). It provides grants of up to $500,000 over five years to community organizations that facilitate citizen participation in local drug prevention efforts. Coalitions are comprised of community leaders, parents, youth, teachers, religious and fraternal organizations, health care and business professionals, law enforcement, and the media. The List of Grantees section provides state-level data for the current fiscal year on grantees (regular, mentor new, and mentor continuation).

611 *Drug-Violence Prevention National Programs.* Washington, D.C.: Office of Safe and Drug-Free Schools, U.S. Department of Education [online only, 2001–date].

<http://www.ed.gov/about/offices/list/osdfs/programs.html#national>

612 *Drug-Violence Prevention State Programs.* Washington, D.C.: Office of Safe and Drug-Free Schools, U.S. Department of Education [online only, 2001–date].

<http://www.ed.gov/about/offices/list/osdfs/programs.html#state>

State-level data is provided on awards for various discretionary and formula grant programs authorized by the Elementary and Secondary Education Act of 1965 (P.L. 89-10, 79 Stat. 27), as amended. The programs focus on developing and maintaining safe, disciplined, and drug-free schools and institutions of higher education.

Research Note: Data for all programs does not extend back to 2001. Award amounts are not provided for all programs.

613 *Edward Byrne Memorial Justice Assistance Grant Program.* Washington, D.C.: Bureau of Justice Assistance, Office of Justice Programs, U.S. Department of Justice [annual, online only, 2005–date].

<http://www.ojp.usdoj.gov/BJA/grant/jag.html>

The Edward Byrne Memorial Justice Assistance Grant (JAG) Program was created when the Violence Against Women and Department of Justice Reauthorization Act of 2005 (P.L. 109-162, Title XI, 119 Stat. 2960) merged the Edward Byrne Memorial Grant Program with the Local Law Enforcement Block Grant Program (LLEBG). The grants assist states and local governments in providing personnel, equipment, supplies, contractual support, training, technical assistance, and information systems to improve the overall criminal justice system.

Research Note: The JAG program is administered by the Bureau of Justice Assistance, while the JAG formulas are calculated by the Bureau of Justice Statistics. Award data is presented by fiscal year.

614 *Fiscal Year [year] Report on the Paul Coverdell Forensic Science Improvement Grants Program.* Washington, D.C.: National Institute of Justice, Office of Justice Programs, U.S. Department of Justice [online only, 2002–date].

<http://www.ojp.usdoj.gov/nij/topics/forensics/nfsia/welcome.htm>

The Paul Coverdell National Forensic Science Improvement Act of 2000 (P.L. 106-561, 114 Stat. 2487) authorizes funding to states and local units of government for expenses related to improving the quality and timeliness of forensic science or medical examiner service through facilities, personnel, equipment, computerization, supplies, accreditation, certification, education, training, administrative expenses, and backlog reduction. Seventy-five percent of total annual allocations are "base" (formula) awards to State Administering Agencies (SAAs) based on individual state populations. The remaining 25 percent are direct "competitive" awards to states and/or local agencies that do not pass through SAAs. Each fiscal year report includes a state-level funding table that lists the SAA and local units of government, the amounts awarded (total, base and competitive), and brief project descriptions.

615 *Harold Rogers Prescription Drug Monitoring Program.* Washington, D.C.: Bureau of Justice Assistance, Office of Justice Programs, U.S. Department of Justice [annual, online only, 2003–date].

<http://www.ojp.usdoj.gov/BJA/grant/prescripdrugs.html>

The Harold Rogers Prescription Drug Monitoring Program was established by the Departments of Commerce, Justice, and State, the Judiciary, and Related Agencies Appropriations Act, 2002 (P.L. 107-77, 115 Stat. 748). The program was designed to enhance the capacity of regulatory and law enforcement agencies to collect and analyze controlled substance prescription data. It focuses primarily on providing assistance to states that want to establish a prescription drug monitoring program or to expand their existing programs.

Research Note: Award data is presented by fiscal year.

•616 *Homeland Security Funding in Texas*. Austin: Legislative Budget Board [annual, online only, 2008–date].

<http://www.lbb.state.tx.us/Federal_Funds/Federal_Funds.htm>

Beginning with the 79th Texas Legislature, the General Provisions (Art. IX) of the General Appropriations Act have contained the following reporting requirement: "All state agencies and institutions of higher education shall include in their operating budget reports to the Legislative Budget Board: (1) an estimated amount of federal homeland security funding received by the agency or institution of higher education and used for the operation and administration of state homeland security programs; and (2) the amount of federal homeland security funding received by the agency or institution of higher education and passed through to other agencies, institutions, or local units of government." This report provides data on historical award amounts, the program purpose, funds allocation, allowable uses, and the state agency operating the program in Texas. The final part describes the process for distributing homeland security funds in Texas, provides a list of pass-through funds by region, and includes examples of federally funded local projects. It contains the following six sections: Homeland Security Grant Program (Part I), Infrastructure Protection Program (Part II), Border Security (Part III), Health Preparedness Grants (Part IV), Other Homeland Security Grants (Part V), and Regional Distribution of Homeland Security Funds (Part VI).

Research Note: The Governor's Division of Emergency Management (GDEM), which is housed within the Texas Department of Public Safety, is responsible for making recommendations regarding the distribution of federal homeland security funds; administering applications for local and state entities applying for federal homeland security-related grant funds; auditing and tracking homeland security funds; and coordinating implementation of the state's Homeland Security Plan. Homeland security funding distributed directly to local entities (e.g., the Commercial Equipment Direct Assistance Program grants and local transit security funds) is not tracked by the LBB and is therefore excluded from the report. Also excluded are homeland security expenditures made by federal agencies based in the state (e.g., U.S. Customs and Border Protection), and funding streams devoted to natural or man-made disasters, such as hurricanes or chemical plant accidents.

617 *Justice and Mental Health Collaboration Program*. Washington, D.C.: Bureau of Justice Assistance, Office of Justice Programs, U.S. Department of Justice [annual, online only, 2006–date].

<http://www.ojp.usdoj.gov/BJA/grant/JMHCprogram.html>

The Justice and Mental Health Collaboration Program (JMHCP) was established by the Mentally Ill Offender Treatment and Crime Reduction Act of 2004 (P.L. 108-414, 118 Stat. 2327). The program's goal is to increase public safety through facilitating collaboration among the criminal justice, juvenile justice, mental health treatment, and substance abuse systems, as well as to improve access to effective treatment for people with mental illnesses involved with the criminal justice system. Applicants are limited to states, units of local government, Indian tribes, and tribal organizations, which must apply jointly with a mental health agency. Data is provided by fiscal year on grants in the categories of planning, planning and implementation, and implementation and expansion (state, grantee, and award amount).

618 *Lists of Awards.* Washington, D.C.: National Institute of Justice, Office of Justice Programs, U.S. Department of Justice [online, 1995–date].

<http://www.ojp.usdoj.gov/nij/awards/welcome.htm>

The National Institute of Justice is the research, development, and evaluation agency of the U.S. Department of Justice. This website reports fiscal year NIJ awards by solicitation as follows: project title, grantee, amount, award number, category, and solicitation title.

Research Note: Geographical locations are not specified, although this can usually be gleaned from the grantee name. The Audit Division, Office of the Inspector General, U.S. Department of Justice, reports on the expenditure of federal funds by selected recipients of NIJ grants. Executive summaries of these audits are available on the OIG's website, arranged alphabetically by state. <http://www.usdoj.gov/oig/grants/_ojp.htm>

619 *National Criminal History Improvement Program (NCHIP).* Washington, D.C.: Bureau of Justice Statistics, Office of Justice Programs, U.S. Department of Justice [online, 1995–date].

<http://bjs.ojp.usdoj.gov/index.cfm?ty=tp&tid=47>

The National Criminal History Improvement Program (NCHIP) provides direct funding and technical assistance to states to improve the quality, timeliness and immediate accessibility of their criminal history and related records. NCHIP implements the grant provisions for a number of federal statutes. The State-by-State Information section reports NCHIP funding for 1995–date (cumulative total) and 2006–date (yearly totals).

Research Note: For additional information on this program, see Gerard F. Ramker, *Improving Criminal History Records for Background Checks, 2005* (NCJ 211485). <http://purl.access.gpo.gov/GPO/LPS73225> For a GAO performance audit of this program, see Eileen R. Larence, *Bureau of Justice Statistics Funding to States to Improve Criminal Records* (GAO-08-898R). <http://purl.access.gpo.gov/GPO/LPS96847>

620 Parent, Dale, and Liz Barnett. *Juvenile Accountability Incentive Block Grant Program: National Evaluation* [Final Report]. Cambridge, Mass.: Abt Associates, 2003. NCJ 202150

<http://www.ncjrs.gov/pdffiles1/nij/grants/202150.pdf>

The Juvenile Accountability Incentive Block Grants (JAIBG) program was established pursuant to Title III of H. R. 3, the Juvenile Accountability Block Grants Act of 1997, as passed by the U.S. House of Representatives on May 8, 1997. It is currently administered by the State Relations and Assistance Division, Office of Juvenile Justice and Delinquency Prevention, Office of Justice Programs, U.S. Department of Justice. It awards federal block grants to assist states in implementing reforms designed to reduce juvenile offending through accountability-based programs focused both on the offender and the juvenile justice system. States (grantees) must pass through at least 75 percent of these funds to units of local government and tribal governments (subgrantees). State-level data is reported as follows: JAIBG allocations, FY1998–FY2002 (Table 2.1); percentage of subgrant awards representing regional coalitions (Table 2.14); and JAIBG funds allocated and returned and percentage spent by the act's deadlines, FY1998 (Table 2.19).

Research Note: The word "incentive" was dropped from the title in 2002 when the 21st Century Department of Justice Appropriations Authorization Act (P.L. 107–273, 116 Stat. 1758) reauthorized and modified the program. See also the OJJDP report, *Status of the States: Implementation of the JAIBG Program* (2002). Datasets are available through the National Archive of Criminal Justice Data, Inter-university Consortium for Political and Social Research (ICPSR), Institute for Social Research, University of Michigan.

<http://dx.doi.org/10.3886/ICPSR04046>

621 *Project Safe Neighborhoods.* Washington, D.C.: Bureau of Justice Assistance, Office of Justice Programs, U.S. Department of Justice [annual, online only, 2002–date].

<http://www.ojp.usdoj.gov/BJA/grant/psn.html>

Project Safe Neighborhoods was authorized by the 21st Century Department of Justice Appropriations Authorization Act (P.L. 107-273, Title I, 116 Stat. 1758), which stipulated that "The Attorney General shall establish a program for each United States Attorney to provide for coordination with State and local law enforcement officials in the identification and prosecution of violations of Federal firearms laws including school gun violence and juvenile gun offenses." The funding is used to hire new federal and state prosecutors, support investigators, provide training, distribute gun lock safety kits, deter juvenile gun crime, and develop and promote community outreach efforts as well as to support other gun and gang violence reduction strategies. Annual allocations are reported by federal judicial district and annual awards are reported by federal judicial district and grant recipient.

622 *Residential Substance Abuse Treatment for State Prisoners (RSAT) Program*. Washington, D.C.: Bureau of Justice Assistance, Office of Justice Programs, U.S. Department of Justice [annual, online only, 2005–date].
<http://www.ojp.usdoj.gov/BJA/grant/rsat.html>

The Residential Substance Abuse Treatment for State Prisoners (RSAT) formula grant program assists states and units of local government in developing and implementing residential substance abuse treatment programs in state and local correctional and detention facilities, and to create and maintain community-based aftercare services for offenders. Allocations to states are reported by fiscal year in the Related Information section.

623 *Screening, Brief Intervention, and Referral to Treatment*. Rockville, Md.: Center for Substance Abuse Treatment, Substance Abuse and Mental Health Services Administration, U.S. Department of Health and Human Services [online only, 2003–date].
<http://sbirt.samhsa.gov/>

The Screening, Brief Intervention, and Referral to Treatment (SBIRT) demonstration program is a comprehensive, integrated, public health approach to the delivery of early intervention and treatment services for persons with substance use disorders, as well as those who are at risk of developing these disorders. SBIRT cooperative agreements are designed to expand a state's substance abuse continuum of care to include screening, brief intervention, and referral to treatment providers in emergency departments, community health clinics, and a wide range of healthcare settings (ambulatory, primary, and specialty). Awards are made under the authorization of 42 U.S.C. § 290(bb) (2003). The SAMSHA Grantees section provides data on college and university grantees and state cooperative agreements.

624 *Solutions for Safer Communities: FY[year] Annual Report to Congress*. Washington, DC : Bureau of Justice Assistance, Office of Justice Programs, U.S. Department of Justice, 2003–date.
<http://bja.ncjrs.gov/publications/#S>

Appendix II provides state-level fiscal year data on BJA awards as follows: Edward Byrne Memorial Justice Assistance (JAG) Grant awards (Table 1); Residential Substance Abuse Treatment Formula Grant awards (Table 2); discretionary awards (Byrne and other funding) and total active grants (Table 3); and discretionary awards (Byrne and other funding) program descriptions and funding (Table 4).

Research Note: Published under varying titles prior to the 2003 edition. The Audit Division, Office of the Inspector General, U.S. Department of Justice, reports on the expenditure of federal funds by selected recipients of BJA grants. Executive summaries of these audits are available on the OIG's website, arranged alphabetically by state. <http://www.usdoj.gov/oig/ grants/_ojp.htm>

625 *State-by-State Grant Activities.* Washington, D.C.: Office on Violence Against Women, Office of Justice Programs, U.S. Department of Justice [online only, 2006–date].
<http://www.ovw.usdoj.gov/grantactivities.htm>

Provides state-level fiscal year data on all grants provided through the Office on Violence Against Women, Office of Justice Programs, U.S. Department of Justice (form name, legal name, award amount, and state totals).

626 *State Contacts & Grant Award Information.* Washington, D.C.: Grant Programs Directorate, U.S. Department of Homeland Security [online].
<http://www.dhs.gov/xgovt/grants/index.shtm>

Provides a interactive United States map that allows access to state-level fiscal year data for the Homeland Security Grant Program (SHSP); Urban Area Security Initiative Allocations (UASI); Metropolitan Medical Response System (MMRS); Citizen Corps Program (CCP); UASI Nonprofit Security Grant Program (NSGP): Regional Catastrophic Preparedness Grant Program (RCPGP); Operation Stonegarden; Interoperable Emergency Communications Grant Program (IECGP); Emergency Operations Center (EOC) Grant Program; Driver's License Security Grant Program (DLSGP); and Buffer Zone Protection Program (BZPP).

Research Note: State-level data on grants awarded under various DHS transportation security infrastructure programs can be found in the annual fiscal year *Overview* on the FEMA website. <http://www.fema.gov/government/grant/index.shtm>

627 *STOP Program: Service–Training–Officers–Prosecutors: Annual Report.* Washington, D.C.: Office on Violence Against Women, Office of Justice Programs, U.S. Department of Justice [2005–date].
<http://www.ovw.usdoj.gov/reports-congress.htm>

The STOP Violence Against Women Formula Grant Program, also known as the STOP Program, was authorized by the Violence Against Women Act of 1994 (P.L.103-322, Title IV, 108 Stat. 1902), and subsequently reauthorized and amended by the Violence Against Women Act of 2000, Division B of the Victims of Trafficking and Violence Protection Act of 2000 (P.L. 106-386, 114 Stat. 1464) and the Violence Against Women and Department of Justice Reauthorization Act of 2005 (P.L. 109-162, 119 Stat. 2960). Appendix A reports state-level fiscal year STOP Program funding allocation and distribution as follows: allocations (Table A1); funding awarded to subgrantees (Table A2); funding returned unused by subgrantees (Table A3); number of awards and amount allocated to victim services (Table A4); number of awards and amount allocated to law enforcement (Table A5); number of awards and amount allocated to prosecution (Table A6); number of awards and amount allocated to court (Table A7); number of awards and amount allocated to administration (Table A8); number of awards and amount allocated to other (Table A9); and percentage distribution of allocation, by type of victimization (Table A10). Appendix B reports state-level fiscal year STOP Program-funded activities and victims served as follows: number of awards reported by activities funded (Table B1); number of subgrantees using funds for victim services and victims seeking/receiving services (Table B2); race/ethnicity, gender, and age of victims receiving services (Table B3); number of individuals with disabilities/limited English proficiency who are immigrants/living in rural areas receiving services (Table B4); and victim's relationship to offender (Table B5).

Research Note: Each edition reports data back to FY1999.

628 *Title V Community Prevention Grants Program: Report to Congress* [OJJDP Report]. Washington, D.C.: Office of Juvenile Justice and Delinquency Prevention, Office of Justice Programs, U.S. Department of Justice [annual, 1995–date].

<http://purl.access.gpo.gov/GPO/LPS31301>

The Title V Community Grants Prevention Program was established in 1992 when Incentive Grants for Local Delinquency Prevention Programs Act amended the Juvenile Justice and Delinquency Prevention Act of 1974 (P.L. 93-415, 88 Stat. 1109) by adding the following new title: Title V—Incentive Grants for Local Delinquency Prevention Programs (P.L. 102-586, § 5(a), 106 Stat. 5027). To date the program has provided grants to over 1,700 communities for developing collaborative three-year programs aimed at reducing risk factors associated with juvenile delinquency and enhancing protective factors that support healthy personal and social development in their juvenile populations. The program also provides training and technical support to help communities design, implement, and evaluate these programs. This report contains data on the allocation of Title V Community Prevention Grants Program funds by state, the number of Title V subgrantees by state, and the number of subgrants per state.

Research Note: Reports are available online back to FY1995.

Chapter 12

Polls and Rankings

Polls

•**629** *Texas Crime Poll.* Huntsville: Survey Research Program, College of Criminal Justice, Sam Houston State University [1977–2007].

These annual polls of Texas residents cover selected topics relating to crime, criminals, juvenile delinquency, victims, law enforcement, courts, legislation, corrections, parole, community supervision, and capital punishment.

Research Note: The Survey Research Program disbanded in August 2010.

Rankings

•**630** *Crime State Rankings: Crime Across America*, edited by Kathleen O'Leary Morgan and Scott Morgan [CQ Press's State Fact Finder Series]. Washington, D.C.: CQ Press [annual, 2008–date].

Provides state rankings based on governmental and private statistical sources (including unpublished FBI data) in the following categories: arrests, corrections, drugs and alcohol, finance, juveniles, law enforcement, and offenses.

Research Note: Previously published under the title *Crime State Rankings: Crime in the 50 United States* (Lawrence, Kan.: Morgan Quitno Corp., 1994–2007). Researchers are advised to review "Variables Affecting Crime," the FBI's caution against ranking that accompanies each edition of *Crime in the United States: Uniform Crime Reports* (see entry 002).

631 *Education State Rankings: Pre K–12 Education Across America*, edited by Kathleen O'Leary Morgan and Scott Morgan [CQ Press's State Fact Finder Series]. Washington, D.C.: CQ Press [annual, 2008–date].

Provides state rankings based on governmental and private statistical sources for school crime, safety, discipline, and substance use.

Research Note: Previously published under the title *Education State Rankings: Pre K-12 Education in the 50 United States* (Lawrence, Kan.: Morgan Quitno Corp., 2003–2007).

632 *Health Care State Rankings: Health Care Across America*, edited by Kathleen O'Leary Morgan and Scott Morgan [CQ Press's State Fact Finder Series]. Washington, D.C.: CQ Press [annual, 2008–date].

Provides state rankings based on governmental and private statistical sources in categories that include the following: deaths by motor vehicle accidents, deaths by firearm injury, deaths by homicide, deaths by suicide, alcohol-induced deaths, alcohol consumption, beer consumption, wine consumption, distilled spirits consumption, adults who are binge drinkers, and illicit drug users.

Research Note: Previously published under the title *Health Care State Rankings: Health Care in the 50 United States* (Lawrence, Kan.: Morgan Quitno Corp., 1993–2007).

633 *State Rankings: A Statistical View of America*, edited by Kathleen O'Leary Morgan and Scott Morgan [CQ Press's State Fact Finder Series]. Washington, D.C.: CQ Press [annual, 2008–date].

Provides selected state rankings extracted from *Crime State Ranking, Education State Rankings,* and *Health Care State Rankings* (see entries 630–632).

Research Note: Formed by the merger of *State Rankings: A Statistical View of the 50 United States* (Lawrence, Kan.: Morgan Quitno Corp., 1990–2007) and *CQ's State Fact Finder: Rankings Across America* (Washington, D.C.: Congressional Quarterly Inc., 1993–2007).

Appendix

Data Archives and Repositories

Behavioral Risk Factor Surveillance System (BRFSS) Annual Survey Data: Survey Data and Documentation. Atlanta, Ga.: Division of Adult and Community Health, National Center for Chronic Disease Prevention and Health Promotion, Centers for Disease Control and Prevention, U.S. Department of Health and Human Services.
<http://www.cdc.gov/brfss/technical_infodata/surveydata.htm>

CDC WONDER [Wide-ranging Online Data for Epidemiologic Research]. Atlanta, Ga.: Centers for Disease Control and Prevention, U.S. Department of Health and Human Services.
<http://purl.access.gpo.gov/GPO/LPS18322>

Compendium of National Juvenile Justice Data Sets. Washington, D.C.: Office of Juvenile Justice and Delinquency Prevention, Office of Justice Programs, U.S. Department of Justice.
<http://ojjdp.ncjrs.gov/ojstatbb/Compendium/index.html>

Consolidated Federal Funds Report. Washington, D.C.: Governments Division, U.S. Census Bureau, U.S. Department of Commerce.
<http://purl.access.gpo.gov/GPO/LPS18322>

Data Analysis Tools. Washington, D.C.: Bureau of Justice Statistics, Office of Justice Programs, U.S. Department of Justice.
<http://bjs.ojp.usdoj.gov/index.cfm?ty=daa>

Fatality Analysis Reporting System (FARS) Encyclopedia. Washington, D.C.: National Center for Statistics and Analysis, National Highway Traffic Safety Administration, U.S. Department of Transportation.
<http://purl.access.gpo.gov/GPO/LPS38001>

Federal Assistance Award Data System. Washington, D.C.: Governments Division, U.S. Census Bureau, U.S. Department of Commerce.
<http://www.census.gov/govs/www/faads.html>

Federal Justice Statistics Resource Center. Washington, D.C.: Bureau of Justice Statistics, Office of Justice Programs, U.S. Department of Justice.
<http://fjsrc.urban.org/index.cfm>

Federal, State, & Local Governments. Washington, D.C.: Governments Division, U.S. Census Bureau, U.S. Department of Commerce.

<http://www.census.gov/govs/index.html>

InfoBase of State Activities and Research (ISAR). Washington, D.C.: Justice Research and Statistics Association.

<http://www.jrsa.org/database/index.html>

Inter-university Consortium for Political and Social Research (ICPSR). Ann Arbor: Institute for Social Research, University of Michigan.

<http://www.icpsr.umich.edu/ICPSR>

Research Note: Access to datasets is restricted to consortium members only.

National Addiction and HIV Data Archive Program (NAHDAP). Ann Arbor: Inter-university Consortium for Political and Social Research, Institute for Social Research, University of Michigan.

<http://www.icpsr.umich.edu/icpsrweb/NAHDAP/>

Research Note: NAHDAP and sponsored by the National Institute on Drug Abuse, National Institutes of Health, U.S. Department of Health and Human Services. Access to datasets is restricted to consortium members only.

National Archive of Criminal Justice Data (NACJC). Ann Arbor: Inter-university Consortium for Political and Social Research, Institute for Social Research, University of Michigan.

<http://www.icpsr.umich.edu/NACJD/>

Research Note: NACJD is primarily sponsored by agencies within the U.S. Department of Justice. Access to datasets is restricted to consortium members only.

National Data Archive on Child Abuse and Neglect (NDACAN). Ithaca, N.Y.: Family Life Development Center, College of Human Ecology, Cornell University.

<http://www.ndacan.cornell.edu/>

National Juvenile Court Data Archive. Washington, D.C.: Office of Juvenile Justice and Delinquency Prevention, Office of Justice Programs, U.S. Department of Justice.

<http://ojjdp.ncjrs.org/ojstatbb/njcda/>

Open Data Center. Austin: Texas Comptroller of Public Accounts.

<http://www.texastransparency.org/opendata/catalog.php>

Substance Abuse and Mental Health Data Archive (SAMHDA). Ann Arbor: Inter-university Consortium for Political and Social Research, Institute for Social Research, University of Michigan.

<http://www.icpsr.umich.edu/SAMHDA/>

Research Note: SAMHDA is sponsored by the Office of Applied Studies, Substance Abuse and Mental Health Services Administration, U.S. Department of Health and Human Services. Access to datasets is restricted to consortium members only.

Terrorism & Preparedness Data Resource Center (TPDRC). Ann Arbor: Inter-university Consortium for Political and Social Research, Institute for Social Research, University of Michigan.

<http://www.icpsr.umich.edu/icpsrweb/TPDRC/>

Research Note: TPDRC is sponsored by the National Consortium for the Study of Terrorism and Responses to Terrorism, University of Maryland, and the School of Criminal Justice, Michigan State University. Access to datasets is restricted to consortium members only.

TRAC [Transactional Records Access Clearinghouse]. Syracuse, N.Y.: S. I. Newhouse Communications Center; Martin J. Whitman School of Management, Syracuse University.

<http://trac.syr.edu/index.html>

Research Note: Includes the following components: TRAC-Reports, TRAC-Fed, TRAC-FBI, TRAC-DEA, TRAC-Immigration, TRAC-DHS, TRAC-IRS, and TRAC-ATF. Access to detailed datasets is fee-based; open access is provided for summary data, which is provided by federal judicial district.

UCR Data Tool. Washington, D.C.: Federal Bureau of Investigation, U.S. Department of Justice.

<http://www.ucrdatatool.gov/>

USASpending.gov. Washington, D.C.: Office and Management of Budget, Executive Office of the President.

<http://purl.access.gpo.gov/GPO/LPS91044>

Where the Money Goes. Austin: Texas Comptroller of Public Accounts.

<http://www.window.state.tx.us/comptrol/expendlist/cashdrill.php>

WISQARS™ [Web-based Injury Statistics Query and Reporting System]. Atlanta, Ga.: National Center for Injury Prevention and Control, Centers for Disease Control and Prevention, U.S. Department of Health and Human Services.

<http://www.cdc.gov/injury/wisqars/index.html>

Title Index

-B-

-C-

-F-

-G-

-H-

-I-

-J-

-K-

-L-

-Q-

-R-

-S-

-T-

-U-

-V-

-W-

-Y-

Subject Index

-A-

-D-

-E-

-H-

-I-

-J-

Juries, 186, 196–197, 220, 222, 412
Justice and Mental Health Collaboration Program, 617
Justice Prisoner and Alien Transportation System, 310
Juvenile Accountability Block Grants Program, 620
Juvenile alcohol abuse, 003, 020, 544–545, 549, 560–561
Juvenile arrest statistics, 001–003, 072–075, 374, 377
Juvenile arrest trends, 072–073, 075
Juvenile capital punishment, 373, 378, 427
Juvenile correctional education, 367
Juvenile correctional facilities, 003, 378–379, 396
Juvenile correctional population projections, 368
Juvenile corrections, 003, 073, 075, 228, 395–408
Juvenile courts, 003, 073, 075, 198–202, 220
Juvenile delinquency, 003, 072–076
Juvenile delinquency prevention, 620–621, 628
Juvenile designated felonies, 072–075, 200–203
Juvenile drug abusers, 073, 369, 381, 404, 406, 544–545, 549, 560–561
Juvenile drug use, 003, 020, 073, 408, 544–545, 549–550, 560–561, 563
Juvenile inmate fatalities, 370
Juvenile inmate statistics, 003, 073, 075, 371–373, 396–397, 400, 402
Juvenile justice system, 003, 073, 075, 080–081A, 374–379, 620
Juvenile mental health services, 380–381
Juvenile murderers, 001–003, 021, 072–075
Juvenile offense statistics, 001–003, 072–075
Juvenile probation, 003, 226, 366, 382–391
Juvenile prostitution, 017–017A
Juvenile Residential Facility Census, 372
Juvenile sentencing, 199–202, 204
Juvenile suicide, 021, 057–058
Juvenile victims, 055, 057–058, 073, 075, 450–451

-K-

Ketamine, 544–545, 549, 568
Klonopin® (See Benzodiazepine)
Ku Klux Klan, 046

-L-

Land sale fraud, 077
Larceny, 001–003, 019, 072–075, 097

-M-

-Q-

-R-

-S-

-T-